Walk A Mile in MY Shoes
by
Bonnie Lou Oliver

Faithwalk
by

Bonnie Lou Oliver

Perspective by
Gregory Oliver

xulon PRESS

Xulon Press
11350 Random Hill Center
Suite 800
Fairfax, VA 22030
(703) 279-6511
XulonPress.com

Illustrations by Bonnie Lou Oliver

Edited by: Verlyn Verbrugge

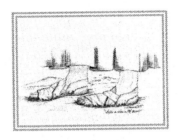

This book is dedicated
to my sons, Bill and Bob,
my parents, and my sister Barbara,
who never gave up on me
while on my *"Faithwalk"*

All Stories and conversations
are as I remember them
and some of the names have been
changed to protect their identity.

Table Of Contents

❖

Acknowledgments
❖

I owe a debt of gratitude, first to God for His forgiveness, mercy, grace, and faithfulness to His Word. Through this testimony, I began to understand some of what is required for disciples to "Walk A Mile in HIS Shoes." Next, special thanks goes to <u>all</u> my family, especially my sons, Bill and Bob, my parents, and my sister, Barbara, who endured and never gave up on me when the trials were almost unbearable. Where others might have thought I was going off the deep end, they remained faithful.

To Cheryl Thompson, who spent hour after hour with me during my first editing process. We often prayed, laughed and cried together while trying to put together a readable manuscript. To Verlyn Verbrugge, a shepherding friend, who during his edit managed to challenge my grammatical skills and on occasion my theology before submitting it to be published. To my proofreaders, Barbara Keefer, David Keefer and Penny Rice whose keen eyes found many of the last minute corrections.

To my ex-husband who, through his brash drive and tenacity throughout our marriage, instilled in me the tenacity to stick it out and survive, using many of the skills he taught me. It was God who had me draw upon some of those skills during difficult seasons of my life. I thank all of my benefactors who saw God's hand moving in my life and kept me going when the road seemed to be nearing an end.

And last but not least to Gregory Oliver, the man God put in my life to show me the way to Him and to clarify my needs and to help me see I was a person who had value and self-worth. This work actually belongs to them. The errors, mistakes and lessons learned belong to me.

Preface

❖

In writing this book, I believe the Lord wanted to use my life and struggles as a sign of His victory in a person's life. It is not just a story of being born again and receiving the victory. It is a story of the struggle to learn to discern God's voice, and to walk in the obedience necessary to put in motion the faith required that would move mountains in our lives.

I made many mistakes in my walk, but the Lord's mercy always carried me through. Christians need to be aware of the fact that they are vulnerable to the things of the world even though they are Christians. They are not immune to fleshly desires and spiritual weaknesses. As a matter of fact, it seems the reverse is true. I have observed that Christians are more exposed to the temptations of the world, partly because non-Christians don't see worldly things as "temptations." I also think Satan works harder on committed Christians than non-Christians; he already has the latter in his camp.

Through making my own mistakes, I discovered that I, too, can be judgmental, lack compassion, be critical and be many other things that the flesh wants me to be in this world of self-indulgence. I'm guilty, I know it; but I also know that with the blood of Christ I can and will be made new and whole.

When reading through the following pages, keep in mind my spiritual, emotional and intellectual struggles during my growing season. See how the spiritual cleansing and growth of a believer "with the washing of water by the Word" (Ephesians 5:26) can be compared to a garment in the "washing machine of life"—a garment that is being spiritually cleansed, inside and out, by the tumbling and agitation of the life's experiences. By doing this, you will be able to see how the Lord revealed to me the truth that is uncovered during my personal faith walk.

CHAPTER I

Wedding Bells

After fourteen years of being single and not dating, I was getting married again. There weren't a lot of plans to make because nothing could be fancy. My sister, Barb, was a godsend through this whole wedding. She volunteered to come with me when I went down to Missouri to marry Gregory. My feelings were mixed. They were probably like those of a mail order bride in the days of old when women traveled cross-country for the promise of marriage. The difference between those women and me was that I was traveling across country to marry a black inmate serving a life sentence in prison, and then I was going back to Michigan to live after the wedding.

Barb and I were able to split the expenses on the trip, which helped tremendously. She also helped me find a wedding dress and new shoes, plus she made my bouquet, Gregory's mother's wrist corsage, and Gregory's boutonniere. She was the photographer also.

Our plan was to visit Greg at the prison that morning so Barb could finally meet him in person. Up until then, she had only talked to him on the phone and received cards and letters from him through the years. Then we would leave, come back to the motel to get dressed for the wedding and return to the prison for the ceremony.

All went well on the visit. Barb recognized Greg from his pictures when he entered the visiting room and they hit it off beautifully. Greg even sang her a couple of gospel songs that he had written. We all had a good time.

Back at the motel, however, we had a little problem. After dressing for the wedding, we packed the car and were going out to lunch. I had left the car keys in the hatchback lock of Barb's mini van, so she was struggling to get the key out while the hatch was up with one hand while holding clothes in her other hand. While doing so she was getting frustrated with me. I was in the middle of getting Greg's ring out to make sure it was handy and give it to her for safekeeping. Barb's predicament caused me to set the ring on top of the van so I would have both hands free to help her. Then we finished loading the van and went to lunch.

It was during lunch that I remembered the ring—on top of the van. To my sister's surprise I didn't panic. We just drove back to the hotel to look for it. As we neared the hotel, we began scanning the road for the little gray box that held Greg's wedding ring. When we reached the hotel we got out and paced up and down the long steep incline that led to the motel, looking for the ring. We tried everything we could think of including checking the lost and found at the office.

It was hot that day and I was beginning to perspire. I was afraid of getting perspiration marks on my dress, which would be terrible for a bride to look like she had been overexerting herself. Also, time was beginning to close in on us now, and I still had to stop downtown to pick up the marriage license before heading to the penitentiary. The deadline for getting back into the prison was 3:00 P.M. If we were late, we couldn't get in and the wedding would be off.

I began to seek God for direction. "Lord, where is the ring?"

"Down a little further," I heard in the Spirit.

I went a little further checking thoroughly along the side of the highway, but with no success. Time was running out, so I called to Barb and we got back in the van and headed towards the county building where I was to pick up the marriage license. I drove because I knew my way around Jefferson City due to all my trips there through the years. I had just pulled onto the two-lane highway that ran in front of the hotel, when I saw it—a little gray box lying crushed in the middle of the road—not the side where I was looking. Pulling over, I ran back to where I thought I saw it. Sure enough, there it was! It was so badly crushed it couldn't be opened. I knew God had directed my eyes to that particular spot on the road.

We headed toward town as Barb continued trying to open the box. Not meeting with success, we stopped at an auto parts store to ask one of the men if he could pry it open. I wondered what he thought about a woman in a wedding dress running into an auto parts store so we could break into a crushed ring box. Success! The clerk got it open—but no ring!

Barb wanted to stop and get a new one, but time was running out. I just wanted to get to the prison. I agreed to stop if we should happen to see a convenient place to pick up a ring on the way. We saw a department store, and pulled in.

The woman at the jewelry counter must have thought I was rude because of my aggressiveness. She came out from behind the center island after hanging up the phone.

"I'm getting married in half an hour and I lost my fiancée's ring. I need a size 12, cheap and quick."

"Just a minute, I'll be right back." Then she went over to a woman at the counter and began discussing the spreadsheet that was on the counter. As the moments passed, my anxiety grew. I was nearly frantic now.

Barb walked over to the clerk to ask if she could get us some help. She appeased us by paging someone.

"If someone isn't here in two minutes, we're going," I impatiently told Barb. I still had to pick up the marriage license before going over to the prison.

Two minutes went by. "Okay," I said loud enough for the clerk to hear, "Let's get out of here. They obviously don't want a sale." I turned to walk away, and the clerk responded by quickly leaving the other employee.

"Now I need a size 12, plain gold ring, cheap." I said impatiently. The clerk pulled out a size 12 for $99.00. "I said cheap, size 12, quick! Do you have it or not?" I didn't want to play games. I would have called myself rude, but Barb assured me I was direct and assertive, leaving no question that I didn't want any delays (She is a supportive sister.) The next ring was a size 12 and only cost $60.00. I don't know why she didn't pull it out first.

Barb took care of paying for it while I went out to get the van so we wouldn't waste anymore time. We had only twenty minutes left to pick up the license and get over to the prison.

I pulled up in front of the county office building and jumped out. Barb got behind the wheel and waited with engine running while I ran in to get the license. Once inside there was another delay. "Devil, get out of my way. You are not going to stop this, in Jesus name," I said under my breath.

License in hand I ran out to the van. Barb drove. The prison was only a few blocks away. I kept hoping there would be a parking spot right in front so we wouldn't have to walk up the *big long* hill leading up to the prison. As we approached the prison, a truck pulled out of a spot right outside the front door—what a blessing! We made it inside just in the nick of time.

Greg's mother, youngest brother and sister were already there. They had been there for a couple of hours and were not allowed to see Greg.

We waited for about ten minutes for Greg. In the meantime, the chaplain who had refused to marry us married two other couples; one of them a black man and white woman. The only reason that I can think of that he refused to marry us was that he knew that Greg and I were solid Christians. He was thinking spiritual yoking of mixed races was taboo, and told Greg so. In the secular world, however, that spiritual yoking is not the issue. The Scripture is very clear on this. In spiritual things it says,

> *"There is neither Jew nor Greek, there is neither bond nor free, there is neither male nor female: for ye are all one in Christ Jesus.*
>
> (Galatians 3:28) *Where there is neither Greek nor Jew, circumcision nor uncircumcision, Barbarian, Scythian, bond [nor] free: but Christ [is] all, and in all."* (Colossians 3:11)

Greg arrived with his best man, and so did the chaplain who agreed to marry us. Barb taped the boutonniere on Greg's visiting room T-shirt (straight pins were not allowed in the prison), and we took our position for the ceremony. Gregory had his best man read the "virtuous woman" in Proverbs 31, then he read a poem he had written just for me. I began crying and cried all the way through the ceremony. I don't even know what Greg was saying in his poem to me.

At those times when I needed strength, I looked Greg in the eyes and was able to draw upon his strength, because that is the only way I could say my vows. When my vows ended by saying, "In the name of the Father, Son and Holy Spirit," I knew what I had done was permanent. Gregory Oliver was now my husband, and I was fully aware of the covenant that I had just made to "love and honor till death do us part."

I was married again, but it wasn't going to be a normal marriage. There were times I questioned myself. *What are you doing, Bonnie? What brought me to this stage? I'm a middle-aged, educated, middle class white woman. Why would I even consider marrying this exceptionally charismatic black prisoner who was twelve years my junior and whom I got to know through letters, monthly visits and phone calls?* This book answers the question why, and a lot more!

CHAPTER II

Spiritual Embryo

As I heard the heavy electric doors close behind me that first day at St. Louis City Jail, an incredible fear raged inside me. I was wondering what I was doing there, yet I just knew that I had to be there. The guard directed me to the Social Service Office where I would find Pete, the man who was assigned to the GED program, and Vaughn, the man who was to be my immediate supervisor in that program. The route I had to travel consisted of the guard station to my right, which had a holding tank on either side, and a wall on the left, forming a kind of corridor. The first holding tank appeared to be full, with about 20-30 men in it. From my quick observation, they appeared to be drunk or drugged; some were half-naked, and all were black. I was terrified when I saw them.

I was led down to City Jail via a "tug" in my spirit. That experience began a journey that I would have never thought possible, as I was becoming aware of God's plan and purpose for my life.

❖

Looking back over nearly half a century, I am beginning to understand the "whys" of life. God has placed in each one of us, from conception, a divine purpose. The Lord told Jeremiah, *"Before I formed you in the womb I knew you, And before you were born I consecrated you...."* God's infinite call and knowledge of life began before physical life. We do have a choice, however, and that is where I begin. The choice I made at eleven years old.

When I was little, my parents let me go to the corner church for Sunday school. I heard all of the teachings of the Bible and memorized the usual John 3:16 *("For God so loved the world....")* and the Lord's Prayer. I had a hard time believing some of the stories, however. There were stories about a man living in the belly of a fish, a boy killing a giant, a man being resurrected, and so forth.

I remember my parents investigating numerous churches and denominations in the Detroit area. They eventually settled into a United Methodist Church.

Then I discovered it—"the truth"—in my science class. My teacher began teaching astronomy. I was fascinated, and it was one of the few scientific subjects I was able to really absorb. I learned so well at my elementary level that when Captain Video visited the Detroit area, I was the child in the crowd who was able to shout out all the right answers about the planets and their locations. My parents were proud of me. "That's my kid!" they would say when someone asked whose little girl had the answers.

My interest in astronomy was the beginning of a walk that would ultimately lead me back to the basics I learned in my Sunday school class. Astronomy was also my introduction to evolution, which fascinated me. It all made sense to me, so I grabbed hold, because I could picture everything my teacher taught me.

As I grew, so did the distance between the teachings of the Bible I had as a child and my belief in evolution. Childhood memories of God were of a condemning God, not of a God you reverenced. I was taught that nearly every move I made was a sin and put a black spot on my heart. My biggest act of rebellion against my family came when I began smoking at the age of thirteen. That made the condemnation even worse. Now even God, if there was one, wouldn't have anything to do with me.

My evolution theology kept growing. Years later, at a dinner at the Fort Rucker Officers' Club, my husband, others and myself were talking about religion and God. I had held so strongly to my belief in evolution through the years that I stated, "I don't believe in God."

Shocked, my husband said, "That's the dumbest thing I have ever heard."

I was as surprised by his comment as he was about mine, because he made no effort to bring religion into our household. From my perspective, he did not practice any form of religion nor did he really acknowledge God. All I knew was that his military dog tag read "Religious Preference: Protestant."

❖

I took an English Literature class at Enterprise Junior College near Ft. Rucker, Alabama, where my husband was stationed. The teacher was very impressive and had my undivided attention. As with most English Literature courses, the stories revolved around the struggles the

Christian church was having. One of the main controversial issues was the struggle between the belief in free choice and predestination. After studying many literary works, only two remained unforgettable to me: *Paradise Lost* and *Dr. Faustus*. *Paradise Lost* was about the fall of humanity in the garden of Eden, and *Dr. Faustus* was about a learned doctor who had reached the highest levels of academia except for the area of black magic. For that knowledge, he was required to sell his soul to the devil and deny Christ in his life. Once he did so, the devil granted his desire to be trained in the art of black magic. Faustus traveled Europe casting spells and freely exercising his newfound powers, only to end his life crying out for just one drop of Christ's blood—the only thing that could save him, but it was too late.

Through studying English literature, I learned of different sects and ideologies that were developing in the church. One ideology was Deism, and the Deist philosophy drew my attention. They believed in a God of creation, but held that when creation was completed, it was left for humanity to have dominion. I liked that ideology, because the Sunday school version did not make sense to me—it required me to believe in the supernatural. I grabbed hold of the Deistic philosophy, thinking I had progressed from being an atheist, though I still believed God used evolution.

As my education continued, I took a basic Physics course through Troy State University's extension program at Ft. Rucker. It was a boring class until we began studying the molecular structure of the atom. I was really getting into all those protons and neutrons orbiting the nucleus. Then it hit me. *"Wow!"* I thought. Something I learned nearly twenty years prior was unfolding before my eyes. This tiny atom had exactly the same form and structure as the galaxy I learned about while studying astronomy as a child.

Hard evidence was unfolding before my eyes about the possibility of the existence of a master planner in charge of creating the universe. Surely this perfection I was witnessing could not have happened by chance—could it?

I was remembering my childhood teachings about the universe, the largest thing known to humanity, while my professor was explaining what was, at that time, the smallest thing known to humanity. These two scientific facts meshed together so perfectly, and one functioned as a minute part of the other, to form the whole. How fascinating this all was.

I began to rationalize: "Of course, that's it—the orbital motion of swirling masses of gas could catch the particles needed to form the larger masses, couldn't it? But where did the gases come from?" I was beginning to realize it was taking more faith to believe the evolution theory without a plan than to entertain the possibility that there was a God—or a Master Planner. My cosmic faith required that one of those planets be placed so climatically perfect in its orbital path that various life forms could evolve by chance.

I was twenty-eight and had already spent seventeen years believing in evolution; now this current information was causing me to question my beliefs. The seeds of information I had just acquired generated reservations about my original theory, but it would lay dormant for many years as I went on to finish my education. Revelation was birthing inside me, but I didn't want to get too carried away with this religion stuff.

CHAPTER III

Intellectual Struggles

"Mediocre" would best describe my level of academic achievement when I graduated from high school. At the end of fourth grade, teachers and administrators at my elementary school decided to split up my large pre baby boomer class. I was a little behind many of my classmates, but above the designated "slow learners" and trouble-makers. I had hindrances the other students didn't seem to have, such as my glasses and my speech problem, and I was academically one of the slower, if not the slowest, girl in the class.

I was the only girl in my class to have compounded problems. I had a "lazy eye" problem—that is "My left eye thought my right eye was so pretty that it kept looking at it." The doctors at Henry Ford Hospital in Detroit put a patch on my right eye to strengthen my left. Fortunately, it worked, although it did not eliminate the farsightedness. I started wearing glasses at a very young age—I wasn't allowed to start first grade without them. At this time in history, kids who wore glasses were usually called names and picked on. Children can be incredibly cruel! I still had to go through the harassment of having my glasses being pulled off my face as the other children mocked me—the typical children's harassment of something or someone different. The wounds from those early years of harassment went deep. I still struggle when I have to wear my glasses, because through the years my vision has gotten worse and my lenses looked like the bottom of Coke bottles.

Furthermore, I was one of the only girls who had to take speech therapy because I could not say my "s" correctly. I struggled with keeping my tongue behind my teeth. That therapy too, worked its way out, but I was still labeled abnormal. To make matters worse, I was placed in a part of my class that was considered to be slow learners—even losers.

The combination of my scholastic mediocrity and inferiority complex played a major part in the decision to place me with the section of the fifth grade that had the slow learners and troublemakers, and that was taught in a fourth-grade classroom. My classmates who went to the fifth-grade classroom moved along normally. In sixth-grade, the whole class was brought together again, but there was a noticeable difference in the two sections. My section had stagnated. I was the best of the worst, so the teachers tried to put me in the faster group, but I couldn't keep up. I had lost too much ground. The times the teacher worked with the slow group I was overlooked again—because I was the best of the worst. Consequently, my reading and grammar skills never got above the fourth-grade level. But unlike others who had difficulty in school, I did not become a troublemaker. Instead I withdrew, and my complexes grew. I wouldn't understand until years later how God would use my feelings of inferiority to help people that society considered losers.

❖

My parents were never aware of the struggle I had with my reading and writing. But the fact was I did as little reading as possible. When I embarked on a college education as an adult, I had the reading ability of a fourth-grader. Auburn University accepted me because my husband was attending full time on the government Degree Completion Program for Military Officers. The counselor in the admissions office pointed out, as graciously as he could, that I did not have the credentials to attend Auburn or any other college. He told me my test scores were not acceptable for college work.

"I am surprised," he said, "at a woman who has such poor reading and writing skills in comparison to her math and science skills. It's usually the other way around—women are usually stronger in the language skills." Continuing cautiously he said, "Because your husband is a student here, we will allow you to enroll in school on probation—I'm not saying, however, that we will accept any of your credits. That will have to be determined by your performance."

I wasn't surprised at my score, but my husband was. I only took the test because he insisted and had set up the appointment. I think at that moment I felt even more inferior to my husband and his abilities than I had ever felt before. He was an honor student, and to my knowledge had never failed a test in his life. It was humiliating to think that a university would accept my admission based only upon the credentials of a smart husband.

Another school quarter passed before I decided to enroll in classes. I realized during that quarter that there had to be more to life than what I was experiencing. I took the chance and went to school part time, enrolling in courses any basic curriculum would accept. My dream from childhood had been to be on a drawing board as an architect. This previously undisclosed desire surprised my husband. He wanted me to get a degree in Business Administration; but not wanting to compete with him, my beginning years at college were directed towards architecture. My yearning to become an architect remained through six transfers in the eight years it took to earn my Bachelor of Science degree. All through college, I avoided reading. It wasted time for me, because I got so little out of it. The proof of this was in my test scores. My salvation was in extra credit papers and any listening skills I could develop. I would do just enough research reading (which wasn't much) to write a paper. Fortunately, my under-graduate professors did not insult my grammatical skills. Occasionally, a professor would tease me about the spelling ability of my typewriter, but overall they seemed to grade my work based on content, not presentation.

Prior to entering Kansas State University in 1975, I concentrated my studies in the area of math, because the architecture curriculum I had been enrolled in at Auburn was heavily laden with math courses. One of my math professors told me just before transferring that I had more math credits than many math majors.

As I was getting more and more educated there were changes taking place in mine and Bill's relationship. I was growing more and more in love with him. When we first married, I would ask him a question and he could usually satisfy me with *one* answer. Now, however when I asked a question and he answered it I would come back with another question. I thought this was wonderful because this is the reason that he wanted me to go to school so that we could communicate on a higher level. It was working!

I entered the architecture program at Kansas State University at the pre-design level. Their program was a five-year curriculum, and it viewed architecture more artistically than Auburn's Curriculum. I was able to attend school full time through the next months, and finished the pre-design portion of the College of Architecture's curriculum. Then another career advancement for my husband made it necessary for us to transfer once again, this time for a nine-month duty at the Commanding General Staff College at Ft. Leavenworth, Kansas.

While at Ft. Leavenworth, I commuted to Kansas City, Kansas Community College for a couple of courses. Then it was back to Kansas State, where my husband received his Master's Degree in Industrial Engineering on a six-month military program. Due to the circumstances of his career, I was forced into changing my curriculum to Business Administration so I could accomplish my goal of graduating by the time I was 34 years old. The change was brought about because I had too many credits built up that were not transferable anymore, plus I knew I had only one year at Kansas State University before we were going to move again.

During my last year in school, my husband planned to spend six months in Washington, D.C., in the Project Managers' School offered by the military. On the home front, I was faced with twelve months to complete 67 hours of credit, although I would be alone for six of those months with the duties of mother and father to two healthy, active boys. My husband insisted I could do it because he had done it at Auburn to receive his Bachelor's Degree in Business Administration. With Bill's support I was up for the challenge, but apparently he was unable to handle it himself. As I became more engrossed and spent more time in my studies, he became more engrossed in other women. Needless to say, my undergraduate education was the beginning of the end of our marriage.

CHAPTER IV

The Army Wife

"Ladies and Gentlemen, may I present WO and Mrs. William Stuck." The day of our wedding, July 8, 1965, I became an "Officer's Lady." Little did I know what that would mean for the years ahead. Bill gave me my first *assignment* as a new bride. I was to read the book *The Army Wife*, which (to say the least) was antiquated.

I was unaware of the potential long grueling Vietnam War that loomed over our head and would be a household word for the next ten years. Bill owed the government three years after his flight training in Warrant Officer Candidate School. Then he would decide whether he would get out and become a civilian again or make the Army a career.

Bill had lived a restless and, in some ways a reckless youth. He was asked to drop out of school when he was on the honor roll! Academia bored him, because it couldn't move as fast as his mind would work. Necessary subjects like history, English, and social sciences bored him. He had a mathematical and statistical mind. I think that is why he liked gambling so much because of the odds of the wins and losses. Craps for example, fascinated him because when he was winning there was an exponential accumulation of money. The reason he was asked to leave school was because; he wouldn't go. He kept cutting class, and often times it was to gamble. I seldom cut class, but on this one particular day we both skipped school and wound up in the same place—that is how we met. Shortly after that Bill and I started going together. We went steady for about six months.

Bill became a high school drop out while we were going together. Shortly after that, however, is when I broke up with him, mainly because of his aggression including sexual aggression, which was beginning to scare me. I was thinking and responding to things that I shouldn't have been responding to or doing! Then three and a half years later I received a letter from Bill while he was in Warrant Officer Candidate School at Camp Wolters, Texas. By this time, he had been to Korea as a Private, and Germany as a SP 4 and SP 5 in the Combat Engineers.

Now he was a Warrant Officer Candidate because of a dare. One of the men in the unit heard about the Warrant Officer Candidate Flight Training School beginning to increase in its scope and he took the entrance exam and failed. Bill couldn't believe that anyone could fail an Army test so he took it on a dare—cold turkey. He got one of the highest scores anyone made on that test at that time. That dare was to establish the direction of his career.

This is when I came into Bill's life again. While he was home on Christmas leave we started seeing each other. At the end of Warrant Officer Candidate School we got married. Now his direction in the military included me.

We went on a short honeymoon with the money we received from our wedding, and then we were off to Ft. Rucker, which was Bill's first assignment as a warrant officer. While on our honeymoon I learned who was in charge. My next *assignment* was to learn all about the ranking structure patches, emblems, and the general ornamentation of a military uniform—not to mention the different uniforms. Bill wanted to make sure I wouldn't embarrass him. And, being a new bride, I wanted to learn.

I blew my first opportunity to impress Bill with what I had learned when we were getting my Military ID card. The man helping us was a Staff Sergeant. Trying to make an impression on Bill, I boldly said, "Now he is just a Sergeant!" in front of the man. Bill quickly recovered by saying to the man. "She is new and just learning." That was the wrong thing for me to do! Boy did I get it outside. That is when I learned what a debriefing was.

"He's not just a Sergeant! You never say 'just a Sergeant.' That man probably has more military experience than I do and you are calling him 'just a Sergeant'!"

"I'm sorry. I was just trying to let you know that I was learning."

❖

Bill's written orders were to report to the First Calvary Division at Ft. Rucker, Alabama. Once at Ft. Rucker we discovered that Bill's orders were wrong. He was assigned to the First Calvary Division all right, but he was supposed to be in Ft. Benning, Georgia.

I also learned during the first two weeks of our marriage that old Army saying, "If the Army wanted a man to have a wife, then they would have issued one" was true. Families of the military man had low priority in the scheme of things—though they were *well* provided for.

We rented a brand new furnished apartment in downtown Columbus, Georgia. I was so excited. My very first home as a married woman. Bill of course didn't want me working so I didn't. Officer's Ladies don't have to work: they have other responsibilities, as I was soon to learn.

When Bill came home after just a couple of days he let me know what the First Calvary was slated for.

"Where's Vietnam?" I asked. I had never heard of it and I thought I was pretty good in geography.

"It is in the Far East."

"So what is going on over there and why are we getting involved?"

"They are trying to stop the spread of Communism. It is not certain whether or not we are going, but if we do, they will give the wives a briefing on what to expect."

While we were waiting for the news about the First Calvary's activities, I learned how to spit shine boots and polish brass. Brasso, boot polish and I became very good friends during those days. I would sit on the floor for hours and wax up all of Bill's boots and low quarters (shoes). Then I would take a cigarette lighter and melt the wax into the boot. Immediately after that, I would take a rag (old T-shirt), cover three fingers with it, and wrap the rest of it around my wrist. I would dip the rag in ice water so that the cold against the hot wax would set the polish and I would shine away. The next day my job was rolling all of Bill's T-shirts, shorts, towels, washcloths, and socks. This is what he told me military wives do. Eventually I even learned to press military creases in his uniform, but I didn't have to do that very much. I got a lot of experience sewing patches on uniforms, too. I wanted so much to be a good military wife and make Bill proud of me.

One evening after the reality of the First Calvary's assignment to Vietnam, Bill came home and told me that I had to dye all of his fatigues OD green. "But they are already OD green. Why do I have to do that?" I asked.

"The patches on them aren't and they don't want any bright colors in the jungle."

I didn't have a washing machine except for the public one in the basement of the apartment but we were not allowed to dye clothes in it. Therefore, I did the next best thing. I filled the bathtub up with hot water and dye. One piece at a time I dyed all of his uniforms. Bill had a lot of uniforms—both regular fatigues and flight suits. Then I would lay them out on the small strip of lawn owned by the apartment complex to dry. When I had all of his uniforms dyed I really felt good about the job I had done until I went into the bathroom and saw all of the green grout in the floor. I had a tough clean-up job ahead of me. I took bleach, cleanser, and a toothbrush and scrubbed the grout lines with the toothbrush. By the time Bill got home that night, his fatigues were ready and the bathroom was clean.

I was not happy when he told me I had to dye all of his underwear OD green also. "But there is no more of that color dye anywhere in Columbus." I whined in exasperation. He told me to do it anyway— and somehow I managed to find what seemed to be the last package of dye in downtown Columbus and got the job done.

I wanted to make a lasting impression on Bill one night before he left, so I fixed an Italian meal and had my plan ready. His normal routine was to come home, take off his uniform, hang it up and change into civilian clothes. That would give me enough time to set the stage. I had everything ready. As soon as he came home and went into the bedroom, I got out the candles and lit them. Then I put the meal on the table. I was ready for a romantic evening. Bill sat down to eat, and then suddenly he jumped up, flicked on the lights and blew out the candles saying, "I want to see what I am eating." I was crushed and the bruise that made on my heart kept me from making candlelight dinner, for him again. I tried to blame it on the tension of going to Vietnam but over time I discovered this was just Bill. Romance and Bill were poles apart.

The day came for Bill to leave. I was scared, not knowing what was going to happen to him. He had told me he would never be a POW because, he would say, "They are going to have to shoot me in the ass trying to get away."

The First Calvary moved out August 15, 1965—just one month and seven days after we were married. I decided to drive to Wisconsin to live with my sister instead of moving back to Michigan. But after four months I moved back to my parent's house for the remainder of Bill's tour. We wrote everyday and I know my letters were often times more depressing than uplifting to him. I was suffering much self-pity. Vietnam was such an unpopular war that the well-meaning people on the civilian side were insensitive to the soldiers doing their job and their families. I tried to avoid telling people that Bill was in Vietnam. Occasionally I would write a good letter that not only helped him, but it helped me also. His letters were brief not really saying too much and he always said, "I have a busy day tomorrow." I didn't find out the stories about the "busy days" until he got home though.

One day, out of the blue, I received a "Purple Heart" in the mail.

Bill told me not to worry; it was a cheap one. He took some rounds on a reconnaissance mission. The enemy rounds hit the radio and shattered it. Some of the shrapnel hit him in the face. Bill's original assignment in Vietnam was with the 1/9th Calvary. He was one of the 19 original pilots assigned to the unit. Of those 19 only 3 survived Vietnam.

Mid tour in Vietnam they opened up the men's chances to receive direct commissions. Bill, wanting to be first in line for one, asked his commander to recommend him for it. His Lieutenant said abruptly, "No, you can go through OCS (Officer Candidate School) like I did." Not wanting to go through another candidate school, he asked for a transfer and got it. He asked his new commander for a recommendation for a direct commission to Second Lieutenant and received it. Bill had told me once shortly after we got married that the Warrant Officer rank was just one step closer to becoming a RLO (Real Live Officer).

❖

I was getting excited. It was time for Bill to come home. He was to arrive August 15, 1966. I made a new dress to wear to meet him at the airport. August 15 came and went and no word from Bill. The next day we received the reason via Bill's sister. Bill had extended and wasn't sure when he would be back. In a letter that followed a few days later, he explained that his direct commission went through and he was extending to get sworn in so he would not lose any time in grade. The morning of September 10th I received that wonderful call. "I'll be in tonight at 8:00 P.M. I can't wait to see you." His homecoming was great, and now I was married to the nineteenth man to receive a direct commission in Vietnam. Moreover, my war hero was wearing over thirty air medals, a Purple Heart, and the highest non-combat medal of valor that the Army gives—The Soldiers Medal. Movies of him and another soldier had been taken as they rescued another pilot from a burning aircraft just in the nick of time, saving the man's life.

Now that Bill was an RLO Second Lieutenant he owed the government another two years for the promotion. He selected the Field Artillery as his branch. All aviators still had to have a branch affiliation. Consequently, we needed to spend two-months at Ft. Sill, Oklahoma in the Field Artillery Basic Course.

Bill ranked in the top three in his class scholastically when he graduated from the basic course. I discovered this was the norm for him—always succeeding and scholastically on the top with everything he did. He was indeed a high achiever. From there we went to his next assignment in Germany.

❖

On the home front, I couldn't meet his standards as a housekeeper, and my wardrobe wasn't quite right for the functions we went to. I made most of my clothes. The stress was such that I developed severe tension headaches while at Ft. Sill. There were certain things he expected, and I couldn't seem to pass the test. I was always in need of correction. No "atta girl" for me—ever.

I was apprehensive about our next assignment in Germany. The first week after arriving in Katterbach, Squadron Headquarters was having a party. Col. Black, the Squadron Commander, loved partying so he could get to know his men and their wives better. I got all dressed up. I even had new shoes for the occasion. All the way there Bill was giving me instructions on what to expect and how I was to conduct myself. I just knew I was going to make him proud of me. As soon as we arrived, I excused myself to use the ladies room. In the meantime, Bill linked up with the colonel. When he saw me coming out, he motioned for me. I hurried, but my new shoes were slippery, causing me to slip and fall. There I was laying flat on my back looking up at the colonel. He helped me up and was very sweet about it. That set the stage for my night of embarrassing moments.

I wound up falling twice that night in front of the colonel. Then as the party wore on, the colonel had this game he loved to play called "Under the Sheet." All newcomers were the guinea pigs. Bill was the guinea pig that night. The colonel said, "You two can't leave until you play 'Under the Sheet.'"

I innocently but boldly responded, "With who?" Everyone laughed.

"Bonnie," the colonel said chuckling. "You are the star performer for tonight. You made the best entrance and you got the biggest laugh. It is a pleasure meeting you."

The story was different on the way home, however; I was an embarrassment to Bill—again! The more functions we went to, the more I disliked going because of the debriefing I would get on the way home. I tried not to show it, however.

Bill went to night school in Nuremberg. He had gotten his GED as an enlisted man and was taking courses to get his education so he could apply for an RA (Regular Army) commission. Even with the Vietnam War being only one and a half years old, Bill was telling everyone that he was getting his RA commission and then when the RIF (Reduction in Force) came down, he would be sitting comfortable. They used to tell him, "Stuck, you're nuts; they aren't going to do that again." But Bill knew better and pursued his education with that purpose in mind.

Consequently, the evenings he was home were spent studying. He didn't want me visiting my friends and getting out of the house to give him quiet. I couldn't listen to the radio because it distracted him. He really didn't like me sewing either because, as he found out when I was making all the drapes and curtains for the apartment, it made a mess. So because reading was not my thing, I went to bed early nearly every night.

Abnormal Psychology was one of his classes. He would come home and begin to tell me everything that was wrong with me. I was paranoid. I was psychotic…. I began to think I was totally worthless.

My correspondence with my family went through Bill's APO mailbox. He would read all the mail before he brought it home, and many times he would proof the letters I would write.

Living in a foreign country was tough. I couldn't work, didn't have money, and was not allowed to take the courses to learn conversational German. Bill took the car everyday to the airfield across the highway, so I had no transportation. There was a small PX (Post Exchange) with a little snack bar area just outside the entrance to the airfield so I would walk over there frequently just for the exercise.

Finally, I figured that to help my frustration I needed to have a baby. So that was when I got pregnant with Lil' Bill. I thought, with the pregnancy, Bill would not be as critical of me. Little did I know how sick I was going to be. By the time I was six months pregnant I had lost 30 pounds and went from a size 14 to a size 12 that I could button at the waist. But Bill would tell me my sickness was all in my head and to take a shower. On top of it, whenever one of the military women did something he didn't like I would get reprimanded for *their* actions. I was so sick and frustrated at the time that if I had had money, I would have left Germany, pregnant or not.

❖

The women's group at Squadron Headquarters' was having a special election of officers, but I was too sick to go. Mary, the CO's wife, called me to check on me. "Bonnie, we want you to come."

"I can't, I feel horrible. I get so sick whenever I get up and move around."

"Look, you can sit the whole time. You'll sit in the front seat of the car and the rest of us will help you at the luncheon."

"I'm afraid I will get sick as soon as I eat something."

"We'll take care of that. You need to get out and get some fresh air."

Finally I agreed. I left Bill a note telling him where I was, because he always came home for lunch. I went to the luncheon and the fresh air was good for me. We had just gotten settled for lunch when the waiter told me I had a phone call. It was Bill. "What do you think you are doing there?" he said abruptly.

"They are having a special election and the girls wanted me to come."

"I came home and there were dirty dishes in the sink. If you are too sick to do dishes, then you are too sick to party with the ladies."

"But it is when I stand or exert myself that causes the sickness. I'm OK if I am sitting or laying down."

"I'm coming up there to pick you up. Be ready."

"Mmm."

I didn't know what to say to Mary except the truth. "Was it an emergency?" She asked.

"No," I said sheepishly. "Bill is coming up here to pick me up and take me back to Katterbach."

"Why? What for?"

He wasn't happy when he came home to the note instead of lunch. There were dirty dishes in the sink from morning, which made him very angry. So angry that he told me that he was coming up to Squadron Headquarters to get me and take me back home so I could take care of things at home.

Mary and the colonel's wife were mad. I told them to stay out of it—that if they interfered it would only be worse.

Bill arrived and I left. I was debriefed all the way home.

❖

About six months into my pregnancy the aviators were beginning to receive their orders for second tours to Vietnam. The turn around time was anywhere from 12–18 months. One by one the people that I had gotten to know were packing up and going back to the States. I wondered, *What if Bill got orders while I was still pregnant? What would I do then?"* I had become very dependent on Bill as I began to lose my own identity.

Orders for a second tour did come down. Bill was scheduled to leave around my due date, December 15, 1967. Because of my pregnancy he was able to get a deferment until the baby was six months old. That deferment didn't really help the emotional strain because the inevitable second tour still loomed over us.

❖

December came and it was Mary and Dick's turn to leave. Dick was going on another tour to Vietnam. With his departure there had to be a change of command ceremony because he was Troop Commander. I had just gotten a new camel color car coat with a fake fur collar and a new pair of knee high suede boots to match. I was so excited. It was the nicest winter outfit I ever had. Even though I was nine months pregnant, I felt good in the outfit. I arrived early and took my place in the front row as the Operation's Officer's Wife. The Troopers were lining up, readying themselves for the presentation phase of the ceremony. There were still a lot of people to take their places, and Mary and the colonel's wife hadn't arrived yet. I was watching all the commotion when Bill came up to me and said, "I want you to go home—now!"

"Why?"

"You look like a tramp in those boots."

"What?" I said, totally shocked. This kind of insult was becoming normal.

"Get out of here now, you are embarrassing me."

I got up as though I was going to the restroom and tried to slip out inconspicuously. As I put my hand on the door to open it, there was Mary and the colonel's wife.

"Oh, Hi!" I said, trying not to show any emotions.

"Where are you going?"

"Home."

"Why, the ceremony hasn't begun yet?"

"Bill doesn't want me here."

"Bonnie, you come back in with us. He won't say anything to us."

"No, I have to go."

"I don't understand, why?" Mary insisted.

"My boots make me look like a tramp to him." I looked down and noticed that the colonel's wife had on black patent leather knee high boots.

"You're kidding."

"Just leave it alone. It's OK. I'll go." I was as humiliated as I have ever been.

❖

Lil' Bill was three and a half weeks late and was a whopping 8 pounds 9$\frac{1}{2}$ ozs. in spite of my sickness. Bill had dropped me off at Nuremberg Army Hospital at 9:30 P.M. on January 6th and drove back to Katterbach. He thought it was stupid for the men to hang around or to go into the delivery room. He said, "You women only want sympathy and emphasize your moaning and groaning just to get it". Consequently, I was alone in a strange hospital, in a strange country having our baby, while Bill preferred to be totally uninvolved.

When Bill visited me on my second day in the hospital, I told him that the baby and I could go home the next day and that he had to be there at 10:00 A.M. to check me out.

"I don't know if I can take off work to come and get you, seeing I took off yesterday."

"Don't bother," I said in a hurt but angry tone. "The baby and I will take the train home."

Ten A.M. that Wednesday Bill did show, though he was armed with two of our neighbors who were excited to see the baby and help me get settled.

❖

Lil' Bill had colic and cried all the time. In other words, not only did I have a tough pregnancy, but the first three months were hard as well. But after that, Lil' Bill grew like crazy. He was thirty pounds by the time he was six months old. It was time to travel back to the states so Bill could go back to Vietnam. As we were getting packed up and planning the travel back home, Bill informed me that he wouldn't be able to help me with Lil' Bill because he was traveling in his uniform and couldn't carry the baby. "But, he's so heavy!"

"I can't carry him in uniform."

"Well, travel in Civies (civilian clothes)." I spouted.

"It's a MATS Flight (Military Air Transport Flight). I have to travel in uniform."

As we traveled, I watched the other men helping their wives with their children, and they were in uniform, too. I have to admit I was angered and envious.

❖

I decided to stay near Ft. Benning, Georgia, while Bill was gone. Therefore, he bought *his* first house in Columbus, Georgia. He didn't want my name on the house because, to him everything was *his*; after all, he insisted, he was the one who worked, so it was *his money*! "If anything happens to me the house is yours anyway, so there is no need for both of our names to be on it."

Bill set Lil' Bill and I up with $500/month in expenses to live in *his* house and a $500/month allotment. That meant no extra for groceries and the niceties in life, yet he didn't want me working. We didn't have much in the way of furniture, because we had lived in furnished housing. There were no carpets on the floor either in this cute three-bedroom slab house with parquet and tile floors. I was concerned about getting some carpeting because winter would come soon and Lil' Bill was reaching the crawling stage and would spend much of his time on the floor.

When I took Bill to the airport to leave on his second tour to Vietnam, I wasn't the sad, boohooing wife—instead, I was relieved to get him off my back for a year. I didn't want anything to happen to him, of course, but I sure welcomed the break. The first thing I did was to go home and shorten all of my skirts two inches as my act of rebellion against his authority and the way he had treated me in Germany. I wasn't his wife; I was his "private no-class." I loved him and hated him at the same time. Even though my emotions were mixed there would never be a Dear John letter to Bill. That, to me, was a horrible thing for a woman to do with a man away at war.

❖

During the second tour, Lil' Bill was sick with a continual cold and ear infection. Every other week when the medicine ran out I was back at Army Hospital and had to see another new doctor to start the routine all over again. Finally, I decided I would go to a civilian doctor who lanced Lil' Bill's ears—then we both got some relief.

The year was long and hard. Money was extremely tight. Occasionally, Bill would send poker winnings to help us out, which was greatly appreciated. The area was flooded with women and families alone—waiting for their loved ones to come back from the war. Consequently, the news and activities around Columbus, Georgia and Ft. Benning area were definitely focused on the war efforts. Daily, new wreaths were placed on the doors indicating another death. I lived in fear of being one of those statistics, because this was his second go around and the odds were increasing with the additional time he had in Vietnam. Many of the women I knew were taking Darvon to cope and calm their nerves. I refused to take it because I knew it was addictive. Cigarette smoking was my only addiction.

It was nearing time for Bill to come home and I was getting excited. The hurt from our time in Germany was behind us. Moreover, after our R&R in Hawaii I was confident that Bill was willing to do some changing. He asked me to have another baby to give him another chance. I had the house looking nice with my inexpensive decorating abilities and I made sure that it was always clean, not knowing when I would get the call. Then it came—but not the one I wanted. "I am extending for a few weeks," he said.

"Why?"

"We are having an inspection and seeing I am Headquarters' Commander I want the inspection to be on my record."

I was not happy—it was always *his* record, *his* impression, *his* this and *his* that, but I accepted it as a good army wife.

After the second tour, I got pregnant with Robert right away. Our first assignment upon Bill's return was back to Ft. Sill for the Field Artillery Advance Course. This pregnancy was not nearly as bad as my first one, which was a relief. We went out every weekend to the Ft. Sill

Officer's Club and had a particular crowd of people that we hung with. As I got bigger and bigger, Bill became increasingly ruder to me. One night when we were at the club we saw a woman come in alone. It was obvious by her dress and demeanor that she was looking to get hit upon by one of the young officers. The first man that approached her was turned down. Bill, being up for the challenge, got up and went over to her and asked her to dance. She accepted and that was the beginning of an evening of me sitting alone like a bump on a log. I was seven months pregnant and unlike my pregnancy with Lil' Bill I was definitely showing. One of the bachelors felt sorry for me and asked me to dance. When the dance was over Bill started to make fun of me.

I waited until the time was right. Everyone was gone from the table. I got up and acted as though I was going to the restroom in case anyone saw me. There was an exit next to the ladies room door so I used it as my escape. I went to the nursery and picked up Lil' Bill then went home and locked Bill out with the chain lock. It must have taken awhile for him to realize I was gone because I was home quite awhile before he got back. He was not happy with me for that maneuver.

It didn't stop there, however. Another woman whose husband was in Vietnam began running with our crowd. Guess who she spent most of her time with. Yup! Bill and she hit it off and the two of them would tease and make fun of me being pregnant.

❖

Robert was born on August 13, 1970, and again I was alone. Bill didn't stay at the hospital. He used the excuse that he had to take care of Lil' Bill, even though three people volunteered that night to take care of him so Bill could be with me. He wouldn't hear of it.

When I woke up from my nap after having Bob, there was a beautiful bouquet of roses. I was thrilled and I just knew they were from Bill. When I opened the card, I was emotionally crushed. The card read, "Aren't babies grand?" and was signed by Bill's Section Leader in the Advance Course and his wife. The flowers were so pretty and appreciated greatly, but they weren't from Bill.

The flowers were our first topic of conversation when Bill came to visit. I told him of my disappointment when I discovered that they weren't from him. When I woke up from my afternoon nap, I had a second dozen roses only this time they were from Bill and Lil' Bill. Unfortunately they didn't have the impact they would have had if he had gotten them without prompting.

❖

Our next move was to Columbus, Georgia again. Bill was going to go to Auburn University for the Degree Completion Program. Upon completion he would have his Bachelor's degree and could apply for his RA commission. That is when I started school, with Bill's encouragement. It was at Auburn that I discovered that I had become a vegetable; that I no longer had an opinion of my own and that I couldn't carry on a conversation without voicing Bill's opinions. It was a startling awareness and I started making some changes. That season in our lives was quite good in comparison to the previous five years. Bill and I began communicating a little for the first time in our marriage; and my getting an education was the reason for it.

From Auburn, where he graduated with honors, we went to Ft. Rucker, Alabama. Bill was branch chief for the Utility Branch. Utility Branch re-qualified POW's or trained fixed wing pilots to fly the UH1-D Huey aircraft. I was going to school part-time and so was Bill. He was studying for his MBA. Life was good in Ft. Rucker. Bill was his usual work-a-holic self and I was busy doing women things and going to school. It was always a challenge, of course, to work my schedule around the boys in school.

❖

Bill was and always has been disrespectful of women. I got used to it becoming the norm in our life, so much that it didn't seem like disrespect anymore. Sometimes, however, he went over the limit. Yearly, there was a dress blues formal affair where the men would sport their miniature medals and ribbons on their dress blue uniform and the women would wear formals and long gloves. There were always reception lines and the formal speeches. On one of those occasions, it was sprinkling out and had been raining on and off all day. We pulled up to the Officer's Club and there were guards assigned to help the ladies out of the cars. This was done under a canopy so no one would get wet. Then the men would park and join their wives. "Oh, why don't you drop me off there?" I said. Bill went ahead and parked quite a ways from the entrance, because the lot was full. He told me, "You've got two legs, you can walk!" So I walked as fast as I could trying to dodge the raindrops.

❖

Vietnam ended while we were at Ft. Rucker, which was a glorious day. Bill almost instantly had the pressure of a third tour lifted off of his shoulders. He suffered his first major career disappoint during our last months in Alabama. The Department of the Army (DA) told him that because he didn't have enough command time that he couldn't go to England as the British Army's Standardization Pilot. This was a position he had been hand picked for. In order for Bill to get that command time in before he made Major, we had to transfer to Ft. Riley, Kansas the only place that had immediate openings for Battery Commanders.

Our time there was wonderful. I was going to school full time while both boys went to school. Our relationship had turned into a solid mutual love and respect for one another. To me Manhattan, Kansas is the best kept secret in the world, and was one of the happiest times of my life.

❖

It was nearing time for Bill to make Major, which meant he would be off to the next career move; Commanding General Staff College in Ft. Leavenworth, Kansas, but not before we took the trip of our lives. While in Kansas, Bill got another bug to do something as a family adventure. He took up motorcycle riding and he insisted we couldn't be a family unless I learned to ride my own motorcycle. I fought it because I had a cousin die in a motorcycle accident when he was thirty-two years of age. I was then thirty-two years old. Bill and I first learned to ride on a Suzuki 360. Then he bought me a Honda 175, which I rode to school nearly every day and loved it. The students called me "Motorcycle Mama." Then came the sidecar.

Once Bill had both bikes rigged he was ready for us to take a short family trip to Six Flags North of Kansas City, Missouri. A Honda 175 in rush hour traffic on the expressway in Kansas City is not a safe place to be, but we made it through. We could only pack a pup tent. Our bed was the ground. I have to admit it was fun, but the saddle sores I got from the Honda were too much. We needed bigger bikes. Bill bought himself a 1976 Honda Gold Wing, got the sidecar painted to match, and then came the trailer that he hooked up to the Gold Wing. He then bought me a BMW 900R fully loaded with only 19,000 miles on it. We now had the equipment to do some serious riding.

Bill wanted to go west on the long trip we were planning. We would spend forty days on a motorcycle, camping all the way. I was afraid to drive in the mountains, but we went that way anyway. Although I was very apprehensive of the trip, it turned out to be the greatest adventure of all of our lives. I felt a freedom I had never felt before as we took on one challenge after another battling the elements and road conditions. Once I made it through the mountains in Colorado, I was a biker. I could leave Bill behind because my bike was much more maneuverable than his with the sidecar. I had learned to lean into each curve just like a pro and began to feel like I was on top of the world when I was up on my bike.

As we crossed each state border, I discovered that there was a personality to each state as we were able to taste, touch and feel the countryside. It was beautiful! Inside of me other things were stirring too. I was falling in love all over again with this country as I sang songs about its greatness. I was also falling in love with the side of Bill that drove me into this adventure. But the greatest stirring inside me was the awareness of God. He wasn't dead to me anymore. He was alive and he was sharing this experience with me! With every turn in the highway I could see His work and feel His presence. Yet I didn't know Him. I wanted to, though.

In Kansas the plains were flat, yet distinct. Colorado had its own beauty and form that revealed itself as I learned to ride the mountains high. What a surprise southern Utah was with its beautiful rock formations and wilderness roads. The tip of Arizona and New Mexico that we passed through spoke even more boldly to me. The desert country of Nevada and its hot, almost blinding, heat told us another story just before we crossed into the northern country of California where the redwood trees reach for the sky. One could never mistake the misty air and cross winds of riding on the coast of Oregon where ferns grow wild and vivid green is the dominant color. Washington state had some of its own overcast beauty where we finally ran into rain. I thought I had seen it all, then we crossed the Canadian border into British Columbia, where camping became a challenge in bear country. The waterfalls, lakes and streams in Canada were an incredibly beautiful jade green. It was thrilling, the whole trip. By the time we got to Calgary, Alberta, I knew nothing could compare to what we had already seen. That is until I saw Glacier National Park with its breathtakingly majestic beauty. We didn't miss the watering hole at Wall Drugs either after riding through the Bad Lands of South Dakota. The cornfields of Nebraska finished our tour before heading back to Kansas and our next assignment.

As we were preparing to move to Ft. Leavenworth, I can't explain the feelings I was having. I was so thankful for Bill's persistence in taking this trip. The wonderful thing was that I was beginning to believe there was a God and that He was alive. I couldn't believe we did it. We spent 39 days on a motorcycle and traveled through a total of thirteen states and two Canadian Provinces. It was the adventure of our lives! The boys still talk about it today. That was the greatest gift we gave them.

❖

At Ft. Leavenworth, we found out that the next year after the Commanding General Staff College there would be more moving. Bill was able to get into the six-month quickie Master's program at Kansas State University in Industrial Engineering, then he was going to Washington, DC to take the six-month Program Manager's School offered by the Military. So instead of uprooting the kids twice in one school year, I would stay in Manhattan and graduate from Kansas State University. The only problem was that I couldn't get my degree in Architecture in that one-year period; consequently I had to change curriculums to Business Administration. The College of Business told me that I could earn my degree if I completed 73 hours of credit in one year, which equates to two years of school work. *Impossible,* I thought, but Bill told me I could do it and that he would help me.

In order for me to get a jump on *all* those credits, I commuted to Kansas City, Kansas Community College and took a couple of business courses before going back to Manhattan, Kansas to help lessen the burden.

Manhattan, Kansas for me was the happiest time of my life. I felt like I was becoming someone, and Bill's and my communication was expanding in every aspect of our relationship. I loved this person that Bill was becoming through his visible and almost daily changes. By the time we were married thirteen years I was hopelessly and romantically in love with my high school drop out who became my war hero soldier boy. I was very proud of Bill and trusted him implicitly.

Our time in Ft. Leavenworth was also good time. Bill was able to punch another career development ticket and occasionally, I would help a friend of mine tutor math at the Post Library. The tutoring service was offered to the support staff on post that wanted to get their GED. Most of the students were guards at the Military Prison there on post. Sometimes there was conversation about the role of the guard in a maximum-security men's prison. It was a time of maturing for both of us and a time for family bonding.

CHAPTER V

The Divorce

Back in Manhattan, Bill and I got to go to school together again as we did in Auburn. This time, however, I had the heavier load. I signed up for 12 credit hours for the summer semester and 22 credit hours of course work for the fall semester. My days were submerged in school-work.

Bill had promised he would help me, but his idea of help and mine were different. During the fall semester, he started going out in the evenings to the local nightclub. He never had to study as much as I did, consequently, he had more time then he knew what to do with. He said he was getting out of my way so that he wouldn't bother me during my study time. That left me, however, not only with the homework, but also the evening routine of getting the boys to bed and the normal things that happen during the course of an evening. I couldn't even begin studying until late, but I figured as long as I got my eight hours sleep, I would be all right.

As the months passed, it became more and more difficult for me. Bill would come home later and later. One night in particular, just before a test, I tried to study, but Bill's late nights were beginning to concern me. I finally went to bed, but couldn't sleep. I wasn't ready for the test and didn't know where he was. The nightclub had already closed. I lay in bed trying to sleep, but sleep wouldn't come. Then I heard the door open. I pretended to be asleep as he crawled into bed. When I knew he was sleeping, I slipped out of bed undetected, got dressed, and got my books together. As I exited the house at 3:00 A.M., I slammed the door, hoping to wake him up. I ran to the car, drove to Denny's, and tried to study for a couple of hours drinking hot choco-late to keep me awake. I was exhausted and could barely concentrate.

I was hoping Bill would be concerned about my absence.

After I figured I had been gone long enough to make an impact on him, I went home. To my disappointment, he didn't even know I had been gone. I was so exhausted that my performance on the test left something to be desired.

Near the end of the semester, things were deteriorating in our relationship. Then one night Bill hit me with it. There was a woman at the nightclub that he went home with. My suspicions were becoming a reality.

"Why?" His bottom line was that my attention was being taken away from him and put on my studies. "I will not let this family be destroyed because of my going to school!" I said emphatically. "I only started it because you wanted me to. You wanted us to communicate on a higher level." I was so hurt. Everything Bill wanted me to do I tried to do, but it didn't please him. Nothing seemed to please him— He wanted more, but I didn't know what. Finally, I told him, "I will quit school!"

"No, you won't quit!" Bill insisted. "You are just months from graduating. You are going to finish! I'm leaving in a couple of weeks for DC, so that episode is over. I promise I will be faithful." We had a few more words, and everything seemed to be smoothed over. Under the circumstances, it was quite easy to forgive him. I managed to survive the semester, passing everything. So far I had taken 12 hours in summer school, 4 hours intercession, received 4 hours credit through CLEP testing, and completed 22 hours during the fall semester. I was also given 4 credit hours for my affiliation with Toastmasters International and other life experiences, and the transfer credits from Kansas City. I had 52 hours completed going in to my final semester before graduation. I only had 21 more credits to go.

I was so drained physically and emotionally. I questioned whether I would make it through the spring semester with Bill being gone. I was also the neighborhood mother, running the neighborhood kids to the roller-skating rink and all the special events that they liked doing. Moreover, the boys often brought their friends over to the house. I was, the boys would tell me, a fun mom to do things with them along with their friends.

❖

Bill went off to DC in early January, 1979 and started the Project Manager's School. At first, he called in the evenings, usually when things were hectic in the house. Then he began calling at 2:00 A.M., waking me up. I fussed at him for that, but he seemed to take pleasure in doing it. "Bill, I have to get my sleep if I am going to do this." So I began calling him instead, but there was rarely any answer. He told me that the phone made a strange noise and perhaps wasn't working right. I should have been more suspicious than I was, but then I was too busy trying to play the role of mother, father and double-time student. For Bill not to have something like a phone fixed or not getting a new phone was totally out of character for him. He always told me he was there in his room, and I believed him.

❖

Spring break came and Bill came home. His next assignment was going to be in St. Louis, Missouri. We were both excited about this next move and took a trip to St. Louis to see what was available in housing. We contracted to have a new five bedroom, two and a half bath, two-story home built. I was so excited! I thought it would make us tight financially, but he assured me we could do it.

❖

Back at school I was feeling the pressure of everything. Then one day at the beginning of one of my classes the secretary of the Business School came in with a message for me that my son Bill broke his hand at school and needed to go to the Emergency Room. I rushed to the school and took him to Ft. Riley Military Hospital. I remembered to bring my books because I had a test that night in International Marketing, but I couldn't study. The remainder of the day we were at the hospital taking Bill to the Lab and the X-Ray Departments and passing time in the Emergency Waiting Room. There was no time for study.

I went to class early that night to stop by the professor's office. Fortunately he was in. I began telling him about my afternoon and how I was unprepared for the test. He had me sit down then proceeded to talk. "Bonnie, this has been a very difficult year for you. We all know that. This is what I want you to do. I want you to go home, draw a hot bath, sit in it for about a half-hour, put on your nicest nightgown and lay around doing nothing all evening—and I mean nothing but relax. Then tomorrow when you are ready to take the test, just let me know and I will let you take it at your own pace."

That is exactly what I did. I went in the next day when I was ready and took the test just outside of his office. I aced the test!

❖

One weekend Bill and I met in Kansas City. He looked so good. He was tanned, had lost some weight, was wearing a gold necklace around his neck and wore his shirt with an extra button undone. He had been playing tennis everyday too. He was upset that I didn't just fall all over him. Taking this particular weekend off was probably the worst one I could have taken off, seeing I had midterms the next Monday and

Tuesday and I knew that he wouldn't want me studying.

Bill was no longer the same person. He had bought me a gold necklace, matching bracelet and earrings. This was the second expensive gift in a couple months that he had given me. During spring break he had bought me my graduation ring—a three quarter caret round sapphire that slipped into a diamond jacket. Now this—what had gotten into him?

Another thing that struck me oddly was that he, who always had wanted me modest in my dress, was now pestering me to go braless. On that weekend, I felt as if he was parading me around like a trophy while he strutted around with his shirt opened wider, exposing his tanned hairy chest and heavy gold necklace. I was so concerned about the upcoming midterms that I was too preoccupied to suspect anything.

The rest of the semester was hectic, to say the least. I was so drained that every time I sat down to study I fell asleep. I had stopped smoking for two years by then. But with all the pressure on me once again I went back to my old habit. I convinced myself I would quit as soon as finals were over.

My family drove down for graduation and Bill flew in for it. My goal of graduating before I was 35 had been reached. It took eight years and six transfers to receive a BS in Business Administration with the equivalent of a minor in Architecture. That weekend Bill managed to make everyone uncomfortable. At one point, he upset Lil' Bill so much that he stormed into the house, calling his father names. I reprimanded him for doing that and sent him to his room. Lil" Bill proceeded to climb out the window and run away. I didn't know it then, but previously when I had sent the boys to Washington for a weekend, their father had introduced them to a female friend of his. While we were looking for Lil' Bill, husband Bill had slipped away to call his girlfriend. In the meantime Bob figured out where Lil' Bill was and took my father there to get him.

When graduation was over, Bill went back to DC and my family went back to Michigan. I was left with moving to St. Louis and closing on the house by myself, and I only had a week to do it. After loading all day, the boys and I drove to St. Louis pulling the motorcycle trailer with all the bikes on it.

The next day I dropped the trailer off at the new house after I inspected it and then ran around trying to close on it. I was functioning on the two hours sleep I had received while catnapping in the car. Once the signing was done, I went to the house and crashed on the floor for a couple more hours of sleep before the truck came with the household goods. Everything was on schedule and so was the unloading.

❖

Bill was due home in a couple of weeks, so I worked like crazy trying to get the house ready. I wanted the time when he returned for us
to be a family again. But as soon as he got home, I noticed a change
in him. He was working in the bedroom hanging wallpaper when
finally I couldn't take it anymore and asked him what the problem was.
That is when he told me about his girlfriend in Washington. I was
crushed. I felt as though my heart had been ripped out of my chest.

He decided he had to go back to Washington to see her and he
asked me to drive him to the airport. I agreed, only for a chance to talk
some sense into him. "Bill, I don't understand, what did I do wrong?"
His answer stunned me.

"I don't like the way you use the word 'irregardless' it is not a word.
The word is 'regardless.'"

"That's a cop-out! Who are you trying to kid? Ruin a marriage after
13½ years because you don't like the way I say a word? That doesn't
even make sense!"

Then he hurled a couple of untrue accusations at me. These events
happened on Father's Day weekend, 1979. It was devastating. I lived on
water and cigarettes, while confining myself to the bedroom. I couldn't
get up. I couldn't look the world in the face. For the boys' sake, I finally
got myself together and called a church—just any church. I had to talk
to someone. I dialed several church numbers before I finally dialed a
church phone number where the Associate Pastor answered. He was
gracious enough to take one hour out of his Father's Day and talked
with me after their morning service. The most profound thing that
came out of that meeting was his reaction to my feeling guilty about my
feelings towards Bill. "Don't ever feel guilty about your feelings," he
said, "because they are your feelings. It is how you react to those feelings that is important." I have never forgotten those words of comfort
whenever I've had negative thoughts or feelings.

When I came home, Bill called and said he was coming home and
was going to be a husband again. I took the boys out to get their father
a special Father's Day present—an ID bracelet with the inscription on
the back saying, "Love Will Keep Us Together." When we picked him
up, I pretended that nothing had happened, and so did the boys.

❖

Bill *insisted* that I get a job for the first time in our marriage, so I
did. It didn't pay much, but I was on the drawing board as a sales engi-
neer for a demountable partition company and I drew the working
drawings for the carpenters in the field and ordered the supplies.

Bill's new job took him all over the country. He would sometimes be gone for a month at a time. I felt that the long TDY's were planned deliberately. I eventually found out that he was building a chain of girlfriends. I kept thinking this would pass, but it got worse instead. Though he traveled so much, he continually kept his controlling hand on the kids and me. His efforts were such that I tried to give my all in reconciling, forgiving him and by trusting him again and again.

Although Bill wanted me working, he didn't like it. This was all new to him. He wasn't the center of attention in my life anymore. I had some things to share at the dinner table outside of the stories about what the boys did that day; we no longer had to listen only to his stories. I was really enjoying it. From my perspective my education was an asset to our relationship, but not to him.

❖

After several months, he told me he was getting an apartment. I found out that his girlfriend from Washington D.C. was coming to town and he had to have a place for her to visit him. I was so crushed over the turmoil building in our marriage that I began doing things that a suspicious wife does. I even staked out his apartment, wanting to get a look at my competition. That proved to be a flop, because my pull to take care of the boys got in the way of my detective work, so I stopped. Inside though, my heart was breaking.

❖

After two months in the apartment, Bill moved back home and was off again on another lengthy TDY assignment. In the meantime, I was adjusting to being a working mother, which I didn't like! I'd rather be home with the boys when they got home. Having latchkey kids now bothered me. I was feeling like a failure in mothering and being a wife at the same time.

Finally one night, when Bill was home ignoring me, I couldn't take it any more. Something inside me exploded—I had had enough. I went into the closet, grabbed an armful of his clothes and threw them down the stairs, hangers and all. Bill came to see what was going on and kept telling me, "Honey, don't do this, please!"

"Get out! If you're not going to be a husband, get out!"

Bill finally moved out for good, but not before he told me that he had contacted a venereal infection. He blamed me for giving it to him and threw awful untrue accusations at me. Apparently, he was accusing me of everything he was doing himself. So I went to the doctor and got a clean bill of health to prove to him that he was the culprit. To Bill, however, I was still the guilty person because he knew where he got it from. From that point on, I didn't want anything to do with him. That is when the battle got tough. I was now the enemy, the adversary! I had finally told Bill, "No, more!" after taking him back several times because he professed how much he loved me.

❖

The thought of another man in my life was the last thing I wanted, but Bill tried to get one for me. He wanted me to go out with a visiting emissary from another country that he was dealing with when he came to the St. Louis area. Bill's condition was that I would have sex with him before I went out with whomever he would set me up with so that I wouldn't be tempted by the other man. Naturally I declined the invitation on all counts. That didn't make him happy.

Once he had me meet one of his girlfriends at a bar, who supposedly was going to teach me the art of picking up men. What an insult! The woman was your typical 40-year-old, not striking but well kept. She didn't have any trouble picking up men. I had remembered years earlier I had asked Bill why some women who might be plain Janes get hit on and the more attractive women don't. He used me as an example and said, "Men don't hit on you because you don't look like you want to get hit on. It is all in your actions." Well, at least I knew I was safe.

❖

It was hard for me to hide what was going on at work because Bill kept making harassing phone calls during working hours. I was working on the drawings for the largest project the company I worked for had ever contracted for, the historic Wainwright Building remodeling project. The man who sold the job and I had to work closely together. The two of us were going over the plan and some of the special application that was needed for the system when I broke down, crying for no apparent reason. "Bonnie," he said. "You need a friend."

"No, I'm fine. I'm OK."

"Do you have any friends in St. Louis?"

"I haven't been able to make any because of my circumstances. Every time I think I might have one, Bill starts harassing them and they tell me to stay away."

"You don't deserve this treatment."

"It's OK. I'll be all right."

"No, you need a friend who is not afraid of Bill Stuck. I'm going to be your friend!"

"You don't know what you are getting yourself in to. He will create problems for you."

"This Marine is not going to let some Army punk walk all over a woman like you."

"Don't, Denny. You have your family to think of."

"You need a friend. I'll be your friend. Don't you ever hesitate to call me day or night." That was Denny Domino; he was Italian and was raised near The Hill in St. Louis. He used to tease about mob connections. Evidently, his father did have some serious connections when he was growing up. Larry's offer seemed almost as if he was looking for a good confrontation.

❖

Every weekend Bill would pick up the boys and take them to his apartment. When they were sleeping sometimes he would come over and harass me. He still had the key to the house, so he came and went as he pleased.

❖

August 13, 1980, was Bob's tenth birthday so I planned an overnight with he and his friends in the backyard. Bill insisted on being there for his son's special day. After the boys were tucked in, I went to bed. Bill took it upon himself to stay the night. As the evening wore on, Bill began to force himself on me. I didn't want anything to do with him. As he was forcing me, I screamed at him, "Why don't you go get one of your whores and leave me alone?"

At that, Bill started slugging me for the first time in our marriage. Back and forth he swung. He suddenly stopped because the phone rang. He answered it, and I took the opportunity to hide. I had to think fast. Where would be the best place? *Bob's closet,* I thought, *under the toys.*

Bill got off the phone and started looking for me, calling my name. Finally, he came to Bob's room. When he found me he was sweet, phony sweet. "I just want to be with you," he said in a crying tone. "I love you."

"Leave me alone!" I insisted and walked out of the house. I left Bill with the boys, went to a local bar and sat outside watching the drunks coming out. It repulsed me so much that I went home and sneaked upstairs to Lil' Bill's bedroom to sleep. Shortly, Bill was crawling in bed with me. "Leave me alone!" I shouted again.

"I just want to be with you. I won't touch you. I promise."

The next morning when we went downstairs to fix the boys breakfast, there was the worst look on Bob's face. It had started raining during the night and the boys had moved inside. All of them had heard the activities of the night. Bill and Bob had never in all their lives seen nor heard their father and I arguing, so that night was total shock treatment for them. *What were we doing to the boys?* I wondered. *How can I prevent them from getting hurt?*

❖

One Saturday, Bob was over at a friend's house and Lil' Bill and I were running errands. I drove by work and saw Denny's car there. I decided to go to the gas station up the road and call him.

I pulled into the gas pumps and Lil' Bill, then 12, got out to fill up the tank. Suddenly the car door opened and Bill leaped in the car, locked the doors, grabbed my throat with his hand and pressed my neck and head against the headrest. I couldn't breathe. He started calling me all sorts of names because he found out that Denny had been helping me.

Lil' Bill started banging on the window, and Bill stopped. Then he snatched my keys and got out of the car hollering at me. I went to pay for the gas, Bill continued to holler and make a scene. Lil' Bill was embarrassed; he had never seen his parents acting like this, especially in public. He walked towards the back of the station. At that moment, Bill threw my keys over the station. Lil' Bill saw them land and picked them up without anyone knowing. I was pacing back and forth trying to get away from Bill because I didn't have my keys. I paced past Lil' Bill and he slipped me the keys.

"Get in the car!" I whispered. So he did. When the timing was right, I leaped into the car and took off. Bill sped out behind me and I headed towards home. Suddenly, Bill whipped his car to the right and drove down the road waving and wearing this silly grin on his face. "He is going after Denny," I said.

"Mom, go home. Denny can take care of himself."

So I listened to Lil' Bill. I was beginning to listen to Lil' Bill more and more. The wisdom that 12-year-old had was incredible.

By this time Bill and I had a separation agreement, *written by him*. I was to live in the house with the boys and he would make the payments. He wrote it exactly the way he wanted it, including rights to his military retirement. The lawyer obviously sided with him in court when the judge questioned it. "Your honor, there is no reason to get carried away about this, it is only a 'Separation Agreement.'" I couldn't bring myself to divorce Bill, but I wanted my independence from him and to let him know I was serious.

I was offered another job with one of the other contractors while I was working on the Wainwright project. I knew I had to make that change when my boss called me into his office one day and told me they were not going to put up with Bill's harassment and advised me to go back to Michigan.

❖

I needed a break and a trip to Michigan sounded good, so while Bill was out of town I decided to go. I wrote him a note and told him that the boys and I were going on vacation to Michigan before school started. While I was gone, I began checking out lawyers and looking into a divorce. The Michigan attorneys informed me that I needed to take the boys back to St. Louis. One of them was good enough to line me up with a St. Louis Attorney.

While still at my sister's house, Bill called begging me to come back to St. Louis and confessed how much he loved me. He also told me that he had patched the holes he made in the wall when he found my note. He had taken everything my mother and sister had given us and smashed it against the wall. He blamed them for our problems.

❖

My first stop back in St. Louis was the lawyer's office to get a restraining order and check into a divorce. Bill was on another TDY assignment already when we got back. The Lawyer initiated a restraining order on Bill. Then that next Monday, I started my new job the same day that the boys started school. Mid morning, I received a call from Bill. "The school called me. Bob is sick, and they didn't know how to get a hold of you."

"Oops! I forgot to give them my new work number."

"It's started already, huh? Neglecting the kids! I'm coming over to get you!"

I had no choice but to tell my boss about my situation on the first day. I told him before I left that I had gone to the court for protection the day I left to go up to Michigan, and that the judge recommended I change the locks on the doors. Then I went on to ask him about the phone call he received from Bill.

While I was gone, Bill had found my new boss, Jim's phone number by the telephone and called him trying to find out why I had this man's number. He was thinking it was a boyfriend.

"I couldn't figure out why he was calling. It was so strange." Jim said. "Why don't you go take care of your son?"

"Well, Bill will be here soon."

"We will deal with it. Bonnie, I am sending one of my men over today and changing your locks."

"Thank you. I don't know what is going to happen, but I can't let any of you get involved." I as much as quit my job, because I knew the problems that Bill was going to start making.

I went to pick up Bob from school. When I got to the house Bill was checking my mail. I stayed home with Bob after Bill left to go back to work. The locksmith came over and changed all of my locks to the one key he had.

❖

When we realized that the separation needed to be a divorce. I was still living in the house with the boys and Bill had an apartment. To let the boys know about our decision to divorce Bill sat the boys down and said, "Your mother and I are not going to make it. We are getting a divorce and you boys have a choice. You can either tough it out with Mom on the street with nothing or you can live with me in the house. Lil' Bill said, "I'm going to take care of Mom." Bob, however, said, "I'm going to stay with Dad."

Bill would do no negotiating with my lawyer. He had a lawyer, then he didn't. When my lawyer refused to call him back and talk with him, Bill harassed me to get what he wanted. I can't remember how many times I called the police on him, but nothing worked.

❖

One evening when I called the police on Bill, the policeman that responded to my call was in the kitchen with me getting the information about the mishap. Bill called 10 times in 10 minutes. The policeman said, "That is terrible!"

"That is what I live with day and night and nobody will help me because he is an officer and gentleman in the United States Army."

"Why don't you get a block on your phone and have the phone company press charges for harassment?"

That is exactly what I did. We caught him for 26 phone calls in 30 minutes. Now it was up to the Southwestern Bell to press charges.

❖

One weekend after the locks were changed, Bill came to pick up the boys. For some reason he went to use his key in the front door instead of going through the garage, which the boys had open. When it didn't work, rage built in him and he charged around through the garage and upstairs where I was. He started hollering about my changing the lock and grabbed me by the throat and pushed me down on the bed still holding me. In the background, I could hear Lil' Bill yelling at his father and charging up the stars. Bill took his hands off of my throat and took my only key to the house. Then he took the boys away for the weekend. I was scared to death after that. Now the only key to the house was in his hands, and I couldn't ask Jim to change the locks again.

Before I went to bed that night I barricaded the door. I wasn't afraid of a thief. I was afraid of Bill. I shoved all sorts of furniture in front of the door. That would give me time to get to the phone and call the police when he came over after putting the boys to bed. I must have dozed because the first thing I heard was him crashing through the door shoving all of the furniture aside. By the time I got downstairs he was in the kitchen and had taken the phone off the hook.

"Get out of here and leave me alone. Where are the boys?"

"They're sleeping."

"They're sleeping and you leave them to come over to harass me? Just leave me alone."

He finally left after we argued for some time, but not without having the last intimidating word. I called the police, now that I had a restraining order. As the officer was questioning me he asked, "What does he do for a living?"

"He's in the Army."

"What rank, Ma'am?"

"Major."

"Oh, I'm sorry Ma'am. This is a military matter. You need to call the Military Police.

"I have a restraining order."

"I'm sorry, Ma'am. I'll take the information if the Military Police want to do something. Then we'll have the record for them."

The next day I called the Military Police. They treated me as though I was a distressed housewife and said, "This is a civil matter. We can't get involved."

That restraining order wasn't worth the paper it was written on, and the MP's wouldn't help either!

❖

It was nearing time for Bill's 36th birthday; I took the boys shopping to get their father a present. My plan was to drop the boys off at his apartment with presents I had them buy. I also gave the boys money to take their father out for pizza. Bill saw us drive up and he came to the door when the boys got out of the car, presents in hand. Bill asked me if I was coming. "No!" I said. He then took the presents from the boys and threw them at the car. The boys ran to the car, jumped in, and I took off. Bill ran to his car and took off after us. I pulled into the drive. We didn't even get out of the car and there was Bill blocking the driveway and getting out of his car. I just sat there, not wanting to get out after seeing his last display of anger.

❖

Bill went away again on TDY and called after the boys were in bed, as usual. In that conversation, he threatened to kill me in such a way that no one would be able to pin it on him; then he would have the boys. I was so scared I turned off all the lights in the house. Bill had been in Vietnam, and I knew that he had killed before; therefore, the danger was real and immediate to me. I called my lawyer and told him. He said, "Are you that scared?"

"Yes."

"Ok, go to Michigan. I'll have him in jail." My lawyer always talked tough, but never delivered.

I called my sister and told her. Of course I could come. It wasn't easy, but I made it to Michigan. Once there, I knew Bill's schedule. My family wanted me to get my things and bring them up there. That would take a large truck, and I had never driven a truck before.

Bill was going to be TDY again for about three days, so we made plans. I was to fly down to St. Louis. Denny would pick me up from the airport. From there we would get a U-Haul and go to the house. Because I didn't have the keys to the house, I called the police to meet me there with the separation agreement giving me the house. He couldn't break in for me, but he could supervise my breaking in through the garage entrance.

Once inside, Denny and I had to work fast. I just told him what had to go, and he loaded the truck by himself in six hours. I left Bill what we had agreed upon. Then Denny took me on a test drive, giving me instructions on driving the truck. It was a stick, which wasn't the problem. The problem was the size. Once he was satisfied with my driving skills he went home. I stayed a couple more hours to get some rest before hitting the road at 10 P.M. I was only able to average about 45 mph, so the trip took 16 hours. I pulled over in a truck stop in the wee hours of the morning to get some sleep.

❖

Bill was livid when he got back to a half empty house. He made three trips up to Michigan—two surprise ones and one planned. The first trip was by car. As usual he made all kinds of noise, but unbeknown to us he had a gun. He found out that the boys were over at Randi (my niece) and Sam's house so he proceeded to go over there. Sam, a large farm boy who doesn't scare easily, came out and they had words. A couple hundred feet away was a Sheriff's deputy that Randi had called watching the whole thing. Bill proceeded to walk around to the back of the car and changed his shirt. While he was doing so, he made sure that Sam saw a handgun that he had in the back of the car. The Sheriff's deputy couldn't see it from his vantage point. He allowed Sam to see him move the gun twice.

Bill made a comment to the Sheriff's deputy after Sam told him to get off his property. "There is nothing you can do. I'm not breaking any laws—I know the law." All the while trying to intimidate Sam.

Sam glanced down the road and spied Bob, he had gone down to the neighbor's farm to buy some fresh butter. When Bob saw his father, he darted across the highway and ran behind the neighbor's house and came around the back way to sneak into Randi and Sam's house. The boys were inside with Randi, scared and cowering not knowing what was going to happen. Intimidating Sam didn't work so Bill tried to intimidate by threatening to go to my parent's house.

I was at my parent's house helping my father build his new garage. We had just gotten the side wall up when my mother came out and told me that Bill was on the way and to get out of there. I fled out of there by taking the back road route to my sister's house. My parents went to the Mason Police Department and spent the afternoon there, informing the police of Bill's irrational behavior.

❖

It wasn't the kids he wanted; it was me. He had been trained to stalk out the enemy and use any type of intimidation he could to flush them out into the open, and I was now his enemy, and I couldn't understand what I had done to become one.

I made it back to the Grand Rapids area, without incident. Bill had to get back to St. Louis for work, so he had to leave Michigan.

Whenever Bill called and talked to the boys, the conversations were upsetting to the boys. While in the same room with the boys when their father called, we could hear him screaming at them over the phone.

❖

One day the only one at my sister's house was Randi. Suddenly she heard the whooping noise of a helicopter overhead, really close. She looked out the side window and there was an Army helicopter close enough for her to recognize the pilot—Bill. He was supposedly getting the flight time required to maintain his flight pay. Another pilot was in the helicopter with him. My brother-in-law reported the incident, but of course the other pilot backed Bill's story that they were near the house, not buzzing it. This was his second surprise visit.

❖

His third trip was at Christmas. He took the boys skiing up North. On their way back to Grand Rapids, I received a call from Bob telling me that he was going to go back to St. Louis with his father and that they were going to drop Bill off on the way. I knew this was another one of Bill's plots to get to me.

It finally worked. New Year's Eve, Lil' Bill and I drove down to St. Louis to try to make it work for the seventh and last time. I was frightened by what I saw when I met Bill. At one point, I looked in his eyes and there was a deep, dark emptiness there. The look scared me. He had been fixing dinner for our return and wouldn't let me help. As he was pealing potatoes, he had a knife in his hand and the way he was handling it as we talked bothered me. I was wondering, *how can I ever trust him again.* I imagined him killing me if I turned my back or refused his advances.

Moments later, Lil' Bill whispered to me, "The car is loaded Mom," and went outside. I followed behind. When Bill realized I went outside he came charging outside with the knife still in his hand. Lil' Bill was by the car. I was halfway there. Bob was in the house watching television.

I was so torn as Bill stood there pointing the knife to himself, saying, "What do you want me to do, kill myself?" In my heart I wanted to help him, but I was so scared of him and the look in his eyes that I had never seen before troubled me deeply.

Out of the dark came Lil' Bill's voice. "Move it, Mom, now!" I immediately ran to the car, and we were off.

❖

The day of the divorce came right after I began working a new job as a sales person for an office furnishings company. I was scared to go to the court because nothing had really been worked out with the lawyer. No formal settlement was made yet. All we had was the separation agreement that needed to be modified and that was it. At the last minute, Bill finally got a lawyer to represent him. So there were the four of us in a room just outside the courtroom trying to negotiate. Because Bill and I had talk about a couple of things over the previous weeks, because of Bill's unrelenting persistence, my lawyer became very unhappy with me and decided to drop me, then and there! He abruptly got up and said, "I have other cases to take care of today." There I sat with Bill and his lawyer; I was stripped of whatever was left including the military retirement tucked away in the separation agreement Bill had written.

When we got into the courtroom, the judge didn't like the splitting of custody of the boys: "Why isn't the mother taking both of the sons?" he asked.

"Because she can't afford to, your Honor."

"Then give the father both sons!"

I turned to Bill and said, "You did it, didn't you? You got the house, the whores and the boys. I hope you are proud of yourself."

Then Bill's lawyer spoke up assertively in *my* defense, "Your Honor, you can't do that to this woman. This man is stripping her of everything—you can't take the last thing she has from her."

The judge relinquished and let me have custody of Lil' Bill.

❖

One day the phone rang at work. It was Denny. He had a sales call in the industrial park that I worked in and spied Bill, so he stopped and called to warn me. While he was talking to me on the phone he suddenly said, "Oh, no, here he comes." I could hear Bill yelling at Denny in the background. Then the phone went dead. I told the office manager. "Get out of here, Bonnie. Take a long lunch hour. I will cover for you," she said.

The office manager, Cheryl called the police as well as John, the warehouse man in back for support. Just moments after I had left, Bill showed up. Cheryl and John met Bill at the door when he came in. Bill had jumped Denny and ripped his toupee off of his head. He had a piece of it in his hand and threw in on the reception desk, hollering obscenities about me at them. Both of them thought it was part of Denny's scalp and were scared half to death.

❖

I really thought the divorce would end the harassment, but I was wrong. Shortly after the divorce, I received a phone call from a Detective Donald Southerland of the St. Louis County Police Department. He had just received a complaint from Southwestern Bell about the harassing phone calls. I talked for the better part of an hour, filling him in on the events of the last two years. When I finished he said, "My God, woman, why are you still sane?" Coming from a police officer I felt maybe I wasn't imagining the terror that Bill was putting me through and getting away with.

"Bonnie, this is what I am going to do," he said. "I am going to call Bill down here about the Southwestern Bell's complaint. I will tell him that he is not to see you, call you or communicate with you in any way. He won't know it, but I am going to arrest him. If he as much as calls you I want you to let me know right away. OK?"

"Yes, sir, but it won't do you any good. That won't stop him," I replied.

❖

The next day Det. Southerland called and let me know that he did as he promised and had Bill come down to the station. He arrested Bill while he was in uniform. Bill removed his military shirt for the ride down to the jail, where they processed him. I don't know exactly where he was, but he had just bailed himself out and was on the phone calling my office. The office manager answered the phone and took the message. "You tell Bonnie that I have her son!" He supposedly was calling from my apartment. I called the police to have them meet me at my apartment. Before I went to the apartment, I made plans for Lil' Bill and me to take refuge in Illinois that night with one of the girls in the office. Bill would have no idea where we would be.

When I got to the apartment, Lil' Bill told me his father had been there and had used the phone. The policeman arrived. After he gathered the information he volunteered to go and talk to Bill. I just laughed, saying, "He was just arrested for harassing me and was told in no uncertain terms to leave me alone. The restraining order isn't worth the paper it was written on, and you're going to talk to him? Good luck!"

Lil' Bill and I did spend the night in Illinois and waited until we heard from Det. Southerland before we left. He finally called about 10:00 A.M. the next day and I filled him in. "OK, Bonnie, this is what I am going to do. I am going to the Army and get this taken care of. We'll let him think he is getting away with this for a day or so. You'll hear from me."

The next thing I knew I heard from Colonel McKenny in charge of the St. Louis' area CID (Central Intelligence Division). He wanted to come down and question the people I worked with about Bill's activities.

The next phone call I received at work in reference to Bill's activities was from the general's aide. "Bonnie," he said. "This is Skip. I want you to know that I am on leave and have been called in for this. Det. Southerland came down here, demanding attention for Bill. The general is in California, but is taking a special red-eye flight in specifically to meet with you and Colonel McKenny. I am trying to coordinate that meeting," he said. "I promise you, Bonnie, Bill does not know the general is coming in early and you don't have to worry about him finding out. Can I tell the general you will meet with them tomorrow morning at 0800 hours at the airport—in the Ambassador's Club?"

I was reluctant about meeting with Bill's commanding officer. I didn't want to get him in trouble, but I was tired of the harassment. So hesitantly I said, "Yes, I will."

"Bonnie, I want you to know something. Bill and I have been jogging on lunch. He has been telling me what he has been doing to you and the kids. I'm have been in yours and the kid's corner all along."

"Thanks, Skip. I appreciate it."

As I was driving to the airport the next morning, I had no idea what I was going to say to the general. After all, he was Bill's Commanding Officer. I finally decided that I'd cry when I needed to cry, laugh when I needed to, swear if the occasion called for it, and just let it all come out. All the while, I was afraid of Bill finding out.

The meeting was in a private room. Both the general and the colonel sat on the opposite side of the table and were stone-faced. As they asked questions and I answered, I could tell they thought me just a distressed housewife. I tried to be as thorough as possible in my stories, but they didn't budge.

Finally the general asked the crucial question: "Did he do any of these things in uniform?"

"Yes, sir, he did." Then I went on to tell which things he did with his uniform on and that he was arrested in uniform.

That did it! He said, "Would it help if I transferred him out of St. Louis?"

"A little, maybe," I said hesitantly.

Bill received the worst OER (Officer Efficiency Report) of his career and though he could not be stopped from making lt. colonel the general promised he would never make full colonel. When Bill found out, of course, he blamed me for ruining his career in the military and going behind his back.

The general did as he promised and transferred Bill to Huntsville, Alabama. Bob, of course, went with him. After a few months, Bob came back to St. Louis to live with me. The phone calls continued for a while even long distance so I called the phone company again for another block. They were unable to do so because of interstate laws. Eventually Bill gave up and left me alone.

Bill remarried and retired two years later from the military. He sent me one third of his military retirement, in addition to child support that he had promised me since I had been his wife during most of his career! He did so for two years, then abruptly quit the retirement money.

❖

I loved the military and the life it offered—the excitement of moving from place to place, the close community, the regamentation, the saluting the flag on post every evening at sundown when the cannon boomed, the National Anthem being played before the movie in post theatres, the nationalistic espirit and just the sense of security that military life offers. The military man is who I had to struggle with. Sadly, that part of my life was over, but the good memories of military life remain dear to my heart.

❖

I plodded along as a single parent. For twenty years I felt the pain of my marriage and break-up with Bill daily—I couldn't allow myself to be vulnerable ever again. I had to be tough and I could not allow myself to care that much again about anyone or anything. And I didn't until…. That is the rest of the story.

CHAPTER VI

The Call

By the time I was 39 years old, I felt like a hopeless failure. I had a job, but I could not make ends meet. It was almost four years after my divorce, and I was still not able to buy Christmas presents for my sons.

My 39th Christmas—I remember it very well. I was going to be alone because I could not afford to drive to Michigan to be with my family. My son Bill and I lived together, and my other son, Bob, lived with his father and stepmother. Both boys were going to spend Christmas with their father.

I was so financially tight I made Christmas presents. I crocheted the boys' facemasks out of some scrap yarn I had stashed away somewhere. When I held it up, it looked like a bra for a one-breasted woman.

My son's father had become successful as a civilian, had married a younger woman who was a high school drop out with two children of her own, and loved planning holiday trips. This was one of those trips. He was taking the whole family to Colorado skiing for a week. They planned to stop by my place, drop Bob off for an hour to visit with me, and then take both boys on the skiing holiday.

The night before the ski holiday, Bill, then fifteen years old, and I were sitting on the sofa together. We were both emotional as I began to apologize for not being able, once again, to provide Christmas gifts. My son spoke up and said, "Mom, I am so afraid for you."

"Why is that, Sweetheart?"

"I'm afraid that you are going to be a lonely old lady."

I burst into tears. "Bill, if I turn into a lonely old lady it is because I choose to do so. I cannot compromise. I don't do things the way others do and—I don't ever want you cheating yourself out of your future because you think you have to take care of your lonely old mother. I am capable of taking care of myself." That moment turned into both of us crying and holding each other for quite some time.

The time came for the boys' father to drop Bob off for his quick visit. Bob was his normal good-natured self as I presented him with his gift of the ski mask. He was sweet and did not make fun of me. Their father returned to pick up the boys to depart for Colorado, but I did not see him. He sent one of his stepchildren to let the boys know he was back. My son told me later that his father questioned whether I gave him a gift because he did not see Bob with one when he went to the car. To avoid embarrassing me over the mask, he told his father, "No."

That holiday week I drowned myself in my work, fighting loneliness and feelings of hopeless failure. All my efforts failed. The agony I went through over my failure was terrible. All I wanted to do was die. I was too cowardly to commit suicide, even though I planned it out so that my attempt wouldn't fail. I kept thinking of my boys and what they would think of me. So instead I cried out, "God, if you're real, take me tonight—I don't want to wake up anymore." Then I went to bed, not totally convinced yet there was even a God.

❖

As I settled in to go to sleep, something unusual began to happen. A vision started taking form. It began with a kaleidoscope going around and around. The shapes and colors were splendid. As I watched, I suddenly became aware that the shapes were starting to take form, and a face slowly came into view. I eventually recognized the face I had seen so many times in my Sunday School class. It was Jesus! I did not really know Jesus, because I had spent so many years as an agnostic/atheistic/evolutionist (my beliefs were uncertain even to myself), but there was no question who this was. Jesus pointed me to a path. I started running on it. I can remember I was so happy, because I thought I was dead, and it appeared I went the right way.

As I ran up the path, I was stopped abruptly and was held suspended in mid-motion. I kept struggling to go further, but I couldn't. I looked up, and was amazed when I saw an angelic form stopping me. Instantly, I realized this angelic form was my Grandma Parker (my mother's mother). She stood there with her hand up, stopping me with her motion.

I cried out to her, "Grandma, take me with you!" She motioned me again to stop, and I cried out again, "Grandma! Grandma, take me with you, please!" She didn't speak as one would expect her to speak, yet the message came directly to me through her spirit.

"Go back, child, go back. Your job is not finished yet."

"What job, Grandma? What job?"
"Go back, child, go back."
"Grandma, I want to come with you!" I cried.
"Go back."

❖

The vision faded, and I fell into one of the deepest sleeps I had ever experienced. The next morning I was refreshed, and felt renewed. I could not figure out what the message, "Your job is not finished yet," meant. I was nobody and had nothing to offer anyone. What on earth could be in store for me.

CHAPTER VII

City Jail

It was January, 1987. Four years had passed since I had the vision of Jesus and my grandmother, and there was still a great emptiness in my heart. I was frustrated and in a rut. I was a salesperson and was selling office interior design and contract furniture. Every Friday night I followed the same routine as I drove home from work, dreading the empty weekend ahead. If I had the money, I would make sure I had two packs of cigarettes, a two-liter bottle of diet cola and, if I was really flush, a two-pound bag of M&M's candy (sometimes I had to settle for a one-pound bag) before I got home. I would sit in front of the television and watch Miami Vice, admiring Philip Michael Thomas.

My parents were charter members of the Michigan Coalition for Literacy and had encouraged me to become involved in volunteer work. I resisted the thought, not wanting to receive anything my mother suggested. I had built a barrier around myself and shut my parents and others out of my life.

It was a cold Friday in January. I had my cigarettes, soda and M&M's, and my post-holiday depression was weighing me down. I was frustrated, too, because Miami Vice was canceled for that night, so I switched to another channel. During the break, an ad came on for the Missouri Literacy Coalition, similar to the one in Michigan. I had seen their ads before, but something was different about this one. The instructor was not teaching reading or writing—he was teaching math.

I didn't know the literacy program taught math, I thought. *I can teach math*. I jotted down the phone number. The next week I called the number and began asking questions about tutoring math. When the lady on the other end found out I was not afraid of the inner city, she was eager to have me involved in the literacy program.

"We have a twelve-hour training program for teaching reading. Would you be willing to go through it?"

"I want to teach math," I replied. "My reading skills are poor, and I don't think I'm qualified to teach others."

"If you can read at all," she said, "you can teach this program. Can I put you down for the next class? It starts in February. If you decide you don't want to do it, you can let us know then."

"Oh, okay, I'll try it," I said reluctantly.

That was the step I needed to take that would begin the change in my outlook and my life.

When I completed the twelve-hour training session in early February, 1987, I was given a list of nearly sixty centers to choose from. I narrowed the list to about thirty centers based on the days of the week. While scanning the list, one of the centers appeared to jump out at me. I didn't want to teach there, so I tried to ignore it, but over and over again I kept being drawn to that particular center.

I finally asked the instructor, "Are women allowed to volunteer at City Jail?"

"They have a woman there now," he said.

"Well, then, would you sign me up?"

"Sure."

I did it. I made the commitment to go to City Jail to work with the male prisoners, but not without a great deal of anxiety. Arrangements were made and I had my schedule for volunteering, but I really didn't want to teach there.

You see, at different stages of my life, beginning at the age of four, I had been a victim of rape, incest (by an older cousin), child molestation, assault, and I was terrorized for two years by my husband while living in the St. Louis area.

When I was four years old, the neighborhood Crazy Charlie was found trying to shove a stick in me. At eight, I was a victim of an overly aggressive older cousin of which I remember the details very clearly. When I was nineteen years old I was assaulted in broad daylight on a Dearborn street when I was walking home from a job interview. Then the most devastating to me psychologically was when my husband turned on me and stalked and terrorized me for two years.

All of this violence against me I kept to myself. I was so filled with fear and guilt feelings thinking I was to blame for every action against me.

❖

My first night at City Jail, I tried to shake my emotions as I continued to follow the guard's directions. I arrived at the office area, where several offices surrounded the perimeter wall. Three men sat in the only lit up office. They all looked up as I spoke. "Excuse me, I'm looking for Vaughn."

"I'm Vaughn," answered an average built, rugged looking, bearded man in his forties.

"I'm Bonnie Stuck. I am here as a literacy volunteer."

"I thought you were going to be here last week, from what they said."

"I'm sorry," I replied. "I wasn't sure from their instructions what I was supposed to do."

On the way to the sixth-floor classroom, Vaughn gave me a quick briefing on what to expect. I was one of three volunteers that night, one of two women, and the only one wearing a business suit.

The building was old, and so was the elevator, so I shouldn't have been surprised when I saw our transportation up to the classroom. The elevator was constructed of old iron bars. Every floor could be seen as we ascended, along with all the activity on that floor. Sometimes we could view two floors at a time. The elevator operator stopped at each floor and handed a list of inmates' names through the iron bars to the guard on duty. I saw many inmates on the trip up to the sixth floor, and they saw me. They would stop and look whenever they saw a woman.

At the sixth floor, we stepped out into a large empty room. In the center of the floor was a trap door, and high above it was the rigging that had been used during the days when hangings were performed in the jail. It is said that the sound of the trap doors swinging open used to echo throughout the whole building, and a gruesome spirit of death would fill the cell areas, affecting all occupants.

Just to the left of the elevator as we stepped off was the multipurpose room, where classes were held. At one end of the room was a gym set with weights for the men to exercise on. A glassed-in guard station was on the center of the wall opposite the elevator, with doors on either side of it that led to the psychiatric wing. Bookshelves with our supplies on them, surrounded with bars, were back in a corner behind the gym set. There were four eight-foot tables where the men sat. Each table seated six men. There were always a couple of minutes prior to the start of class to get the materials out, as the men entered the room one floor at a time.

I soon discovered the men's floor assignments meant something. The men on the fifth floor were the more seasoned men and usually older—if not in age, then in experience. The fourth floor housed the average inmate who had been around, but did not seem to have the same seasoned crust as the fifth-floor inmates. The third floor housed the younger men. Overcrowding was an issue, and they tried hard to keep the population number under the 625 maximum.

As I watched the inmates come in and take their seats, I noticed something that upset me. All of the inmates were black, and I could feel each one of them sizing me up. By the time the men were seated, it felt like each one had undressed and dressed me several times with his eyes—not a comfortable feeling, to be sure.

As I scanned the room, all I could see were eyes looking at me. Feeling like the new kid on the block, I inched myself back, trying to be less conspicuous. The focus was back on me when Vaughn introduced me to the men. I just nodded and smiled politely.

Discovering the statistics of these men didn't take long. Ninety to ninety-five percent of the jail's population were black males and eighty to eighty-five percent of the crimes in question were murder and/or rape. I was feeling uncomfortable and asked myself why I was there. Thoughts like *Don't smile; don't look scared; try not to get too close to the men, etc.*, were flooding my mind. *Oh no!* I thought, *I forgot to wash my perfume off. Definitely, don't get too close now.*

The other volunteers were being asked questions as the class progressed, and I started feeling like a bump on a log. Finally, one of the men motioned me over to ask a question. Wouldn't you know it? It was an English grammar question. Not being knowledgeable in English, I referred the question to Vaughn. The other men saw me trying and began to ask questions too.

One of the volunteers called me over to help with a more advanced math problem. Good! Math being my forte, I obliged. This inmate annoyed me; however. He appeared sharper than the other men did, and I sensed he could make it on the street. I felt he was toying with me and really knew the answers.

The only truly illiterate student we had, Thomas, was being tutored by one of the other volunteers, but I was to begin working with him on Thursday. We would alternate—Brad on Tuesdays, and me on Thursdays.

When I left the jail that first night, I didn't know what I was feeling, but I knew I was going to give it a chance and go back a couple more times before deciding. After meeting and working with Thomas the next Thursday however, I was hooked. I couldn't wait to go back.

CHAPTER VIII

The Parable Of The Sower

Jail is just like anywhere else in the world when it comes to sowing seeds. There are four types of spiritual soil, and my personal contact with four of the inmates will illustrate that the same four types of spiritual soil is found inside prisons, just as they are found on the outside. I have given fictitious names to two of the men, to protect their identities. For each man, I have given the interpretation of why I called him by his fictitious name and the type of ground they represent.

Maynard means Bold in Strength
- Represents the seed sown on the roadside.
- Pleaded guilty to first-degree murder, plea-bargained for time. Eligible for parole in seven years.

Thomas means Twin
- Represents the seed sown on the rocks.
- Pleaded innocent to first-degree murder.
- Found guilty—sentenced to life in prison.

Ralph means Wolf
- Represents the seed sown in the thorns.
- Pleaded innocent to first-degree murder.
- Found guilty (third felony conviction)—sentenced to death.

Gregory means Watchful One
- Represents the seed sown on good ground.
- Pleaded innocent to first-degree murder.
- Pleaded innocent to first-degree criminal assault.

- Found guilty of both—sentenced to life in prison without parole and life with parole, time to be served consecutively.

THE PARABLE OF THE SOWER

A farmer went out to sow his seed. As he was scattering the seed, some fell along the path, and the birds came and ate it up. Some fell on rocky places, where it did not have much soil. It sprang up quickly, because the soil was shallow. But when the sun came up, the plants were scorched, and they withered because they had no root. Other seed fell among thorns, which grew up and choked the plants. Still other seed fell on good soil, where it produced a crop-a hundred, sixty or thirty times what was sown. (Matt. 13:3-8 NIV)

THE SOWER EXPLAINED

Listen then to what the parable of the sower means: When anyone hears the message about the kingdom and does not understand it, the evil one comes and snatches away what was sown in his heart. This is the seed sown along the path. The one who received the seed that fell on the rocky places is the man who hears the word and at once receives it with joy. But since he has no root, he lasts only a short time. When trouble or persecution comes because of the word, he quickly falls away. The one who received the seed that fell among the thorns is the man who hears the word, but worries of this life and the deceitfulness of wealth choke it, making it unfruitful. But the one who received the seed that fell on good soil is the man who hears the word and understands it. He produces a crop, yielding a hundred, sixty or thirty times what was sown. (Matt. 13:19-23 NIV)

By the time I began visiting Maynard and Ralph at the penitentiary I was already a "born again" believer. Thomas' story was from my tutoring reading to him at City Jail, and Gregory I started visiting before I became a Christian. Gregory is who God used to draw me to Himself and become a follower of the Lord Jesus Christ.

MAYNARD – Bold in Strength

Maynard was my son's age. He was dark skinned and clean-shaven, and wore his hair short. He had two daughters mothered by his girlfriend.

As a student, I had little or no contact with Maynard, but the guards had warned me about him. "Watch Maynard, he's mean."

It wasn't until after Maynard left City Jail and went to the penitentiary that I began my contact with him. I needed the guys to go to bat for me by writing letters on my behalf, and Maynard was the first inmate to respond. He sent me a copy of the letter he wrote and included a personal note, which surprised me. He told me what penitentiary he was in and that he hadn't had any visitors, nor did he have any money. Because he was incarcerated near where I lived, I drove out to the penitentiary to get the paperwork necessary to get on Maynard's visiting list. Within a week I was approved, and drove out again to leave him $10.00. His mother could not visit because there was a warrant out for her arrest, so I decided to visit in her place

Maynard was quiet, so I did most of the talking. Later when he finally received money from home, he took some of it and had another inmate draw a 16 x 20 picture of me in pastels.

Maynard loved boxing and would have been classified a middleweight. He would swing at the air like many boxers do. He wanted to compete and win a trophy for me.

❖

I remember three stories about Maynard that illustrate the type of spiritual soil he represents. It was during our second visit that he asked me, "Bonnie, why are you doing this?" Maynard knew I visited a couple of other inmates from City Jail.

"I really don't know," I replied. "I wish I did, because it doesn't make any sense to me why I would even care about you guys, but I do. God has given me a love for all of you that cannot be explained. I feel there is so much wasted talent in prison—so many misdirected souls needing someone to teach them or show them a better way."

"What if one of us falls in love with you?"

"I'm old enough to be your mother—don't be silly."

"You just don't know, do you?"

I didn't pursue the conversation any further. Instead, I changed the subject and asked him about his reputation.

"Maynard," I said in a teasing fashion, "I heard something about you."

"What was that?"

"I heard you were mean. Are you mean, Maynard?"

"Where did you hear that?"

"A guard at City Jail told me you were mean." I paused. "Did you try to intimidate the guards? Are you mean, Maynard?" I don't think he really knew how to answer the question.

"Not to you."

"Are you telling me that I have to give you the nickname 'Mean

Maynard'?" Maynard just grinned.

❖

I had never seen Maynard really smile. Then one day he asked if the visiting room photographer could take a picture of us together.

"Sure," I said.

The visiting room photographer uses Polaroid's, so you can have the pictures right away. Maynard wanted the picture for himself. Who knows—maybe he wanted to prove to the guys from City Jail that I was really visiting him. The smile on his face in that picture was worth a thousand words. He had a beautiful smile.

He was not easy to talk to about anything, least of all the Bible. He would try, though. One day I asked him, "Maynard, what do you want out of life?" His answer shocked me.

"I want a Cadillac Fleetwood that I can drive around with one hand on the steering wheel."

"Is that all you want?"

"Yeah,"

"Why?"

"The dudes in the neighborhood who drive them are cool."

I was left speechless and wondering just how many Maynards there were in the world. I do know there are some in prison.

❖

I will never forget this third story. I had not planned to visit Maynard at all on this particular evening, but I found myself at the penitentiary visiting him because of something that happened earlier that day. I had gone to the park for lunch. It was mid-afternoon and I was not eating, just taking time to study the Bible. While studying, I sensed someone's presence near by. I began to look up slowly and recognized the familiar gray of the state issue penitentiary pants. I wasn't sure if I wanted to look any closer, but I did. Standing there looking down at me was a tall, young black man. He was just standing there, not three feet away. When we made eye contact he just smiled, nodded his head, and said, "Hello." Then he turned to walk away. The path he walked was strange. He skirted the table I was sitting at, then went off towards the lake. I thought it strange, but I just went back to my reading.

A short time later, as I was getting my things together, I looked up and saw the same young man sitting on the top of a picnic table a few yards away. I began to walk to my car, which was in his direction, and a still, small voice inside me kept saying, "Go and talk to him."

I recognized the voice. "Lord, I don't want to go talk to him. What do I say?"

The still voice said, "Go buy him lunch."

I was not sure I wanted to deal with what was happening, so I thought I would seek the Lord some more on this. I got in my car and began to pray, as I drove away from the young man, "Lord, what do you want me to do?"

Try as I might to hear something different, I kept getting the same answer over and over again, "Go buy him lunch." So I went to Wendy's, picked up two salads, and headed back to the park to give the young man a healthy lunch, but I couldn't find him. I looked and looked. I spotted a county police officer, so I stopped him and asked if he had seen a young man with state issue pants on. "No," he replied.

"Is it possible for someone to have just gotten out of prison and be walking around here with state issue pants?"

"Sure. A lot of times that's the only clothing they have."

I blew it, and I knew it. God had wanted me to talk to that young man about Him, and I let fear of the situation scare me away.

"Okay," I thought "if God wants me to talk to someone in state issue gray pants, then I will. I'll go visit Maynard tonight, and he'll let me talk to him about the Lord."

So that is exactly what I did. When I told Maynard the story of the guy in the park, he got concerned. "What are you doing sitting in a park alone?" he questioned.

"I do it all the time."

"What's the matter with you? You could get hurt."

"I do it all the time—besides, I was in Creve Coeur Park, not Forest Park."

I knew the men I worked with wouldn't want to hurt me, and they didn't want anyone else to hurt me either. I can't speak for all of them, but the ones I was the closest to let me know how some of the others felt.

During that visit I asked Maynard why he chose to plead guilty when all the others involved in his case pleaded not guilty.

"They got to serve more time than me. I ain't trying to fool nobody; I killed the guy."

"Maynard, if you had it to do all over again—would you help kill that guy?"

"Yep," he said without hesitation.

"Why? What did he do to you?"

"He killed my buddy."

"But that doesn't solve anything—oh, never mind. I came here to talk to somebody in gray pants about the Bible. Can I talk to you about the Bible?"

"Yeah."

"Good."

"I'm saved, Bonnie."

"You are? How do you know you're saved?"

"This guy came in the jail and asked me to say a prayer and told me I was saved."

"You mean he just led you through a sinner's prayer and told you, 'You're saved'?"

"Yeah."

I was speechless and infuriated. Maynard summed up my suspicion of some of the zealous groups of Christians who take note of the Scripture that says, "You visited me in prison," and they automatically think they have to go into prison to lead someone to Christ. Unfortunately, their motive is often gaining numbers, not nurturing souls. The true prison ministries nurture repeatedly and often go unnoticed by many, but the Lord knows those faithful servants. Maynard was indeed the seed that was sown on the roadside, where the birds came immediately and took it away. My mistake with Maynard was that I wasn't mature enough or knowledgeable enough spiritually to be a true prison minister.

THOMAS – Twin

I remember the first time I cried over a black man. His name was Thomas. Thomas could not read. He could copy other people's writing, but he could not create for himself. When I worked with him one session, he did wonderful; then the next session he seemed to forget most of what we worked on. He didn't seem to be able to retain information. Thomas was twenty-three years old, tall, dark-skinned and clean shaven, with a short-cropped haircut, and he was single. Thomas was awaiting trial for first-degree murder, along with four of his friends.

I was trying to teach Thomas how to read. What a beautiful sense of humor he had. He could make the dullest basic reading story fun. He would add his comic comments and make me laugh. Oh, he made me laugh. Thomas was magnetic and could be a real charmer. I could not stop thinking about his situation.

"My mother," he said, "doesn't want me calling her 'Mom' because it made her feel old."

He had a teacher one time, he told me, who took an interest in him, but then, as is common in the public education system, they passed Thomas up to the next grade. Thomas got promoted at the end of every school year until he was finally in the tenth grade and was old enough to drop out. Get a job? That is something Thomas could not do, because he could not read well enough to fill out a job application. All Thomas could do was to follow the crowd that accepted him and his imperfections.

I ached to be able to reach out to Thomas, but I couldn't. All I could see as I looked at him was a young man who had fallen through every crack in the system, and there was no one to help him.

Who would care for Thomas? I thought.

I cried. Oh, how I cried for Thomas, because I knew he would never be allowed to amount to anything in this life, yet he had such a delightful wit and winning personality.

Most everyone he knew at the jail called him by his nickname. "Hey, Flea Bag," they would say. I hated that name. Thomas had enough problems as it was. He should not have to go through life without any sort of dignity, because of a cruel nickname.

One day I asked Thomas, "What should I call you? What does your mother call you?"

"She calls me 'Man'," he said with a wide grin.

"'Man'? How come 'Man'?" I asked.

"Oh, I don't know, she just likes it I guess. Why don't you call me by my last name," he went on to say, "because I like it, and some other people call me that."

"If you don't mind, I would just like to call you Thomas, because that's your special name; and seeing no one else calls you that, I would like to. Would that be all right?"

His white teeth flashed against his exceptionally dark skin as he replied, "Yeah, I would like that." It didn't take long before Thomas began to wear his name with dignity. I was so proud of him and his accomplishments.

One day Thomas came into class with his buddies and sat down right where I was. He looked up at me as only Thomas could do with, his uneducated, innocent eyes, and said, "Bonnie...." He paused in a sheepish way, then said, "I, uh...I, uh...I think I love you." He put his head down shyly.

"Thomas," I said, as he looked up, "I <u>know</u> I love you, but it is the L-U-V love, not the L-O-V-E love."

"Yeah—that's it."

"Bless your heart, Thomas."

Thomas, like many others, will probably spend most of his life behind bars. I would like to believe, however, that someday someone will be able to take Thomas or others like him under their wing, take that immaturity and ignorance, and make use of it without spoiling the goodness that is there.

Thomas receives the Word quickly and enthusiastically, but he has no roots, so he easily forgets just like he did with his reading tutoring. It was like he had pockets in his mind. If you hit the right thing at the right time he would remember. It took a few weeks for him to even remember my name.

RALPH – Wolf

This is the hardest of the four to write about—not because of any violent or terrorizing act done by him, but because of my own sinfulness. Many past wounds began to surface during my contact with Ralph; some healing began in my life after visiting him.

Contact with Ralph made me realize my vulnerability and revealed to me some of my insecurities and weaknesses. Ralph was more knowledgeable of Scripture than I—that was not difficult seeing I was a brand new Christian and knew little of the Word. I was easily impressed by anyone who had memorized any amount of Scripture and seemed to use it in the right place.

Ralph was one of my more aggressive inmates. He was part of a group of men who would occasionally leave me notes on the table where they sat. They would write things like, "We love you Bonnie." The penmanship on the notes was exceptional, and I discovered it belonged to Ralph.

This aggressive group adapted a popular rap for me. Because of my own lack of spiritual knowledge and self-esteem at this point in my life, when I first read this I was flattered:

LADY "B" RAP
I'm Lady "B," I'm built so fine
I'm 36-24-36 and I'll blow your mind.
I'm 36 inches across the chest; I fear nothing
but the good Lord and death.
I walk through the grave, like a streak of thunder.
Make the tombstones jump, and put the dead in wonder.
I'm one of a kind; I'm hard to find.
Got all the young men standing in line.
I'm a lady of action, the main attraction.
Men call me for satisfaction.
I got the capitalization to rock the nation.
It's Lady "B" running this demonstration
If you don't believe these words I say
I'm certified proud by the USDA.

This is where my wounds began to show. I had never experienced any real respect from men in my life. Let me word it another way. I never received back from men the respect that I tried to show them. Men who might show me respect were turn-offs to me. I thought they were wimps. The more disrespectfully a man treated me, the more I seemed to be drawn to him. I'm not alone in this. Many women have this type of low self-esteem, and sexual child molestation, incest, rape or physical child abuses have victimized most of them. That is my story.

Because of a history of sexual abuse, I was usually attracted to boys who wanted to control or dominate me. The boy I loved the most, who later became my husband even treated me with disrespect as we have seen earlier. Probably to counteract the effects of the early abuse, I was not sexually active as a teenager, but I was not perfect by any means. Although I managed to remain a virgin until I was nineteen, I did get into some pretty heavy "petting" sessions during my teen years. My moral conscience was strong, but not so strong that my lack of self-image didn't challenge my moral stance. In other words, I lacked the moxie or the courage to tell someone to "buzz off" in a compromising situation. I felt like I had to give in a little, and at least do some petting to appease them, because it was "expected". Sometimes men do not realize the pressure they are putting on their girlfriends (and wives) when they want sex.

As I matured in the Lord, I began to develop a new self-image—one that no longer accepted disrespect as the norm. Just now, as I typed the rap for this book, I cringed at the disrespectful overtones and the vulgarity that really mocked God. How could I have thought it was flattering, even for a second? Perhaps now you will understand why I made the mistakes I did with Ralph.

❖

Ralph was a small, dark-skinned man, twenty-six years old, and had attractive features. Occasionally, he would grow some facial hair, which took away from his looks rather than adding to them. While at City Jail he wore his hair in plaits; but he cut them off before his trial, which really improved his appearance. Like so many of the men, he was very sober. He seldom smiled, but when he did he had a cute smile. I really didn't pay much attention to him because the other inmates who shared the table with him monopolized most of the time I spent at his table. They had that male fire going on inside of them, which was typical for young men who had been locked up for long periods of time. I would fuss at the guys like a mother would, and I really did not see them in a sensual light—or I should say, I did not want to.

Faithwalk

When I started working with the men I had been divorced six years, but had lived alone eight years. I did not date, nor did I have or pursue boyfriends. In those six years, I had six dates (if you could call them that), and was also stood up six times. There was no personal life. I wanted someone to care for me, but I knew that was impossible.

I did not want to know what crimes the men had committed. I heard stories, but I would push them aside. I could assume most of them were in for first-degree murder because of the statistics of the jail population, but I really wanted to leave it at that. No details, please!

❖

One day while watching the class, I was standing by Ralph. He spoke up, which surprised me. "Bonnie," he said, "are you afraid of me?"

"Should I be?" I asked.

"No."

"Well, then I'm not. Why do you ask?"

"Because my case involves a woman being killed."

"Oh." I dropped it there.

❖

One morning on the way to work, I turned on the radio just in time to hear the announcer say Ralph's name in reference to his case. He was found guilty of murder and was eligible for the death penalty. Tears flooded my eyes. The reality of the sentences some of my students would receive was becoming frightening to me. Although no one else seemed to be concerned, I truly cared about them. I didn't hear the entire announcement, so I had to wait until the next class night to find out.

The next morning I experienced a repeat performance when I turned on the radio, but this time I discovered more about the case. Again, I began to cry over the verdict. I thought of Ralph and the crime that was committed against an unsuspecting woman, and again, I questioned "why?"

I could not understand what was happening to me. I was feeling compassion for Ralph, even though I knew more about the crime now. I wanted to say something to him, but as could be expected, he was not in class that night. I asked one of the inmates how Ralph was doing.

"He's okay. Did you hear the verdict?"

"Yes, the past two mornings I turned on the radio and that was the first thing I heard. All I could do was cry."

I was working my bread-and-butter job, my job at the jail, for which I was now getting paid, and really developing my prayer life. Because I spent so many hours driving each day, my car became my prayer

64

closet. I had been praying for a _____ including Ralph. I asked him if he wanted me to go to hi _A6 – IU_ reply was, "Yes".

At the sentencing, prior to court convening, I gave Ralph some Scriptures that a friend of mine had given me for another inmate after he received two life sentences. I also had a quick minute to talk to Ralph's lawyer. He indicated the Ralph was going to need a lot of help to get this verdict changed. I should have paid more attention to the lawyer, but I didn't. As usual, I wanted to believe the best, and I thought I was "armed and dangerous" with the Scriptures I had given Ralph and all the praying I had been doing.

The proceeding began, and the judge was either wrestling with this case or was not prepared, because he ruled for an extension and declared another sentencing date. The ultimate decision, though, was for the death penalty. Months earlier I had found out when the inmates' birthdays were, and I would give them a note or a hand-made birthday card. I did the same for Ralph. Before he left for his sentencing, I handed his card to one of the inmates to give to him. Ralph received the death penalty on his 26th birthday, and I was the only one to remember. Even his mother forgot.

Ralph was returned to City Jail to await transportation to Death Row. Before he left for Death Row, he was allowed to come to class as usual. I discovered more things about Ralph and his case in the weeks prior to his departure. His so-called cohort in crime did not receive the death penalty. He was tried separately and received life in prison. But Ralph was considered a three-time loser, having previously been convicted of two other felonies. When the time came, they transported him directly to death row, bypassing the processing center. Ralph sent me the information I needed to get on his visiting list.

Death Row inmates have different visiting regulations than those in general population. They have unlimited visits. Seeing I was visiting other inmates, I made two trips a month to MSP (Missouri State Penitentiary) and alternated visiting Gregory and Ralph. I made sure I told both men what I was doing, so there were no questions.

The first visit with Ralph went without incident. I bought Ralph a nice Bible and sent him some warm clothes because he was complaining about the cold. He would ask for pictures and more pictures of me. Then he started asking for pictures of me when I was young. Ralph could be persistent, so I found a couple that I was willing to give up. But I told him, "The other inmates don't treat me like that."

"Good," he said.

That comment was a possessive one, and I should have been upset by it, but at the time I was flattered. This was a clear case of crossed signals—my response was dictated by the past experiences imbedded in my memory, affecting my mindset.

I cannot say for sure, but I think I visited Ralph six times. I would try to get him to focus on Scripture and to read it through the screen that was between us in the visiting room, but that would wane. The subject would shift to his case or how good he thought I looked that day. That was something I was not used to, and I ate it up.

The death row visiting area left much to be desired. The inmate side consisted of about eight stalls that were about three feet by three feet in size (they have revamped it since then). Each stall was connected to another, and there was a chain link fence gate between the stalls. So the man in the end stall had to go through the other six or seven stalls in order to enter or to exit, or to go to the bathroom, passing back and forth through the other stalls where other inmates had visitors. It was a nuisance, and there had to be supervision so that a ruckus didn't start.

The visitor's side of the fine mesh screening was just a ledge with a chair that could be pulled up to it, and the walls were all concrete block. On the screen you could see lipstick prints where the death row inmates would kiss their visitors through the screen. Perfect lip prints were at all heights and angles on the screen.

The visitors could get snacks from the vending area, but the inmates could not have any. All they were allowed in the six-hour visiting time (if their visit lasted that long) was coffee, and that had to be passed from stall to stall by the inmates.

After a couple of visits, Ralph became more comfortable with me. He flattered me, and I liked it; but as he was becoming more comfortable, the prayers I had while I was driving to the prison were getting more and more difficult. It was a draining spiritual battle for me to get through my prayers before entering the prison. I knew I could not go in unless I had peace, and peace was not easy to come by when visiting Ralph. I would fight through the spiritual conflict I was experiencing and push on, but I did not know to what mark. I became familiar with Ralph's case. He was not shy about discussing it. He said, "I sat in the car" while his partner slashed the woman's throat, and I believed him. He admitted his participation in the disposal of the body, but not the actual murder.

On this one particular visit, we were just talking casually. Ralph was in the end stall. He had a couple cups of coffee and they were working on him. All the stalls were full, so the routine to get to and from the men's room would take a long time, not to mention the frustration of the other inmates who had to stop their visit for him to get through. Ralph opted to urinate in the empty coffee cup he had. I turned my head and was feeling rather uncomfortable about the whole thing. I could hear him in spite of the noise in the room. Thinking he was finished, I looked around, and there was his penis right in front of me.

"It gets bigger," he said.

"Really?" I said. How do you respond to that?

We had a few unfavorable words, and I asked him not to do that again. I tried to make light of it, which was the wrong decision. The tension cleared and we got back to normal conversation.

I tried to chalk it up to him testing the waters, but there was something in me that was responding, although against my conscious will. I did not realize until later that my earlier conditioning caused me to respond in a sexual way to being treated disrespectfully. Without knowing why, I was enjoying what was happening, even though my conscience, now filled with the Spirit, was saying, "NO!"

A month passed, and in the meantime I let Ralph know I did not want that to happen again. On the drive up, I was warring in prayer again. I didn't have that kind of spiritual struggle when I visited the other men, only Ralph; but I thought I was tough enough to break through to him.

To make a long story short, it happened again; only this time, I refused to look until I could hear the zipper on his pants go up and he could assure me all was well. He was actually begging me to look again, but I did not give in. I reminded him again that the other inmates did not treat me like that, and I had no intention of allowing him to do so.

We got back on the subject of his case and appeal. Then he said something that put doubt in my mind about his declared innocence. "Bonnie, I'll never forget that night," he said. "I was looking right in her eyes when she died, and suddenly there was a light, like a spiritual light, shining out of the depth of her. I will never forget it as long as I live." I just took in what he said, but never forgot the impact it had on me, because I just knew she had been born again and had gone to be with Jesus.

I was no longer comfortable visiting Ralph, but I decided to give him one more chance. I really thought I could make a difference for him, because after all, I had the Holy Ghost and I could pray in tongues. And I thought I was tough. But after the third time dealing with exactly the same behavior, I stopped visiting Ralph. I was really upset and ashamed of myself, because part of me was enjoying the vulgar attention, and the other part of me was saying, "No, no, Bonnie."

Ashamed, I replayed the events over in my mind. Then it dawned on me: How could he look her right in the eyes as she died, if he were sitting in the car? *Oh, my God,* I thought, *he did slit that woman's throat!* I realized, too, in that instant, that his whole motivation for trying to compromise me sexually was because his spirit didn't like the Spirit in me.

I later found out from a young man who had been on death row that Ralph was taking the pictures of me that I had given him and making up all sorts of stories about our relationship. Ralph was living in a fantasy world, with my pictures as the motion picture screen.

There are many Ralphs in prison. I'm not proud of my reaction to the Ralph I knew, but I learned a tremendous lesson from it. Even though I had the Spirit of God in me, I learned I was not immune to temptation.

Why do I compare Ralph to the ground that was full of weeds? Simple: Ralph knew right, and wrong, good and evil. He could even spout off what was right, but he made choices to dwell in the middle of the weeds. He knew the Word of God, but his knowledge was in his head and not in his heart. Consequently, there was no fruit.

GREGORY – Watchful One

Toward the end of March 1987, I went to the jail for class and walked in on a conversation between Vaughn and Pete, the Social Service counselor for the GED program. I gathered they were talking about a couple of the inmates. I didn't want to know about the men's cases because it might affect my work with them; but this particular case sounded interesting, so I listened in. It seemed there were brothers in the class. One of the brothers was innocent and the other one was guilty.

My curiosity got the better of me, and I asked, "Who are you talking about?"

"Greg and Ron Oliver," Vaughn replied.

"Are they in the class?"

"Yes. Greg is the tall brown-skinned man with a beard from the fourth floor, and Ron is small dark-skinned one housed in the psychiatric wing."

"The psychiatric wing? Where is that?"

"It's on the sixth floor. You didn't know that?"

"No." I was trying to picture the men, but I couldn't. "I can't picture any two guys who look like brothers. Where do they usually sit?"

"Over by the guard desk."

I started remembering how the men sat in the room. I could vaguely recall them, but would have to take notice of them during class. From overhearing the conversation, I had bits and pieces of their case. I knew one was innocent and the other guilty. But the guilty one was unstable enough that the jail authorities had to keep him on drugs to control him. That is when I begin to notice that medication was given to the men from the psyche ward before class.

Vaughn and Pete discussed some other things, and then Pete realized that I had never been on a tour of the jail. Pete was a tall, slender, attractive young black man who wore his hair short and was clean-shaven.

"You need to have someone take you on a tour of the jail, Bonnie," Pete said.

"No, I don't!" I snapped back.

"Why not? They do it all the time with groups and volunteers."

"No! Those are men, not animals in cages. I will see them as men and treat them as men. I refuse to see them as animals."

"No one has ever refused before," Pete replied. "People are usually curious."

"That tour would cause me to see imaginary bars in front of my eyes when I work with them, creating a barrier between them and me," I said. "No! I don't need to walk in and view them possibly in an uncomfortable position—no I won't do it! Besides, I am totally opposed to guided tours in jails or prisons. If people do not have a purpose, then they should stay out." I realized my response to Pete's offer was strong, but I was offended by even the idea of tours.

Upstairs at class time, I watched the men come in, and took notice of the Oliver brothers. I was shocked! Gregory was the young man who had irritated me the first night in class because I thought he should be able to make something of himself. Greg and Ron didn't look like brothers. Greg was tall, and brown skinned. Ron, on the other hand, was short, wiry, and dark skinned. He also seemed to be very disoriented. I remember having wondered earlier what was wrong with Ron. Now I knew! Authorities were sedating him with drugs all the time in order to control him. Because of Pete and Vaughn's comments about Gregory being innocent, I began to see him in a different light.

Vaughn had Greg working on algebra. Seeing I was the most proficient volunteer in that subject, I often wound up helping him when I was not helping Thomas.

A couple weeks later, I walked in on another conversation between Pete and Vaughn about the Oliver brothers. This time they were discussing their case in more detail. I was concerned about what I was hearing because of their earlier comments about Gregory's innocence. "What happened?" I asked.

"Ron shot and killed one man, and wounded Gregory's ex-girlfriend and another man," Vaughn explained. "Gregory was there, but was not involved in the shooting. In fact, Greg took the gun away from Ron."

"Why did they arrest Greg?" I questioned. "How could that happen?"

"Well, that's just how the system is," Pete replied. "Sometimes it isn't fair."

That's when I began to discover some of the *in*justice that takes place in our "justice system," and how some of these men, even though a small percentage, really are victims themselves. From that point, I began to pay more attention to Gregory. He carried himself differently than the others. He had a sweetness you would not expect to see in prison, with all the tension there. I was more pleasant to him after I discovered more about him. Sometimes we even had some light conversation.

One Thursday I noticed Gregory had left the classroom. Vaughn was not taking students individually that day, and the class was quiet, so I sat down next to Vaughn and asked, "Where did the big guy go?" I didn't remember his name.

"His trial has started, and he's uptight. He asked if he could go down to the law library to study, so I let him go. Bonnie, how can you say 'No' to a guy like that?"

"They have a law library?"

"Yeah, down on the third floor." Vaughn continued. "Greg has been here two years, awaiting trial for something he didn't do. He has a tremendous amount of faith and is active in the church here."

"How come so long?"

"That is longer than normal. Last year I used to let him tutor the other guys, because he already has his GED. One of the guards started causing trouble about having one inmate over another. He tried to get Greg out of the class, but because Social Service and I have the choice, I decided to keep him in class and teach him more advanced subjects."

"That's why the algebra," I observed.

"Yeah. Ron, too. Ron also has a high school education."

Class ended and I went home, but thoughts of Gregory kept nagging at me all weekend. When class began on Tuesday, April 7, I asked Gregory, "How's it going?"

He cocked his head and grinned, and replied, "Good."

"Really?" I questioned.

He nodded.

I went about my business. Later, as I was talking to one of the other volunteers, he started telling me he had been down to the courthouse that day sitting in on one of the other students' trial.

"Really? You can go to the trials?" My mind was already at work.

"Sure, I've gone to a couple."

"I didn't know you could do that."

"Why not? They're open to the public."

"You mean I can just go down and watch any murder trial?"

"Sure."

By Thursday, April 9, I was like a "cat on a hot tin roof." I was so restless I just had to say something to Gregory, but I didn't know what. On Thursdays I worked with Thomas, so I wouldn't have much contact with Gregory unless I rushed Thomas through his reading. That's precisely what I did and still had time left. I took my position near the guard's desk, hoping Gregory would ask me a question. Sure enough, he motioned for help.

Something began to stir inside me that I couldn't explain. I felt compelled to say something to encourage him, but I had no idea what to say. I knelt down to begin helping him with the quadratic formula. As my pencil hit the page, I began crying from way down deep inside me. I didn't know what was happening. I was trembling and losing control. Fortunately, my head was lowered to read the book illustration and my hair blocked the view, so my tears went unnoticed. I knew I had to do or say something—but what? I whispered to Greg, "I have something to say, but I can't say it now." I could not look at him because of the tears. I pressed on to complete the explanation of the problem.

The instant I set the pencil down and began to get up, something strong came over me. I stood over Gregory, looking directly into his eyes. There were no more tears. There was only a courage and strength I had never experienced before.

"Young man," I said quietly, but with bold confidence, "I want you to know you are special and you don't belong here. I'll be praying for you."

What came out of my mouth surprised me, because at that point in my life I never prayed for him. As a matter of fact, I didn't pray at all. I wasn't even a Christian. So why was I saying this to him? As the words were coming out, Gregory looked up at me with his big brown eyes fixed on my eyes. A waterfall of tears flooded his eyes instantly. Then just as quickly, the tears seemed to be sucked back into his tear ducts, so there would be no telltale tears on his cheek.

I didn't know what to do. I just patted him on the shoulder and walked over to the table where my rowdy bunch was seated. All the time, I was thinking, *I don't believe I did that to that man.* I could feel Gregory's eyes following every move I made after that. Finally, I got enough courage to look back and happened to catch Gregory watching me. He just nodded.

When they called Gregory's floor at the end of class, he got up and came over to me. He just shook my hand and said, "Thank you." Then he went to Vaughn and shook his hand as he did every class period. That was the first time he shook my hand though. I couldn't stop thinking about the way tears flooded his eyes and then were never allowed to leave a trail on his face for the others to see.

I knew that was a special moment and a special message for only Gregory—and I knew it was supernatural. I could not explain or understand why I was being drawn to this sweet-spirited young man, though. I felt compassion for men like Thomas, and now Gregory. They were two different men, with two different stories—one of system failure and the other of injustice. I knew I had to be going crazy. That weekend I was agonizing over these men, and I could not wait until the next Tuesday's class.

In the classroom, we waited for the men to come up. When the elevator unloaded I caught a glimpse of Gregory, and there was an extra eagerness in his hop-like step. It was as though he could not get in the room fast enough. He nodded at me as soon as he saw me, and watched me all the way to his seat. As with all the men, Gregory could case the room in a glance and tell you everything that was going on. I don't think I could have made a move without Gregory being able to give a blow-by-blow description.

We didn't have much contact that day. I asked him how the trial was going. It was now in its eighth day. He just said, "Good."

Gregory was one of those inmates who was well liked by staff, guards, other inmates, church groups, teachers and volunteers. He always had a ready smile for everyone. Those who did not like him were usually angry, bitter or resentful people who found fault with everything and everybody anyway.

Gregory is the good soil. While in prison, the seed of the Word that he received grew, and as it blossomed he shared of its fruit with anyone who would listen (and even those who didn't want to listen).

CHAPTER IX

Gregory's Verdict

It was April 15, 1987. I had a business appointment downtown with one of the other salespeople from my regular job. I planned to stay downtown to go to the Oliver brothers' trial, so I made an excuse to take my own car. My anxiety level was high, but I tried to rationalize it away by telling myself, "I am just a public spectator, nothing else."

I arrived at the courthouse about 11:30 A.M. Not wanting to be seen, I took a sneak peek through the glass doors. The courtroom was empty! I turned to walk away, and I ran into the bailiff. "Can I help you?" he asked.

"I'm looking for the Oliver trial."

"This is it. They broke for lunch just a little while ago and will reconvene at 1:00 P.M. They'll begin the summation then."

"This might sound silly—I teach the boys over at the jail, and I have taken an interest in their case. I really don't know why."

"Oh, that happens a lot."

"How is it going?"

"I believe the big guy is going to walk, or at least get a lighter sentence. He got on the stand and testified the other day, and did a good job."

"The big guy is the one I'm concerned about. Rumor has it he didn't kill anybody."

"No, he didn't. I—uh—I really can't say which way it will go; you never know what a jury will do. As soon as you think you have one of these cases figured out, the jury rules differently. It could go any way."

"Is it okay if I sit in on the summation?"

"Sure. It's an open courtroom."

"I really don't want Gregory to see me, if you know what I mean. Is there somewhere I can sit and not be noticed?"

"Well, let's see. The way he is sitting at the table he could hardly keep from seeing you, because his head turns every time the door opens. But you know, if you sit in the back to the far left while facing the bench, you'll be less noticeable."

"Thank you. Are the boys here now?"

"Yes. They're in a holding room, so they have no idea you're here."

"So I can come back and no one will give me any trouble for observing."

"Not at all. They begin at 1:00 sharp."

"Thank you, sir."

I left and went to lunch. I couldn't believe the timing. I'll get there just in time for the summation and closing arguments, so I'll know all the details of the case without having to sit through the whole trial. What a break! I had mixed emotions. I was thrilled about seeing a felony trial in person; yet, because of the situation I was fearful, seeing I personally knew the defendants.

I arrived shortly before 1:00 o'clock. There was a woman sitting where I wanted to sit, so I tried to get seated as inconspicuous as I could.

This particular courtroom was long and narrow. Because of its location, there was only one aisle, directly in line with the door. There were half a dozen wooden bench seats on either side of the aisle, separate from the trial area, for the spectators. Defense and Prosecution were at the same large table, which was positioned so it followed the elongated floor plan of the room. The bailiff's station was to the left and the juror's section to the right. The judge's bench was set at an angle to get a fuller view of the room.

I didn't look as the door behind me opened—it was the boys. I was sure they didn't see me as they entered, and I slouched deeper in my seat, hoping to go unnoticed as they sat down. I saw Gregory's profile. He turned his head to nod to his family. I was several rows behind them. As his eyes met his mother's, he caught sight of me. He twitched in surprise, trying not to react, and then he grinned and nodded. When he sat down, he leaned over to Ron. From my angle I could read his lips as he said, "Bonnie's here." Then he turned and looked at me again.

The summation began. I listened intently, trying not to miss a beat. Ron's lawyer was the most impressive of the bunch, but none of the lawyers really impressed me that much—I was expecting high courtroom drama (too much TV, I guess). Something about the judge was bothering me, though, but I couldn't put my finger on it. Periodically, Gregory would turn and look at me through the summation and closing arguments.

By the time the arguments were complete, there was no doubt in my mind that Gregory did not murder anyone. It was about 4:30 P.M. when they finished and released the jury to deliberate. Once the jury left the room, the boys were ushered out, and they had to walk right past me. Gregory's eyes were fixed on me. I saw a woman a couple of rows ahead of me reach out and grab his hand, and I followed suit. I reached my hand out to Gregory, and he grabbed it tight and didn't let go until he couldn't hold on any longer. My hand was over my head backwards; my arm stretched as far as it could go.

While the jury was deliberating, I went back to work, but I couldn't concentrate on anything. I made an excuse why I couldn't attend the special meeting that evening for our new insurance program, and headed back to the courthouse to wait for the verdict.

I sat in the trial courtroom hoping it wouldn't take too long. But the empty courtroom was eerie and I was restless, so I walked across the hall. I saw a small black woman sitting alone. I asked her if she knew the boys, and she said, "I'm their mother."

I introduced myself and asked if I could sit with her. She said, "Yes." I began to tell her why I was there and had such an interest in her sons.

"I saw you earlier and wondered who you were," she said. I continued talking with her, telling her about making Gregory cry. She stopped me by exclaiming, "You're the woman!"

"What do you mean?" I asked.

"Jay (Greg's nickname, I found out) called me Friday morning and said, 'Mama there is a woman at the jail that told me I didn't belong here.' He told me, 'It was so spiritual, Mama. When I looked into her eyes, I knew God had sent her.' I knew he was right. God sent you." I smiled, and she went on, "You felt it too?"

"Yes, but I didn't know what it was."

"He didn't tell me you were white."

"Does that matter?"

"No."

The hours passed, and I got to know all the Olivers that were present. There was a spell when I felt out of place with the family, so I moved into the courtroom just in time to hear the judge in casual conversation with the bailiff, court reporter, etc. He was telling them about the motion Gregory's lawyer had filed for a mistrial. I listened and watched carefully. Evidently the request for mistrial had 49 points [actually 50; it was mis-numbered] stating why Greg's lawyer thought it should be declared a mistrial. The judge was not pleased about it. "If he thinks this is going to change things," he said, "he's wrong. I'm going to deny his motion."

Viewing this judge as objectively as possible, there was an arrogance about him that was repulsive. Now I knew why he bothered me.

I was concerned with what I overheard. There had to be something wrong if a lawyer, even the worst lawyer, could come up with 50 different points to justify a request for a mistrial. One point is all it takes. *Out of 50*, I thought, *at least* one *of those had to be accurate.*

Everyone in the room had seen me enter, so I couldn't be accused of eavesdropping. But outside of the bailiff, they had no idea who I was because I didn't show up until the last day. This was the beginning of a picture that was going to get bigger for me. I could not believe what I saw happening—to the Oliver boys, to the system, and to myself.

❖

The verdict was in. There was a general scurrying about, trying to get everyone together who had an interest or role in the case to be present for the reading of the verdict. When the jury had been released for deliberation, the court had informed them that a guilty verdict would result in a mandatory life sentence on the murder charge in lieu of the death penalty, and a sentence of life with parole on the first-degree assault charge. In Ronald's case, there was an additional charge of kidnapping, and the court asked for an additional 12-15 years if a guilty verdict was returned on that charge.

Mrs. Oliver took a seat next to me in the courtroom. Anxiously, we all listened for the verdict. The jury only deliberated three and a half hours, and they were all taken out for dinner first, which is not normal procedure. I thought the deliberation time was ridiculously short, seeing the jury had about 26 issues to go over while making their decision.

The judge began reading the verdicts, charge by charge. I sat there dumbfounded; I simply could not believe the jurors' decisions. Guilty on this, guilty on that, and on and on the verdicts went. Whenever guilty verdicts are returned, standard procedure is to rush the defendants from the room, not knowing how they will react. There is supposed to be no physical contact with anyone.

As they hustled the boys down the aisle, Gregory's eyes were riveted on me. I reached my hand out to him, and he reached for mine. The bailiff immediately leaned forward to stop the contact. As he did, his eyes met mine and he slowly backed off to let Gregory's hand grab mine just as he had before, hanging on as long as he could. Something had stopped that bailiff from interfering with our contact. I knew it, but I could not explain it.

Mrs. Oliver just kept saying, "I'm not going to cry...." Well, if she wasn't, I was—and I did.

In the background, I heard one of the lawyers telling the boys in the holding room, "I did all I could do." Who were they trying to kid? Gregory was innocent of murder, and Ronald had a provable mental condition—a condition so bad the prosecutor had to keep reminding the jury to disregard Ron's blank stare in the courtroom because of the medication the state had him on—medicine they give to people who are psychotic. Justice? What justice? I cried most of the way home.

❖

Thursday came and instead of holding class, Vaughn, Pete, Steve (another volunteer), and I went out for pizza. I was livid as I told them about my experience the day before at the courthouse.

"Calm down, Bonnie," Vaughn said.

"What do you mean, calm down? That man is innocent!"

"We know it."

"How can you sit there and say, 'We know it,' and not be affected by it?"

"It happens all the time."

"That doesn't make it right," I protested.

"He'll filter through the system and eventually get out."

"What do you mean 'filter through the system?'" I asked.

"We see these guys come and go all the time," added Pete, as he joined in the conversation. "They eventually get out. Probably seven or eight years he'll get out."

"I can't believe what I'm seeing," I said. "Our system is so fouled up, and that judge—I couldn't believe what I heard him say—and that jury! How in the world could they sit there, hearing the same things I heard, and send that man away for the rest of his life—with no parole? It's not fair."

"We know, Bonnie," Vaughn said.

"Well, how can you sit back, and just say and do nothing?"

"There's nothing you can do."

"There has to be something—it's so unfair."

I went home so angry and frustrated I began to write an essay on racial prejudice, which is something I had always wanted to do. Now I had a reason. That's when I wrote "Wide-Eyed Ronald." There was more to my anger than what was on the surface. I was so tired of being victimized myself that I couldn't stand to see another person being victimized by something that was out of his control.

❖

Wide-Eyed Ronald

For years, I fought in my heart with the social issue that began with the sale and resultant purchase (demand generates supply) of the first slave in this country. Though tremendous strides have been made in eliminating the prejudicial ways that developed throughout our country, there remain strong feelings of racial prejudice today.

In Wallace's Alabama, in the mid-sixties, I was appalled at the many unpainted shacks I saw sitting next to a great house. These small shacks were filled with black farm hands and cotton pickers, while the big house sat proud and none-too-crowded. I was sick at the sight of the filthy restrooms and drinking fountains with the word "colored" written over them. In Alabama, I found myself not afraid of the black man, but of the white man.

In Georgia, in 1971, I violated the unspoken rules by insisting that my black maid sit down at my table and eat my fresh food instead of the leftovers she was used to. I watched her, listened to her as she cowered when she spoke, saw her fear at the thought of being caught sitting and eating with a white person. I was sickened to think this lady had been beaten down to the level of ignorance that made her almost apologize for her existence.

While I was in Georgia, I had a neighbor who used to ask me to go to church. I went a couple of times, but when I discovered the church members had voted to decide whether blacks could join their congregation, I refused to attend anymore. God's intent, according to my childhood Sunday school class, was not to forbid worship because of skin color. I remember singing, "Red and yellow, black and white, they are precious in His sight. Jesus loves the little children of the world." Something inside me, even back then, believed that song was true.

In Kansas, my husband and I offered bed and board for a few nights to a black family who was friends of ours. My neighbors were not happy, but friends were more important than the disapproving glances I knew we'd get.

Now, in 1987, in an "all-American" courthouse, I had witnessed the ultimate in undisclosed prejudice. As I watched, two brothers received mandatory life sentences. They were black; one of them was innocent, and the other was mentally impaired. But at the same time an innocent six-year-old black boy taught me the lesson of my life. His name was Ronald, his mother had been killed in a fire when he was three years old, and his father had suffered brain damage in his effort to save young Ronald's life. Now his father was on trial for murder.

I had become acquainted with Ronald's father and his uncle through volunteering at City Jail. A voice inside me kept nagging at me to go to the trial to see what would happen, and I took the afternoon off work to do it. I arrived just before the summation and had an opportunity to speak to the bailiff. He said he felt one brother would walk, and the other would go to the penitentiary. After hearing the attorneys' closing arguments, I felt confident the bailiff was correct.

The jury went out to deliberate and I went back to work, but I couldn't concentrate. Making an excuse, I headed back to the courtroom to wait for the verdict. When I arrived, the empty courtroom bothered me, so I walked across the hall to a waiting room. A small black woman was there, sitting alone, and I asked her if she knew the boys. "I'm their mother," she said. That's how I met the Oliver brothers' mother.

While we were talking, other members of the family started entering the room, and I met Ronald, a three-foot-tall dynamo. He took a liking to me right away. We talked and played. Then I asked him to draw for me. I was surprised at the talent he had. I knew the boys were still in the building, so I asked the bailiff if Ronald could give his picture to his father. The bailiff agreed to let him. I had Ronald climb up on my lap so we could write his father a message. "Big Bunches Love," we wrote, signed Ronald's name and put down some "xxxooo," hugs and kisses. I could only see Ronald's back and his father's shirt from my vantage point, but I knew the brothers were pleased.

The bailiff then surprised all of us. He allowed the family to go in one at a time. The boys' mother went in first. When she came out, she asked me to go in.

"I can't," I replied. "I'll cry." My emotions were in my throat. "They're under enough pressure without me crying."

"I know they would like to see you," she said.

I felt so accepted by this family who didn't know me, and the fact that I was white didn't seem to matter at all.

When the boys' younger brother, Mark, came out, he told me, "They said 'Hi!' They wanted to know if you were still here, and I told them you were."

I found myself hurting with this family and loving this family, wishing I could do something to erase the bad situation.

As the hours passed, the room the boy's family and I were in got stuffy, so we moved to the corridor. Ronald was showing signs of being really tired, so I had him crawl up on my lap. As he did, it was as though he were one of my own. I held him in my arms and nestled him to my breast.

There is a special feeling that comes from a woman and child together that can be the most beautiful thing. This was not a child of my body or even of my race, yet I could not have loved him more. I began singing the lullaby I had sung so often to my own sons. I held him tightly as I pulled his head up to nestle it to my face. Love was my only feeling. Ronald's breathing became heavy and I just knew he was sleeping, so I gently lowered his head to check. Ronald's eyes were wide open, and he had a big grin on his face. "You're faking," I said, and his grin widened. He knew exactly what he was doing. I pulled him tight again and he eventually fell off to sleep in my arms.

What a beautiful moment that was. This child so unspoiled by racial prejudice, comfortable in the arms I offered him, and me comfortable in holding this beautiful child of God. It was as though he were my own.

CHAPTER X

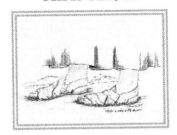

Lights, Camera, Action!

I was troubled by the events I had witnessed both in the courtroom and out, and by the lack of caring I saw. I called Pete and asked him to meet me for dinner. He did and I shared my essay "Wide-Eyed Ronald" with him.

"That's beautiful, Bonnie."

"Can I give it to Gregory?" I asked.

"No."

"Why not?"

"It's too soon after the verdict."

"What does this have to do with the verdict?"

"It's just too soon," Pete insisted.

I didn't like Pete's answer, so I decided to let Gregory make his own decision; but how could I ask him? I began to set in motion the actions that were to change my whole life. The things I did next surprised me, because I didn't know I was capable of being so devious.

I had a car telephone for my regular job that could not be traced to me, so I decided to give Gregory that phone number—but how? "*Of course—that's it—in an algebraic equation!*" I thought. I worked out the perfect problem for Gregory to solve. Afraid to give him the problem myself, I asked Steve, the other volunteer, to give it to him and challenge him with it.

At the end of class, I approached Gregory and asked, "Did you solve it?"

He shook his head, "No."

"Well, let's see," I said, as I picked up the paper. "Did you plug in the numbers correctly?" He had all the right numbers plugged in, revealing my phone number. "That's right," I said. Then I whispered,

"That's my car phone, call me tomorrow at 9:00 A.M." His eyes widened, and he just looked at me. "Can you call out?" I questioned.

He nodded, "Yes."

"Good," I said as I walked away.

The next day, 9:00 o'clock came and went, and no call. After I got to work, I realized I had forgotten to go to the bank. While I was driving to the bank, the phone rang. "Hello," I said. I could hear his voice, weak and hesitating.

"Greg?" I said.

"Yes."

"Are you surprised this is really my number?"

"Yes."

"I wanted to tell you, I couldn't believe what I saw happen the other night in the courtroom, and I want to help you," I said.

"I'm not asking you for help."

"I know you're not; I'm offering it. I don't have money, so I really can't offer that kind of help; but I can offer moral support."

"You don't have to do this," Greg said.

"I know." I paused, trying to figure out how I was going to handle this. Then I began, "I had dinner with Pete last night and showed him something I wrote that was spurred on by what I witnessed at your trial. He thought it was beautiful. I asked him if I could give it to you and he said it was too soon after your verdict, but I decided to let you make that decision. Do you want to read it?"

"Yes, I do."

"Good. I'll bring it to class Tuesday."

I copied "Wide-Eyed Ronald" on paper that wouldn't attract undue attention. Then I went to the post office and rented a box. I put a pen name, "B.K. Williams," and my P.O. box number at the bottom of the essay, hoping Gregory would respond in writing. Because I did not know what I was getting into, I was careful not to let my identity, outside of "Ms. Bonnie," be known.

I gave Gregory the essay with my information on it the next Tuesday. On Thursday I rushed to check my P.O. box before lunch and found a lone letter with the return address of City Jail. I was like a kid with a new toy as I read his letter. I've included the letter, just as he wrote it:

❖

May 2, 1987

To B.K. Williams,

I was so flabbergast to see you sitting in the court-room when we reentered on Wensday that it was hard for me to hold my compossure in tact.

I have struggled with the dilemma of violence, racial prejudice and injustice in this country for many years.

To begin I would first say that I have tried to educate myself with the knowledge of social standards and the betterment of one's community.

At a early age I learned that a hatred was brewing in the black man's community that I could not understand. Being so young and my surroundings so huge and complex, that we could not begin to unfold the purpose and destiny in one's life. I can recall how I would hate the racial slurs, Not just from whites but also from blacks.

This reminds me of the old type wash machines the ones with the roller wringers and open tubs. I can remember standing on a chair watching the agitator working the suds and clothes back and forth. A great lesson comes from that experience, the warning from my mother that if you put your hand inside you're bound to be injured.

Believe in the same sense that an agitated racial disorder will only bring forth social injury. It's pathetic that a country of such great wisdom, honor, pride, and civil ethics could be as naive to the racial degradation being, and becoming a daily practice in this advancing society. To tell the truth, our great nation maybe losing it's saltiness of being a land of Liberty, Prosperity,

And the Pursuit of Happiness, or is that just a fallible illusion created to ellude the multitude by deprivation? God placed man in a land to cultivate it and keep it, But he never said anything about being of greed, and that one or two will control all, given man.

When we learn to live in accordane to God's will then we will know his every blessing, and accept them joyfully because by his grace the veil has been removed to allow his children to see the fulness he will bestow on-to them.

We must learn to stay faithful no matter what the trials we will face in this world. My family and I accepts one's heart. We will not judge one by race or creed, neither will we convict one for another's action. When I saw you in the court-room I knew your heart was of pure nature, and this with many other things have touch me deeply.

This sort of unconditional caring comes of rare existence, Whether you would help me or not, Which I would never want to become an inconvinience in your life because I consider you a beautiful person no matter what the case maybe. I really felt great after reading your testimony of little Ronald because it takes a very special person to read the heart's of others and cut away the crud of worldly demoralism.

Gregory Oliver

P.S. Keep up the good work:

❖

I cried and cried. *This is the most spiritual man I have ever met,* I thought (and I wasn't even saved). After I collected myself, I read the letter again and had the same reaction. I was like a schoolgirl with her first crush on a boy; only this "boy" was a grown man who was, according to the system, looking at spending the rest of his life in prison. (I found out later that Gregory wrote this on his 31st birthday.)

This is nuts, I thought. *He didn't write this—someone else did—or he copied it. That's it—he copied it.* I read the letter again. *Sure, that's it—he copied someone else's work. Plagiarism—that's it.* As hard as I tried, though, I couldn't deny the message and the way it spoke to me. There was no bitterness in his words. There was no anger. There was only strength of character. *Who is this man?* I wondered. I couldn't wait to see him that night, to let him know I had received his letter.

❖

By the following Tuesday, I had sent an answer to Gregory's letter, and he acknowledged receiving it. Thursday came and no Gregory. Vaughn mentioned to me when he walked me out to my car. "Because of the big time the Olivers received, the jail authorities opted to keep them out of class."

"So that's why they weren't in class? I sort of wondered."

"They do that sometimes. Well, goodnight," he said, as he walked away.

I got in my car and headed home. Not two minutes down the road the phone rang. It was Gregory, asking, "What happened?"

"You don't know?"

"No. They just wouldn't let me go to class."

"They wouldn't let you come because of the big time you got."

"I saw you leaving. You looked nice."

"Where were you?"

"In the law library."

"Where's that?" I asked.

"On the third floor."

"You mean the caged area where I saw books is the law library?"

"Yeah, that's it."

"I thought I caught a glimpse of you, but I wasn't sure."

From that point on, we communicated through letters and phone calls after class. Because Gregory's letters were so spiritual, I began asking people, "If you wanted to learn about the Bible fast, what would you do?" Everyone told me to get a good study Bible, but there were so many versions, I didn't know what to get. Finally I decided on the NASB (New American Standard Bible). That was the best money I've ever spent!

I missed Gregory's presence in the classroom, but I was still able to talk to him on my teaching nights as I drove home from the jail. During one of our phone conversations, I asked him if he wanted me to be present at the sentencing, May 20th, and he said, "Yes."

I took my son Bob who had moved back to live with me, to the sentencing so he could see a real courtroom and how things worked. He was a senior in high school at the time. I also took a book I had promised Gregory, hoping they would let me give it to him. Fortunately, the same bailiff was on duty that I had talked with during the trial. He remembered me and gave the book to Gregory for me.

Mrs. Oliver sat with me as we waited for the judge to decide. Both his mother and I wrote letters on Gregory's behalf to the judge asking for leniency.

The judge made no changes and concurred that Gregory and Ronald's sentencing would stand as the jury had decided: mandatory life with no parole for first degree murder, and life with parole for first degree criminal assault. Ronald received an additional twelve years for kidnapping. All time was to be served consecutively. When they escorted the boys out of the courtroom, they let them stop to greet their mother. Gregory leaned over past me to hug his mother and then turned to hug me. He was so tall that when he hugged me, my face went up against the flesh at the bottom of his neck. His skin was so smooth I couldn't resist the temptation, and pecked him on the neck as he said, "Thank you."

❖

"They came 'like a thief in the night,'" Gregory told me later, "to take us to Fulton, which is where central processing is." The boys would spend eight weeks there and then be assigned to a penitentiary. It was a long wait. Once Greg was assigned however, we could visit like real people, not having to be secretive.

Regularly, I would take Gregory's letters, my Bible and my writing material to the park to write and study. Sometimes I would just stroll through the park and thank God for the trees, the grass, and the sky, etc. Often on those walks I could sense a presence around me, but I really didn't know what it was. A couple of times I swore I could see angels in my mind's eye as I walked along the path.

I felt peace coming over me that I could not explain. I didn't know what was happening to me. None of it made any sense. It was contrary to logic and didn't fit "the norm" for my life. I was a businesswoman who was finally beginning to get her act together. Now, suddenly, I was being supernaturally drawn to the jail and actually caring about these guys. I was even "falling" for one of these men—someone who had just received two life sentences for a crime he didn't commit.

This is insane, I would tell myself. *Bonnie, you have just been alone too long. But, no—that isn't it. This is real—I'm real.* I couldn't explain it, because it didn't make sense to me either. All I knew was that there was this "tug".

CHAPTER XI

Commitment

While waiting for Greg's transfer to the penitentiary, I spent a lot of time in the park writing him and studying the Bible. Through our letter writing, a personal, intimate relationship developed. We were physically attracted to each other, and we both knew it. I tried to walk away from the relationship at different periods, but as soon as I was ready to walk, someone would cross my path and confirm that God was putting Gregory and me together.

Shortly after Gregory's transfer to the penitentiary and before my first visit, a situation developed in my life that forced me to make a decision. Gregory's letters were definitely fulfilling the emotional part of my emptiness, yet there was something missing. Gregory and I could never be alone, ever. I cannot say that my physical side was crying out, because it usually didn't—but it sure wanted attention that Gregory could not give it. Then an opportunity presented itself to me for a strictly physical relationship with another young, married man, sixteen years my junior. All the ground rules and boundaries for this affair had been set down; the next step was to plan some rendezvous somewhere. I received a letter from Gregory just prior to taking that final step into a full-fledged affair. I don't even remember what he said in the letter. I only remember that whatever it was, it was just right. I sat down and wrote him the letter that would establish the road I was to follow in my life, not knowing where that road was going to take me.

On the outside of the envelope I wrote, "Read in the privacy of your cell." In the letter, I explained the situation to him and the plans that I had made for this pending affair. I explained the ground rules we had laid out, and I told him that I was looking to him to meet my emotional needs and looking to this other man to meet my physical needs.

I went on to explain that I had received his letter and how it "did something to me." I told him I had decided then and there not to follow through with the affair, that I realized all the physical satisfaction in the world could not compare to the emotional fulfillment and healing I received from our relationship alone. At that point, I made the commitment to be faithful to the man who fulfilled my emotional needs and not allow my physical needs to rule me. It was done. I committed myself to Gregory in June 1987, and have not gone back on my word.

The letter I received back from Greg was worth whatever the decision would cost me. Gregory was his beautiful self. He told me that I deserved better than a married man and a shoddy affair. He wrote, "I did as you asked, and read this in the privacy of my cell. All I could do was cry, because God sent me you. I've never known faithfulness like yours. I love you, Princess." I grinned like a schoolgirl. *No one has ever called me 'Princess',* I thought, as I clung to my letter from Gregory. I just had to read that again. "I love you, Princess."

Eight weeks after Gregory left City Jail, I finally got to visit him—a visit that lasted six hours. It was quite an experience for me, and I'm sure it was for him, too.

One of the most degrading and humbling experiences a person can go through is visiting a prisoner in a maximum-security prison. The security procedures are intimidating. Once I got past the embarrassment of security, I was ushered through two electric doors into the visiting room. The room was divided. There was a section for people visiting inmates in open population, a section for those visiting men in protective custody, a section where people visited over telephones with glass between, and a section for those visiting inmates on death row. Greg was in open population, so we were able to have "contact visits."

I had no idea what to expect or how I should act. I have to admit I was nervous; part of it had to do with how to relate to this man I saw as truly spiritual, but to be completely honest, it was also partly our racial difference. Questions like, *How do I greet him in front of all those people? Do I shake his hand? Do I hug him? Is he going to kiss me? What will these people think?* kept running through my head. Then I saw a young black man come in and greet his wife, and she was white. I began to relax a little. I kept watching for Greg. A half-hour passed—then forty-five minutes turned into an hour. *He wasn't expecting me, so he probably had to get cleaned up,* I thought.

Finally, I saw Greg come around the corner. I stood up to greet him in the middle of a full visiting room. He grinned from ear to ear when he saw me. Then it came, that moment I had been waiting for with anticipation and anxiety. Greg put his arms around me and started to kiss me, but I turned away because of discomfort. I think he was disappointed and hurt.

We sat down and just looked at each other for several moments, then Greg made the first move and leaned over to kiss me. The kiss ended and—I just looked at him. I broke the silence by saying, "Let's try that again." He eagerly obliged me, and we sat back on the sofa, contented. He kept his arm around me for six hours, and he held my hand with his other hand. It didn't take long for a comfort level to form between the two of us. We talked, laughed, cried, and did all those wonderful things that make a relationship real and solid.

The hardest part of the visit was leaving. Greg had to stand at one end of the visiting room and watch me sign out and exit the large electric doors. Already I couldn't wait until I was able to visit him again.

CHAPTER XII

Born Again

I would like to say that all doubt about our relationship ended after that first visit. Not so! Often I mulled over whether I was doing the right thing. There was nothing that Gregory and I had in common. Our backgrounds and frames of reference were totally different. Yet there was something inside me that would not let me turn my back on him, something that kept pulling me to him.

Our letters became filled with the things of God, as I became more familiar with the Scriptures. Gregory was more familiar with the Bible than I was because he had already read it five times.

One day, I was in the park trying to write Gregory a letter. I had my tape player playing Smokey Robinson songs. I was contemplating breaking off this whole thing with Gregory because of our differences. He was black; I was white. He had a basic education; I had a college degree. His roots were poor; mine were solid middle class. He was in prison serving two life sentences; I was free. He was 30 years old; I was 42. "What are you doing, Bonnie?" I kept asking myself, over and over again. I thought I was losing my mind.

There was a picnic table not too far away with a woman sitting at it. Suddenly, I heard the woman getting into my Smokey Robinson music.

"Is it too loud?" I asked.

"No, you can turn it up if you want. I don't mind."

That's all it took to begin our conversation. I shared with her some of the things that had happened at City Jail, my relationship with Gregory, and my frustration.

Then she said, "He's black, isn't he?"

"Yes, how did you know?"

"The Lord let me know."

We talked for a long time and she even prayed for me. I cried and cried, and tried to wipe my eyes, but she grabbed my hands and wouldn't let me. "Let that cleansing take place," she said. "Let those tears flow. God is doing a work in you today."

I felt so much better after she prayed and decided to stick it out longer with Gregory and see what this bizarre relationship was all about.

❖

About this same time, I had two separate, back-to-back "road to Damascus" experiences at City Jail, sort of like the Apostle Paul. After spending several months teaching GED and Adult Continuing Education classes, I volunteered for more. They needed someone to teach a Life Skills class, so I volunteered. That meant I would be going to the jail three nights a week instead of two. I really don't know what made me do it, because I really didn't know what I was doing. I knew by now that I was able to teach one-on-one, but I didn't think I had what it took to teach a whole class.

But I felt this "tug" taking me down to the jail, and I did not know what it was. I just knew I had to be down there. I received more respect, for the most part, from the inmates than I did from men outside the walls. That didn't compensate, however, for the emotional drain I felt from my visits to the jail. Many nights I would leave in tears and swear that I would never come back; but lo and behold, I would be back again for my next class.

All this time my sons were watching the changes take place in me. One night when I came home my son Bill, who was 19, said, "Mom, I think you need to go to the jail more often."

"Why do you say that?"

"Because you're happier than you've been in years. You need to keep getting those happy pills."

My life began to revolve around City Jail and the men I had contact with. I would go to bed thinking about them and wake up thinking about them. I knew their crimes often times were horrible, and I didn't excuse them, but I couldn't shake the reality of the man behind the crime. I figured by teaching the Life Skills class I could gain a little more insight into these men and into my reason for being at City Jail.

❖

It was the first night of class, and I was nervous. Only six men showed up for that class. I had it planned how I was going to begin the class to grab their attention. I began by writing on the blackboard:

The _____ man.

Then I asked the five men who were in the class to fill in the blank. They came back with all sorts of answers,

"Rich," one man yelled.

"Fat," shouted another, and on and on.

But no one answered the way I had expected, which surprised me. I filled in the blank with the word "black." Then I asked another question: "Why am I seeing what I am seeing here at City Jail? Why are there so many black men here? Why is there such an imbalance?"

Again, all sorts of answers came back. "No jobs," said one.

"Poor education," said another.

And the list went on: segregation, favoritism, values, environment, peer pressure, ignorance, cultural hang-ups, crime, prejudice, attitudes (black/white), jealousy, drugs, and "the system."

Once this list of reasons was established, I began to speak, nervously trying to focus on what was next. Suddenly, something came over me. With a boldness I have never known in my life, I began to speak on the subject of racial prejudice and whether people should allow themselves to be controlled by other people's thoughts and actions. I was actually preaching and teaching strongly, very strongly, and with authority. It was as though Bonnie was no longer, and a new self had overwhelmed me. I have never been a person who was confident in front of a group. Now, suddenly, there I was—a powerful speaker who was mesmerizing my small audience—and myself.

As quickly as it started, it stopped, just before the hour was up. I was left dumbfounded over this new Bonnie. "What was that?" I asked myself all the way home. I was almost anxious for the next class, to see if it would happen again.

The week passed quickly. I went to the classroom excited about finishing the discussion. As I was writing the information on the blackboard from the last week's discussion, I could hear the men entering the room, but I didn't look around. When I finally did, to my surprise I had a full house. While I wasn't looking, the class had grown to 24 students, the maximum for the jail. I couldn't believe it.

"You guys did some talking, huh?"

"Yeah," Thomas said with a grin.

"Okay, let's continue from where we left off," I said as we began that week's discussion. The subject of racial prejudice led into the topic of anger and how when people discover what triggers another person's anger, they sometimes deliberately push that button. Then we talked about how to control anger and how to keep people from discovering your "triggers."

Suddenly, it happened again. I was outside of me, listening to me preach and teach these men as they watched me with awe. Again, it continued right up until the end of class time, and then stopped as quickly as it had begun.

The third week, I got there just as one of the cooks was leaving. I had never seen him before, but he spoke up and said, "I know who you are."

"Oh, you do, do you?"

"Yeah! You're that dynamic teacher the men have been talking about."

"I don't know about dynamic, but I am their teacher."

"We all know about you."

The compliments and attention I was receiving stunned me. The third week I taught the class, that "preaching" thing didn't happen, but Week #4 was a blessing; I taught on sowing and reaping, and how what you do to people has a way of coming back to you. It was after this fourth class that one of the guards told me I sounded like a good old Baptist preacher. I was complimented, because I had a definite respect for "men of the cloth"—and I sort of felt like one at that point.

The events of the previous few weeks were exciting to me, but I was somewhat confused and nervous, because I didn't know what was happening to me. I could not comprehend where this boldness was coming from.

❖

I was nearing my 43rd birthday, September 18th. I went to GED class and was sitting with Vaughn by the door. Thomas came over and handed me a card. I opened it. It was a birthday card, and there was a handwritten poem on the inside with all the guys' signatures on it. It read:

The School Teach Poem
You are my school teach who I love so dear,
I get such a beautiful feeling,
whenever you are near.
I love you more than words can express.
Out of all school teachs you're
good, better and best.
You are school teach, yes you are,
you are my bright and shinning star.

I couldn't contain myself when I read this, and I darted out of the room. Pete saw me and didn't know what had happened, so he darted out after me.

"Are you okay?" He said.

"Yes," I said tearfully as I handed him the card.

"Is that what you're upset about?" He said after reading it.

"Yes." I cried.

"Bonnie, I don't think you realize how much those guys in there love you—we all do."

❖

The weather was nice enough at this time of year to spend a lot of time in the park. I would go there to write to Gregory and read the Bible I bought in order to keep up with his letters. I would search the Scriptures for answers to the many questions I had and the feelings that I was picking up from Gregory's letters. The park had become my church, and it was here that I could sense the presence of angels as I strolled along my familiar paths seeing angels in my mind's eye. The only prayers that I knew how to pray were prayers of thanksgiving for all of nature.

It was Saturday, September 26, 1987. I went to the park to read my Bible, but I couldn't get into it, so I took a walk. A ways off I could see a young woman sitting at a picnic table alone reading. I decided that if she was reading the Bible I would talk to her. As I neared her table I could tell it was a Bible.

I spoke first. "I came here to read, too, but I just couldn't get into it."

"Really? Come on and sit down."

We introduced ourselves and began talking. Her name was Patty. We shared stories, but there was something different about hers. She would say, "God told her" this and "God told her" that. I had never heard anyone talk like that before.

"What do you mean 'God told you?' You mean He speaks to you?" I asked.

She began to explain and teach me from the Scriptures how God communicates with His children, and how much He wants to communicate.

Then she said, "You know, Bonnie, I've always wanted to meet someone with a prison ministry."

"I don't have a prison ministry."

"Yes, you do. You go down there and share your love with them, don't you?"

"Well, yes."

"Then you have a prison ministry. But you need some help."

"What kind of help?" I asked.

"God's help, through the Holy Spirit."

"What do you mean?"

"You know those experiences you had while you were teaching?" Patty questioned.

"Yes."

"Well, that was the Holy Spirit, using you to get through to the men down there."

"I don't understand."

"Oh," she said suddenly, "what time is it?"

"5:30."

"Good. Do you want to go to church?"

"On Saturday?"

"Yes, we have Saturday night services for people who work on Sunday."

"Gee, I like the sound of that. What kind of church is this?"

"It's non-denominational."

"Oh, well, okay."

"Where's your car?" she asked. "You can follow me."

I didn't know what to expect, but I went. The building didn't look like a church from the outside. It was a large metal building. And the inside, though done tastefully, didn't remind me of any church I had ever been to. They even had drums set up.

"What kind of church is this?" I asked again as I took my seat.

"It's Charismatic."

"Oh," I said. "I had a Catholic friend who introduced me to a Catholic Charismatic group. One lady even spoke in tongues. Do you know about that?"

"Yes, the majority of members here speak in tongues."

"You're kidding!" I remembered Gregory telling me he spoke in tongues and had been doing so in the holding room at the courthouse during the jury's deliberations after his trial.

"Just watch," she said.

The music started, and so did my tears. I cried all through the music part of the service—a type of music I had never heard before in a church. I didn't think I was ever going to get my composure back. I had never seen a church like this. It had a seating capacity of 5,000. The pastor was a young man in his mid-thirties, and the members just called him "Pastor Ron."

I was overwhelmed by it all, and then Pastor Ron got up to preach. The sermon was just for me. I clung to every word. He told a story during his sermon that really spoke to me:

There was a line of saints at the pearly gates waiting to get in. Each one was bringing their offerings to the Lord, and telling Him about their deeds. Among the saints was a woman who was very humble and had nothing to offer. She knew she would be rejected at the gate as her turn came. "Lord," she said, "I have nothing to offer you."

The Lord then told her, "Look, my child." As she turned to look, there was a mob of people telling about and praising the numerous things she had done for them. Because of this, that woman received a higher reward than anyone else.

Oh, I thought, *those are my guys.* And I began to cry some more. At the end of the sermon, the pastor asked if anyone wanted to receive Jesus. I raised my hand for the pastor to pray for me, and I prayed a "sinner's prayer" with total conviction and commitment in my heart. I was now born again.

❖

When we were dismissed, Patty asked if I wanted to go get something to eat. I was curious about everything that was happening to me. She taught me more as we ate our dinner. When we finished, she asked if there was some place we could go. I had the key to my office, which was close. It was common for the local police to see my car there at ridiculous hours of the day and night. So we went there and sat in the lunchroom.

She continued to teach me about the Holy Spirit, things I had never heard before. I was fascinated. Then we prayed. I prayed for the gift of prayer, meaning tongues, so I could pray for my guys better, but nothing seemed to happen outwardly.

On the way home, I kept thinking about how all this was phony. Yet I knew I had heard people speaking in another language. It was a wrestling match going on in my mind.

I woke up early the next morning, because it was my Sunday to visit Gregory. I said, "Good morning, God." Then all of a sudden something came out of my mouth that I could not figure out where it came from. "Che-de-pit." Out loud I said, "Where did that come from?" I remembered that Patty had told me the night before that I would have to open my mouth and begin saying sounds in order for the Holy Spirit to work. He could not work if I did not give Him an avenue. I questioned again, "God what is that? Che-de-pit," I said again. *This is ridiculous,* I thought. *I have to get ready to go visit Gregory. I'll worry about this later.*

I could not wait to see Gregory and tell him about the night before. As I was telling him, I was still questioning whether this was real or not.

"I got up this morning," I began, "and right after I said 'Good morning, God,' I said 'Che-de-pit.'"

Gregory grinned from ear to ear and said, "You got it."

"I do?"

"Yeah."

"Are you sure?"

"Yeah, you got it. Now let God use it."

That night I was in my bedroom saying my prayers, and my son Bob was watching television. I asked the Lord, "God, if this is real, then let me have it full force." I opened my mouth to make a sound, and the next thing I knew it was all I could do to keep quiet. When Jesus said rivers of living water would flow forth, He wasn't kidding. I was beginning to get concerned, because I couldn't stop. I walked out of my bedroom and into the living room to tell my son what was going on, and I was speaking in tongues as I entered the room. I stopped long enough to think of what I was going to tell him. I opened my mouth again to tell him what was happening, and though I was thinking in English all that I could vocalize was this loud language that I couldn't understand.

"Mom!" my son yelled. "Be quiet! You're ruining my TV show."

I paused, then tried again to explain what was happening. Again all that came out was this language. I could not, as much as I tried to, speak English. What a horrifying feeling that was, not to be able to communicate with my son.

"Mom!" he yelled again, "if you're going to keep that up, go in your room and close the door. You're ruining my show."

I went back into my room and closed the door and kept speaking in tongues until somehow I knew the Holy Spirit was finished. I didn't know then what a "release in the Spirit" was, but I just knew that the prayer was done.

After I finished praying, I could speak in English again. I calmly went into the living room to try and explain to my son what happened. He didn't want to know. I found out later that he was scared to death of what had happened. Without the knowledge that God shares in the Scriptures, it is scary. I didn't understand until years later that God was showing me how difficult it would be to try to communicate spiritual things to people who didn't have a relationship with Him, even with family members.

The next morning when I got up, the first thing I did was ask God, "God, if this is real, let me have it again." Sure enough, the Holy Spirit came on me again and the same thing happened; only this time I wasn't scared.

When I would speak in tongues, there would be a tightness inside that would begin from the depth of my stomach area, and it would work its way up to my chest and throat until I yielded and began to let the Holy Spirit use my vocal cords. Often when I was speaking in these tongues, I would see visions, as though I were seeing the people I was praying for. I became concerned about whether I could control it in front of people who didn't understand, like the experience I had with my son Bob.

Tuesday came, and I went down to the jail. I began to tell my story to Pete when a Catholic brother who came down to minister to the men walked in on our conversation.

"This sounds interesting," he said. "Fill me in."

"Oh, I don't know. I don't know that you would understand." In my ignorance, I said, "You know, Catholics don't see things necessarily like Protestants."

"Come on, tell me anyway,"

So I did. I went through the whole story again, and then I said, "I speak in tongues."

"Praise the Lord!" he shouted.

"You know about that?" I asked, surprised.

"Bonnie, if anyone had told me that story eight years ago, I would have told them they were crazy. Then it happened to me."

"You speak in tongues?"

"Yes, and I had a similar experience."

"Wow! I'm concerned as to whether I can control it or not, though."

"You'll be able to control it."

Not only was I born again as John 3 tells us we must be, but now I was also baptized in the Holy Spirit and had the evidence of speaking in tongues.

A hunger for the Word of God rose up inside of me such as I had never known before. I began to read everything I could get my hands on. Television no longer appealed to me. I even moved it into my son's room so I wouldn't have to hear it. Nothing that I used to like appealed to me except Gregory and the men at City Jail, and I even had some-one I could bounce things off of in Brother Brian. Now when I went to the jail, instead of talking to Pete or Vaughn I would go talk to the Lutheran chaplain or Brother Brian, whichever one was there. Questions, questions. Questions that had never been answered were now being answered! And all I had to do was to confess Jesus as my Savior and acknowledge that the power of the Holy Spirit was already working in me, as a real force in my life. I knew I had to become yielded to this Holy Spirit that I had begun to know intimately. I also discovered the source of the "tug."

CHAPTER XIII

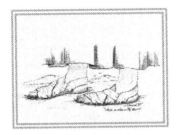

The Spiritual Whirlwind Begins

Satan works hard on those who have just turned to Christ and experienced the power of the Holy Spirit. I expected now to be riding high, drinking in God's Word, and living a life of God's blessings. But such was not to be. It was as though I got hit from every direction. My new Christian walk was indeed filled with severe testing.

The first area of testing was financial. I had gotten to the point on my job where I was finally making enough money to pay my bills, and for two years my ex-husband kept his promise and sent me the portion of military retirement that was due me for fifteen years of marriage. I was finally on course, and things were looking up.

But on September 1, 1987, Bill turned his most recent financial strain into anger towards me. He vented his anger in a letter containing the last retirement check that I was to receive. The letter was full of bitterness, anger, hate and insults. Losing that money hurt me financially, very seriously. To compound the problem, I had been in a sales slump and had no bonus checks to look forward to in the immediate future. All the signs were pointing to financial ruin—for the second time in less than ten years.

God had used the Life Skills Class to prepare me to recognize His Spirit, and then He forced me to turn to Him in a desperate financial situation. I had nowhere else to turn. That's when He brought Patty across my path and used her to lead me the rest of the way to Him.

❖

Away from the jail, suddenly I was having men hit on me everywhere I went. I had never had a problem with that before. I've never thought of myself as beautiful, nor do I present a flirtatious air with men. Consequently, men didn't hit on me.

Now men were crawling out of the woodwork—young, old, fat, slim, white, black, married, and single. I knew Satan was trying to get at me in my new commitment to Christ and in my commitment to Greg. But I had made my commitments, and I was not going back on them. I have to admit, though, the attention was flattering. After all these years, men were finding me attractive. For someone with no self-esteem, it boosted my ego.

I was doing fine turning these men down, until a young single man entered the scene. He was the manager at a local fast food restaurant I went to. His name was Mike, and he was seven years younger than I was.

I don't go to lunch during normal hours because I don't like crowds and I like to study. Often, when I ate at that place, I would get into conversations with Mike. One day he asked me to go to dinner and a show. I hesitated. But he begged me because it was his birthday. I gave in and went out with him. We had a nice evening and I was definitely attracted to him, yet there was something that troubled me. After we parted with one *very* short good night kiss, I felt for the first time what the Scriptures meant when they said, "Do not grieve the Holy Spirit of God." My insides felt like they were being pulled down, or out, or something. It was horrible. I kept thinking of Gregory and my commitment to him, and I wrestled in prayer all the way home. This internal struggle was to be something I would become familiar with as the Lord began His work in me. The flesh does not die easy and because I wanted to follow the Lord, the Holy Spirit in me was very willing to fight my flesh to gain spiritual victory in my life.

Everything seemed fine the next day. Mike was supposed to meet me at church, but he didn't show up. Monday he called me at work to see if I was coming by for lunch. When I got there, my lunch was all ready and on the table waiting for me. I was flattered by the attention. I went back to work and that evening, while I was going to a special prayer meeting at church, my car phone rang. It was Mike. He wanted me to come over to his house.

"I'm on my way to church."

"I thought you would come over to visit me."

"No, I never said that. I've made plans."

"Can't you break them so we can spend some time together? I assumed you would."

"You assumed, did you? I never indicated that I would spend this evening with you. What makes you think you can call me at the last minute and just expect me to change my plans?"

"Well, far be it from me to get between you and your God."

At that comment, I knew for sure that this was a diversionary tactic of the devil. "You're right—I won't let anyone do that. I think we'd better end this conversation now. Good night." I was relieved as I hung up the phone.

"Thank you, Lord. Now I understand why you were grieving my spirit the way you were." Then I shouted, "Devil, if you couldn't get me to play your games as a non-Christian, I don't know what makes you think you can win in this area now that I'm a Christian. Buzz-off, Devil, in Jesus' name."

A confidence and strength was building in me that I had never known before. I was beginning to see myself in a different light. My prayers got deeper and more consistent. I could not get enough of God and His Word. Day and night, I hungered for the Word. I would even get up an hour early to go to church and pray before work. During that time, there were a lot of tears and cleansing that needed to take place in me, from all the years of hurt and pain. This was a time of growth with God that I desperately needed.

In the meantime, Gregory's and my communication got deeper and deeper. God was the center of our relationship. We didn't deny, however, that Gregory was a virile, healthy man and I was a woman, and that the feelings between us were growing tremendously. I loved this gentle giant of a man, who would sing gospel songs to me on our visits. An occasional love song now and then didn't hurt either, but Gregory didn't like singing secular songs anymore.

❖

Another area of testing came through my teaching at the City Jail. I kept getting closer and closer to the men, yet I wanted to quit. I was drained and burning out. I felt as if I couldn't do anything about it. I was getting careless and allowed too much of my human side to show through. Christmas was right around the corner. I wanted to do something special for "my guys," so I planned a Christmas party. Approval was granted. I made each of the men a few sheets of personalized stationary with matching envelopes, packaged in a paper folder. I let the men know I was planning a Christmas party, and I wanted them to let the others know to come.

Two weeks before the party I sent all the men, including the guards I worked with regularly, personalized Christmas cards. They all received them about ten days before the party.

The night of the party came, and I let the men watch the second part of the video *The Cross and The Switchblade*. When the movie was over I began to hand out the stationery by calling the men up one at a time, giving them their present with a little hug.

After the second man came up, the Lieutenant came up and whispered to me. "I forgot to tell you, no Christmas hugs."

"Whoops. Sorry, guys, no more hugs." The thing that stuck in my mind was the "I forgot to tell you..." part of the message. To me, that meant, "set up". I knew then that I was being closely watched that night. I knew that both Warden Jackson and a few of the guards didn't really care for me.

At the end of class, the Captain of the Guard entered. I could see something around this man, in the spirit. It was as though he brought a black, oppressive cloud into the room with him. I ignored it and walked toward the guards, who were rounding up the men to file back to their cells. The tables were set up in a U-shaped arrangement. I always taught either from the open part of the U or in the U itself. I heard the Captain say to the Lieutenant, "How's it going?"

"Fine," he replied.

Then it happened! One of my younger inmates leaned across the table and said, "I'm getting my hug, Bonnie," as he hugged me from across the table. The position I was in, and the way the tables were situated, made it difficult to escape.

"You guys are going to get me in trouble," I said.

The inmate next to him said, "I'll just shake your hand, Bonnie."

Then I turned to get out of the U, and here came one of my more aggressive inmates, with his arms open ready to swoop me up.

"Don't, Jerome. You're going to get me in trouble." He didn't heed my warning, and gave me a big hug anyway.

The Lieutenant came over to me and said, "You got me in big trouble." That black cloud of oppression the Captain had brought in with him indeed brought problems with it, which proved to be my doom there at City Jail.

After clean up, which was very subdued because of the circumstances, one of the guards escorted me out to my car with all the "party fixings" I'd brought in. We entered the elevator without speaking, because we both knew this was it for Ms. Bonnie at City Jail. The elevator stopped abruptly on the fifth floor. When I looked through the bars on the door, there was Sam, a guard that hated women especially me and took pleasure in intimidating the men. He was glaring in at me with his insidious smile. It was as though I were looking into the eyes of Satan himself. Sam spoke in a tone that could send shivers up your spine.

"You thought you were going to get out of here without saying Merry Christmas to me, too, didn't you?"

"No, Sam, I didn't. Merry Christmas." I said gently.

"Well, I got you this time," he said. I can't describe the awful grin he wore, which could penetrate right to the core of a person.

"Merry Christmas, Sam," I repeated, and the elevator started down.

I cried most of the way home, knowing I had blown it, and also knowing I had committed the cardinal sin of getting too close to the men at City Jail. I could see visions of Sam's face and the evil around him. "God, what is happening to me?" I cried out in my heart.

Several days later the phone rang. It was the director of the Social Service Office for the jail. He let me know, "This is the hardest thing I have ever had to do, but the Warden doesn't want you to come back to the jail."

I began to choke back tears as I said, "I know; I understand. I knew it was going to happen." My voice was quivering as I said, "Good-bye." I began to cry. The next day in the mail, I received a letter from the Public School District removing me from the program because of my deplorable conduct.

During the first week in January, 1988, I received a phone call from Pete. I was glad to hear from him.

"Pete, I didn't do anything wrong, really."

"We all know that, Bonnie. We really miss you here."

I became silent and the tears began to flow.

"You're crying?" Pete asked.

I choked. "Yes, but I'm okay. What's up?"

"The authorities beat up on Thomas, because he didn't want them to take the paper you gave him. Jerome was thrown in the hole and blamed for your dismissal."

"Oh, no. Pete, I've been praying so hard," I said, crying.

"That's not all. Sam was found dead of a heart attack in his car the day after you left."

"You've got to be kidding! Do you know what happened that last night with him and me?" I began to tell him the story about the elevator. When I finished, he told me there was more.

"The director of the Social Service was so upset that he single-handedly went to your defense at the meeting with Security, Social Service and Warden Jackson the Monday after. Bonnie, he doesn't go to bat for anyone as he did for you. Security just wanted to slap your hand and tell you to back off. My boss told them to leave you alone, because you were the best thing that ever happened to the jail. But the Warden got the last word in: 'That woman will never set foot in this building again.'"

"They actually went to bat for me?"

"Yes, they did," Pete replied. "But there's still more. The Warden was found last Tuesday, slumped over his desk with a heart attack. He's in the hospital having surgery. They don't expect him to come back to work."

"I didn't pray for that. I didn't want anything to happen to any of the guys, or the Warden, or anybody."

"I know. It's not the same without you. Vaughn was upset when he came in and found out you couldn't come back."

"What can I say? I love you guys, and that's what got me in trouble. I didn't want anything to happen to anyone. Did they hurt Thomas?"

"He's tough; he'll be all right."

Needless to say, it was a rough day for me. I kept asking the Lord to tell me what was happening to me. Then my boss called me into the office. My sales had been down, and there was a cash flow problem with the company. He asked me to take a $500 per month decrease in draw. I really didn't have any choice, seeing my personal sales were down. So between my ex-husband, the dismissal from the Literacy Program and the decrease in draw, I lost about $1,200 per month income. It really crippled me. I was just beginning to come out from under financial stress, and got slapped down again.

I kept crying out to God. One night I asked the Lord to show me what was going on. I didn't expect the answer the way I received it, but I was glad it came the way it did, because I was able to understand a lot more of what had been happening for the past several months. My answer came in the form of a vision. It was as though God rolled back the spiritual curtain and let me see into the spiritual world around me, just as He did in the Old Testament (II Kings 6:17). In this vision, I saw demons coming after me and laughing at the destruction that was coming down on me. Then, out of the center of this group of demons, came Satan himself—and he was jeering at me as Sam had been jeering at me. It scared me and I shouted out loud, "Jesus! Jesus!" The vision disappeared as fast as it had come. I knew then that my problems were spiritual, and I could only trust in God to deliver me from this.

Shortly after the vision, I took my car to the dealership to have it worked on. A lady came up to me and said, "I saw the fish and dove on your car and knew I just had to talk to you." We spent the next hour in the waiting room alone, talking without interruption. I began to tell her my story and expressed my confusion over what was happening.

"Do you know the story of David and Saul?"

"No, I've been a Christian such a short time (four months), I don't know the Bible stories," I replied. I had my Bible with me, so we found the story where Saul was chasing David. David was hiding in the cave and cut the corner of Saul's cloak off. He felt so guilty for touching an anointed vessel of God that he had to tell Saul what he had done.

"That's your story for this situation," she said.

"I don't understand."

"God anointed you to be down at the jail—first, to get born again, and then to minister to the men. When those in authority came against you, against God's will, God removed them for touching an anointed vessel of God."

"No!"

"Yes. You were anointed and called by God to be at the jail, and He removed those who got in your way. Vengeance is God's alone."

I began to understand, but I was still questioning, "Why me, Lord? What are you doing to me?" It was almost frightening, and yet I was peaceful at the same time. My peacefulness could only be attributed to that familiar "tug" that seemed to be leading my life now in every area.

CHAPTER XIV

After The Call—Then What?

One Tuesday night in February, 1988, the leaders at church were teaching about going boldly before the Lord for our needs. I told the group I didn't have a problem praying for the needs of others, but when it came to me, I couldn't do it because it was selfish. They told me, "God knows your needs before you have them, but sometimes you have to ask for them to be met." I had a hard time with that teaching, because I didn't think of myself as being self-centered, and I thought going boldly was a form of idolatry. The next night I was awakened suddenly with a loud voice coming out of my spirit.

"Ask Me!"

"What?"

"Ask Me!" it said again.

"Okay, God. You know I have 120,000 miles on my car and some repair that's needed. I need a new car. I also want a computer for correspondence and for writing my book. I know you know my financial condition; I need help there, too. In Jesus' name, Amen. Goodnight." I did it. The only reason I prayed that way was because I felt God woke me up and asked me to. I didn't even think about it again; I had asked, and that was it. I laid my head back down and went off to sleep.

While I was driving in my car one day, the Lord began to show me things about my call and to give me ideas about the men in prison and about how to bring them back into society successfully. This wasn't the first time I had seen these visions or thought those thoughts. I would always rebuke the devil, when I came to my senses, for putting pride in me. Time and time again I rebuked the devil. On this particular day when I was getting those thoughts and visions, I began rebuking the devil again. A voice came out of my spirit that clearly said, "I'm not the devil." Tears began to well up in me as I began to realize the work the Lord had ordained for me to do. Who was I, that the Lord would put such dreams and visions in front of me—a nobody, a loser? No one ever listened to me before; why would anyone listen to me now?

A week or two later, one Wednesday evening in February, when I was at the office after working hours, I received a strange phone call from my mother. She told me to spend three days seeking God, not to read anything heavy and to avoid large groups of people. I had to ask her whether I could read my Bible because that was pretty heavy reading, and I had to ask her about church. She seemed to hedge a bit on both questions, which bothered me considerably. I knew in my heart that God would never tell me not to read my Bible or study His word, but I was not sure about keeping away from large groups or church. I wrestled with this. I knew my mother was spiritually sensitive, but I also knew to check it against the Bible anytime someone gave me spiritual direction.

The next day as I was still wrestling with it, I asked the Lord directly, "What do you want me to do?" The answer that came up out of my spirit surprised me: "Go to Michigan and see your mother." I really didn't want to go, and I began giving God my reasons. "God, I have a balloon spare tire I'm riding on, and it already has 150 miles on it. There is no way I can make that trip on those tires. Besides, this is my weekend to visit Greg."

I continued to wrestle, and I kept getting the same message. Finally, I gave in. "Okay, Lord. If I go home and there's a check in the mail, I will get two new tires, take a vacation day, and leave tomorrow morning for Michigan."

I went home to check the mail and guess what? My state income tax check was there—only two weeks after I filed. I went to a tire place and got my new tires. I went back to work and cleaned up what I needed to clean up so I could take the next day off work. I was still wrestling, though, because of the resistance (or should I say the rebellion) I had towards authority figures in my life, including my mother. I was tired of always being wrong, being told I was wrong, and always being criticized. Although my family has always told me I take criticism well.

The next morning I prayed, to confirm what I was doing. Then I took my time about hitting the road. I was led by God to stop by a Christian bookstore to pick up a couple of books. While I was strolling through the bookstore, I was drawn to a small book about the discerning of spirits. I knew nothing about discerning spirits (I Corinthians 12), or so I thought.

I propped the little book up on my steering wheel, and as I drove, I would glance down at it to skim the pages. Wow—was it enlightening! The devils that I saw when I asked God to show me what was going on around me was indeed a form of the spiritual gift called "discerning of spirits." And some of the other experiences I had at the jail were also the gift in operation. I began to realize I had a special gift.

I prayed a lot on the trip, but I was not expecting what happened as soon as I crossed the Michigan border. Up out of my spirit came the most gut-wrenching travail I had ever experienced to date. I prayed and prayed. I prayed so hard that I thought this would never leave me. Finally, in Kalamazoo, I received a release in my spirit. "Lord," I asked, "what is going on? I can't stand this!"

"Call your mother and ask her how she is. Let her know you're on your way."

"Okay, Lord." I pulled off to call. My mother answered the phone. "Mom, how are you feeling?"

"Oh, hi, Bonnie. I was feeling pretty punk, but within the past hour or so I've been feeling better."

"Good. I'm in Kalamazoo. I'll be in Lansing in about an hour and a half."

"You're in Michigan?"

"Yes, I felt the Lord told me to come."

That was a shock to her. I didn't understand why until after I arrived in Lansing. She was glad to see me, but I had thrown her off balance a bit by coming unexpectedly.

After my dad went to bed, my mother began our conversation with, "Have you ever thought about becoming a minister?"

"Well, yes," I answered. "God has been dealing with me on that." I was more than a little surprised by the question.

My mother began to tell me her vision. She said, "Do you remember the vision I had of the building with the columns that I told you about, and I thought that it had something to do with a change for you?"

"Yes."

"Well, after that, I had another vision." I listened attentively as my mother shared her vision with me. "I saw this wheat field and the wheat was swaying in the wind. Then the speed of the swaying wheat picked up and I kept getting wheat—on, wheat-on, wheat-on. Then I put it together and realized that there was a school named Wheaton. I quickly called the library for the information." It was clear that my mother had received the name of the Bible College she felt I should attend. Frankly, I had never heard of Wheaton College. She had requested information about the school when she had called. She pulled out all the literature to show me. "I talked to the graduate school and asked about the possibility of you going there. Wheaton was started by the Methodist Church."

"Mom, I can't just quit my job and go to school full time. There is no way I can do that with my debt structure."

We kept talking until I could no longer stay awake. It was almost 4:00 A.M. when I finally dropped off to sleep on the couch. The next day, Saturday, Mom and I spent the day just visiting, more or less avoiding the subject of school.

I knew I had twelve hours of driving to do, fourteen if I wanted to go see Gregory, so I left that evening. I knew I could get my rest on the other end before I had to be back to work on Monday. I prayed a lot about the visit to Michigan and about the school. *I can't go to school,* I thought. *There is no way I'm graduate school material. I could never get in.*

I wanted to visit Gregory that weekend because he was expecting me, and I couldn't get a message to him otherwise. If I didn't visit then, it would be a month before I could visit again. I drove hard, stopping only for bathroom breaks and catnaps at truck stops. As I neared the penitentiary, around noon, I was praying and singing in the Spirit. The last road going to the prison was a winding, two-lane highway. As I was driving along, I asked the Lord to let me sing with my understanding so I would know what I was saying. Suddenly, the most beautiful song came from me, and I am not a singer. I was caught up in the song, but then a feeling of a binding came in my throat. It was as though something just had to get out, so I yielded to the Spirit to bring forth the message. The message was, "Oh, my God, I know now what I am to do. I am to teach; I am to preach." Then the sensation in my throat left as fast as it had come. Tears began to flow from the depths of my spirit. This new revelation was running around in my mind.

Suddenly, a sense of alarm came over me. I kept hearing the message, "Slow down, slow down." Not knowing what was going on, I was getting concerned. I slowed the car down. My speed had crept up above the speed limit. *Maybe there's a speed trap ahead,* I thought. It was more than that. My speed crept up again. "Slow down! Set your cruise control," came the urgent message. I began to set my cruise control, concerned about what was going on in my spirit. I fumbled with the cruise control. Consequently, I slowed down well below the speed limit for a spell. Then I saw it. A car was coming at me head on. Its driver had decided to pass on a curve. If I had not fussed with the cruise control and slowed the car down below the speed limit, I would have had a head-on collision. Our cars missed by inches. As soon as the danger of collision passed, so did the urgency in my spirit, and I had peace again.

My visit with Greg was short because of the trip, but I did get to share with him everything that happened. I asked him to pray about all of it, because it seemed so bizarre to me. I thought it had to be God because I couldn't, in my wildest imagination, have concocted such a story. From the first day I felt the "tug" to call the Missouri Coalition for Literacy, right up to that day with Gregory, I could look back and see confirmation of the call.

CHAPTER XV

What Would You Give?

I was wrestling with all that had happened to me. I didn't know what to do—about school, or about the rest of my life. So I sought the Lord, prayed and read my Bible and prayed. I would get up at five o'clock and go to church to pray before going to work. It was so peaceful in the church. I would walk and pray, sit and pray and read my Bible. One February morning, I was sitting peacefully waiting on the Lord. Then I heard something, clearer then I have heard before. "Bury your past, get rid of your possessions, give ten percent to the church." It startled me, so I questioned it. "Bury your past, get rid of your possessions, give ten percent to the church," came the message again.

I heard it twice, distinctly. I just sat there weeping, knowing it was God. I knew I needed to bury my past, because it was choking me. I also knew that moving on with God would be impossible until I did. I didn't jump to obey the message, however. I had learned that if it were God, He would confirm the message to me two or three times.

Through wrestling in my mind, I kept getting the same message. I decided to make an appointment with the pastor because of the nature of the request I believed God had given me. I explained to him some of what had happened to me so far as a Christian, and shared the message about burying my past and getting rid of my possessions. He responded with a question. "Bonnie, do you know the difference between anxiety and peace?"

"Yes."

"When you first received that message, was the feeling anxiety or peace?"

"I wasn't anxious. I knew I had to do it, to rid myself of the past."

He gave me several Scriptures about the peace of God to meditate on. He told me God would show me what to do next and take me step by step through it. I read the Scriptures, and I knew I had peace, not anxiety. I knew deep down inside me what I had to do, but we were talking about everything I owned!

One Saturday afternoon I was pondering this issue of my past. I decided to pray, so I sat down in the middle of the living room floor and began to talk to God.

"Lord, this is heavy, what I believe You are asking me to do. I understand that it's necessary, but I have to know that it really is You. If I know it's You, then I know it will be all right, but if it isn't You, I don't want to make a mistake. I don't want to miss it, Lord. God, if this is You, would You please give me a sign." I paused to figure a sign. "Lord," I said, "I'm going to reach my hands up to You. My right hand is 'yes' and my left hand is 'no'. Would you give me a sign, please." At that prayer, an electrical charge went through my right hand and arm. *Wow!* I thought. "Thank you, Lord. I believe it's You. But you know how heavy this is for me. I have to know it's You and not a pinched nerve or something in my right arm. So I'll lift my hands again, only this time my left hand is 'yes' and my right hand is 'no.'" As soon as I finished that prayer, I lifted my hands up and the electrical charge went through my left hand and down my left arm. "Thank you Lord. I know it is You." At the time, I had never read the story about Gideon in the Bible, so I didn't know that what I had done was to "throw out a fleece," but I knew in my spirit that God was showing me what to do.

It was an awesome thought, getting rid of everything I owned; I hadn't ever heard of God asking anyone to really do that. People talked about it, but to do it was something else. Yet the confirmation was too strong to deny, so I yielded. "God, I'm willing, but you are going to have to show me how."

❖

Not long after I asked God for that sign about my possessions, I was in a restaurant for lunch. There were a couple of women at the next table talking. I didn't hear anything in their conversation except the word "auction." That was it—the Lord was telling me to have an auction.

I searched the local phone book, but found only a couple of auctioneers. Only one answered the phone. I explained what I wanted, and he came over to see what I had. Initially, I just wanted to auction the antiques I had spent hours refinishing and the Bavarian china we got in Germany—only the things of real value except for my diamond sapphire ring that was given to me as a graduation present from my ex-husband. The thought of everything was still too overwhelming to me.

This auctioneer, however, convinced me to get rid of everything, period—even the mobile home. I had thought before he had come over that God was prompting me get rid of everything, and everything around me seemed like confirmation.

Under normal circumstances, this auctioneer would be the last person I would trust with anything of mine. I was totally unimpressed. He was obnoxious, arrogant, rude and unprofessional. I had all I could do to keep from kicking him out of my house, but I had a peace about me inside that I could not explain. I knew he was the one to use.

As I was preparing everything for auction, I was looking around the living room. I had a nice stereo system that was relatively new. My son Bob was there. He was due to graduate from high school in a couple of months, and I didn't have anything to give him.

"Bob," I said, "do you like the stereo?"

"Yeah, I like the stereo."

"Well, seeing I can't give you anything for graduation, you can have that to take to college with you."

"Really?"

"Yes."

"Wow! Hey, Mom, seeing you don't watch television anymore, can I have the TV too?"

"Sure, you can take that, too."

"Mom—can I have the electric typewriter, too?"

"Well, if this is real and I do wind up going to school, I'm going to need it myself. Unless, of course, you want to give me a computer," I said jokingly.

"Sure, I'll give you a computer."

"You don't have one to give."

"Not now, but I will. Dad is giving me an IBM compatible with a hard drive and color monitor for graduation."

"You're kidding. That is exactly what I've been looking at for the last four years. I don't necessarily need a color monitor, but I'll take it. Are you serious? I've been pricing them for three years."

"Yeah, I know. Dad's getting a deal from work."

I suddenly remembered that night in February when God woke me up and told me to "ask Him." One of the things I had asked for was a computer, and now here it was!

❖

In the meantime, my mother sent me a picture of herself standing in front of one of the buildings at Wheaton College. The picture represented the vision she'd had, only in the vision it was me walking up to the building. Then my mother called me and asked if I could meet her and my dad up in Wheaton.

In mid-April, my parents and I met in Chicago and went to Wheaton's graduate school to talk to a counselor in the admissions department. We didn't have an appointment—we just went. What a day that was. Everything we attempted to do, we got done. One of my fears was alleviated when the counselor told me that because it had been nine years since I'd received my Bachelor's Degree, I wouldn't need to take a GRE (Graduate Record Exam). What a relief that was, because I knew I couldn't pass it. Amazingly, all the doors seemed to be open for me to walk through that day. After that trip, I went through the actual application process for Wheaton. I had to wait six to eight weeks for acceptance, which would not be until mid-June.

❖

We had a beautiful spring day for the auction. The auctioneer managed to get two other people's things merged with mine and rented a hall for the occasion. Ads went in numerous newspapers, and we were expecting to make a haul, especially with all the beautiful things I had. My fine things were what the crowd seemed to be waiting for.

Finally, they began to pull my treasures out, one at a time. When that happened I could not believe what I was seeing. God had rolled back the spiritual curtain again, and all I saw was vultures picking at my old life. They were tearing me apart. My treasures were being bought up for practically nothing. I couldn't stand it anymore, so I went outside. There was a lunch wagon there, and the man in charge had no activity because the prime items were finally being auctioned off.

I started to dump on the poor man. "That is twenty-five years of my life, going for nothing in there, and there is nothing I can do about it." I paused. "Do you believe in God?" I asked.

"Yes," he said. "When I saw the ad for this auction, I figured it would be a good place to set up, but I'm doing lousy." He went on talking. I don't even remember what he said, just that it was something about God clearing out the old things in people's lives to make room for the new. All I know is whatever he said, it was what I needed to hear.

"God sent you to tell me that, thanks." I walked off to pray.

When it was all over and everyone was taking my treasures to their homes, I sat in the car with a friend of mine. Suddenly, I started laughing hilariously.

"What is the matter with you?" She said.

"Don't you see what just happened? Those people are going home thinking they got a real steal, and they did—but none of them will go home like me. I'll go home tonight financially wiped out, and sleep on the floor, but I'm going to be happy and peaceful, and they will never know what I know right now. Don't you see what God just did for me?"

"Bonnie, you need to see this movie I have. It's called *Out of Africa*. It's about an English woman who lost everything."

"I don't want to watch it."

"I think you need to."

So I went to my friend's house, and she got the video going. It was a good movie. The woman suffered many of the things I had with my ex-husband and finally wound up auctioning off everything she owned to return to her homeland. I had just auctioned off everything I owned to get where I felt God wanted me to be. For me, that was the emotional equivalent of my "homeland." I left after the movie, feeling even more confident and peaceful in knowing that I was right where God wanted me.

Gregory called later that day to find out how the auction went. His response wasn't exactly what I expected; he sounded sort of matter-of-fact about it. Years later he told me he'd been wondering if I had really heard from God. He didn't question me about it, because he didn't feel he knew me well enough to know if I was hearing God's voice. There is no doubt in his mind now that I was walking in obedience to the Lord.

❖

While on my way to work Monday, I was seeking the Lord saying, "Lord, two people are going to ask me how the auction went, and I don't like the answer I have to give them. Help me, Lord." Out of the depths of my spirit came Matthew 16:24. I quickly pulled the car over to the side of the road, grabbed my Bible and turned to that Scripture. I had no idea what it said beforehand, because I was biblically illiterate at the time.

The NASB has section headings over blocks of Scripture to summarize and identify thoughts, parables, etc. The heading over Matthew 16:24 read "Discipleship Is Costly."

"Praise the Lord!" I shouted. "I was hearing Your voice!

Then Jesus said to His disciples, If anyone wishes to come after Me, let him deny himself, and take up his cross, and follow Me. For whoever wishes to save his life shall lose it; but whoever loses his life for My sake shall find it. For what will a man be profited, if he gains the whole world and forfeits his soul? Or what will a man give in exchange for his soul? For the

Son of Man is going to come in the glory of His Father with His angels; and will then recompense every man according to his needs.

I cried the rest of the way to work, knowing in my heart that when God had required my possessions of me, the ultimate expression of who I was, I gave them obediently. Now my wrestling was over concerning my possessions and nothing anyone could say would make me doubt anymore whether I was hearing the voice of God.

Only one person asked how the auction went, and when he did, I placed my Bible on his desk, opened to Matthew 16:24, and walked away.

I netted enough from the auction to pay off one bill, auto insurance for my son and myself and give ten percent to the church. That was the sum total of twenty-five years of my life. What is a life worth? Ask yourself!

CHAPTER XVI

Finally Accepted

It was nearing the end of June, and I still did not know whether I was accepted to Wheaton. My sales were horrible. Over the course of the past couple months I had lost all my "bread-and-butter" accounts to competitors. No matter how low I cut my profit margin, the competition came in lower. I quoted more jobs that month than I had quoted in any other month in my seven-year career with the company. Out of more than $1 million in quotes, I did not get one order. My sales for the month were so low they were embarrassing, and nothing had shipped for me either. I could do nothing right. I had orders on backlog, but either shipments were late coming in to us, or the customer was not ready to receive them yet. Consequently, my record to the sales manager for the second quarter was at the point where something needed to be done with Bonnie, and I knew it.

I was beside myself, not knowing where to turn. I was seeking the Lord diligently, but with my debt structure I didn't feel I could quit my job and go to school full time. And yet, with the way my job was going, I wasn't sure how much longer I was going to have a job. My living conditions weren't much better either. I still had my mobile home, but there was no furniture at all. Both my son and I were still sleeping on the floor in an empty house.

I had to find out what direction I was going, so I called Wheaton College to see if they had made a decision on my application. The secretary I talked to was very nice. She got the file out and informed me the letter was in the mail.

"Could you tell me now whether I have been accepted."

"I'm not supposed to do that," she replied hesitantly, "but I will. They have denied your application."

"Does the letter state a reason? My GPA from Kansas State University was 3.02. Do you have any idea what the problem might be?"

"No, I don't know."

"I don't believe they read my transcripts," I said. "If they had, they would have seen I completed 67 hours of credit in one calendar year while raising two sons, and still maintained a "B" average. Are they saying I can't do the work? My transcripts prove differently."

"Bonnie, I don't normally do things like this, but I think you need to come up here and talk to someone. Can you take the time?"

"Yes. Who do I need to talk to?"

The secretary gave me the names of some people to see who she thought might be able to help me. As a rule I am not an aggressive person, but prior to the Life Skills class at City Jail, I had never been one who could speak in front of a group either. Now, even speaking with the secretary, that same boldness was there. The next day I called and set up an appointment for the following week with one of the women in Admissions. I would take two vacation days and make the trip.

On the day of my appointment, I sat in the Admissions Office asking why my application was denied. The Admissions Counselor was sweet and tactful in her approach with me. I can't remember her exact words, but what it amounted to was that I had no Bible background— which was true. I would need to take undergraduate courses in Bible and Theology in order even to be considered. She did, however, tell me about an equivalency test that was offered at the beginning of each semester. If I passed it, they would waive the requirements for the Basic Bible and Theology classes. There were three tests: New Testament, Old Testament and Basic Theology. I knew right then there was no way I could pass the three tests. I just do not test well. Besides, I didn't even know what theology was.

She proceeded to tell me that Wheaton College had standards that had to be met, and I did not meet those standards. Unless I could pass the equivalency tests, I would not be approved for admission to their school.

Then I had my turn. For an hour or more I shared with her the things that had happened to me since I became born again. I shared some of my vision with her. By the time I finished, she couldn't deny that there was a call on my life—and we both knew that fulfilling that call would require more education.

"Have you thought about applying at another school?"

"No!" I persisted. "The vision was of me attending Wheaton. I don't need to apply anywhere else. I'm supposed to be here." I could not believe the boldness I displayed.

"Bonnie, why did you apply for the Education curriculum?"

"Because that's what the other counselor told me to do," I answered. "Education was not my choice."

"I see. I thought that had been your decision."

"No! Does that change things?"

"I think so." She paused to collect her thoughts. "We have a program that awards an Advanced Certificate of Bible and Theology. It's a one-year program, consisting of 24 credit hours of designated courses. At the end of the year, if the student maintains a 3.0 minimum average, they can enter the Master's program under the Interdisciplinary Studies curriculum. This is also a one-year program, but it requires 48 credit hours and the student designs his or her own curriculum. The neat part is that the credits earned for the Advanced Certificate are Master's level credits, and are transferable into the Interdisciplinary Studies program.

"This program was designed to accommodate missionaries who work in countries that scrutinize their curriculum course work. That's why the students design their own programs. This way, if the students need psychology courses, they can request them; if they need theology, they can do the same, etc. It's a flexible program. The total time it would take on a full-time basis is two years."

"I don't know that I have two years."

"Well, that's the program. I'm not saying I can get you into it, but it looks like the only option we have. If you think you have the time to complete the program, I'll see if we can talk to the Dean of Admissions to get his approval. Now, I must tell you—if you *are* accepted in this program, it will be strictly on a probationary basis."

"I understand."

Probation again! That seemed to be the story of my academic life, because I simply did not meet the standards—EVER.

We went to talk to the Dean, who happened to be available at that time. The meeting went well; I felt better when I left. At least I had a chance, now. My poor sales performance did not seem as devastating to me any more; now there was a glimmer of hope.

July 15th came, and I had still not received formal confirmation of my acceptance, so I called the Admissions Office to check on my application. The answer was different this time. I was accepted to begin classes at Wheaton College in the fall semester, which began in late August, 1988.

With this information in hand, I went to a meeting the Sales Manager had scheduled with me. I knew he wanted to talk to me about my poor sales and lack of orders invoiced, but I really wasn't prepared for what he actually said. He began by asking me to take another $500 per month cut in my draw, which made my total income loss in less than one year $1,700 per month. He worked out a commission program that would enable me to pay the draw back sooner; I could still receive regular bonuses in the meantime, so it was a little easier to take.

I understood where he was coming from and I was not offended, but after he presented the new pay program, I spoke up. "I need to be fair and honest with you," I said. "I just found out I've been accepted into the master's program at Wheaton College. I've decided to go back to school full time to prepare for the ministry. I have a month to clean up my backlog and take care of any outstanding problems, so you won't have to deal with any of those headaches after I leave."

There was light conversation for a spell, then he asked, "Will you agree to this program for the last month?"

"Yes, I will."

It was done. My notice was in, and I didn't even feel bad. You'd think after being with a company for seven years there would be some feelings, but I had none. I finally had focus and a place to go with something to do.

❖

In the meantime, Gregory's case was scheduled to go to Appeals Court. I had obtained a copy of his trial transcript, all 1,300 pages of it, and I began to study it. I wrote my first letter to the Appeals Court on Greg's behalf. I got a nice letter back saying that my letter was received and went into the file, per the Supreme Court rule that deals with extra correspondence. In my innocence, I had imagined my letter would have some impact. I soon discovered that because Gregory had filed a 29-15 motion for ineffective assistance of council that the appeal process would drag on until a decision was made on the motion.

❖

August came, and suddenly my entire backlog started shipping. I was able to clean up my messes and invoice them. It was wild—I could not believe it. I was even able to stop working earlier than I thought.

I did not have a phone because of my financial condition, so I had to call my son collect. Bill was nineteen years old now and living in Connecticut. I told him I was moving to Wheaton and needed help moving. Could he come to help his brother move me?

"Mom," he asked, "how is your car?"

"It has 130,000 miles on it. I just put $1,200 into repairs, and it needs another $600 worth of work from what I can see, and it's only two and a half years old."

"How much do you owe?"

"$3,000."

"Mom, I have a better chance of getting a pay-off for you here in Connecticut than you do in Missouri. I have $1,000 I can put down on a car, and I have a good job. I make more money than I need. I'm going to buy you a car and bring it when I move you. Then I'll bring your car back here to sell it."

"Bill, you don't have to do this."

"I know, but you need a good car. You're going to be alone. How much are your car payments?"

"$230 a month. Bill, I don't need anything more than a pregnant roller skate, so don't get carried away."

"You let me handle it. When do you need me down there?"

"August 15th. I don't have much to move, just enough to set up housekeeping. You know, dishes, pots and pans and the aquarium. The aquarium is going to be a problem, but I think we can do it between the three of us." The aquarium was 75 gallons, and I had fifteen fish—each approximately twelve inches long.

I made a quick trip back up to Wheaton to see about housing. I went to the Housing Office first and they only had one-bedroom apartments with roommates.

"No—no! You don't understand. I'm forty-three years old, I am the head of a household just like any man with a family, and I have to have a place for my sons to visit me. I don't need a roommate there; besides, I don't share a bedroom with anyone. Can you understand where I'm coming from? I'm not a kid away from home for the first time."

"Yes, I do. But every two-bedroom I have is designated for foreign students who are on their way." She paused. "Why don't you do this. Go and see what you can find in town, but check back with me before you leave town. Will you do that?"

"Yes, I will. Thank you."

I shopped around town and was disgusted with what I saw. Having been a "military wife" for fifteen years, I'd gotten used to leaving a set of quarters that had passed a white glove inspection, and anything less is not too appealing. I went back over to the Housing Office, disappointed. Mrs. Sullivan asked how it was going.

"Not too good. I was not impressed with what I saw for the price."

"Well, Bonnie, I believe God has called you to the ministry, but your family situation is a little unusual, so I've decided to give you a two-bedroom apartment by yourself."

"Praise God! He knows, doesn't He? Thank you."

She gave me the instructions for checking in and sent me to the building coordinator so I could be shown my apartment. My apartment was better than anything I had seen on my own, and it was furnished.

I was starting to get excited now. I was going to Wheaton College! Even though I had never heard of Wheaton before, I was finding out it was the "Harvard" of evangelical colleges. The Admissions counselor hadn't been kidding when she said I didn't meet their standards. Well, maybe I didn't fit according to human standards, but God had decided otherwise.

Now I needed to get a crash course in the Bible. If I could take and pass those equivalency tests, I would not have to take the additional undergraduate courses. And God, as God will do, provided the way. I had learned, just before moving to Wheaton, that Marilyn Hickey was coming to our church to teach her *Bible Encounter*, which was a complete summary of the Bible in a three-day seminar. It was just what I needed. I did not miss a session. I had the overview of the Bible I needed that would help me when I entered Wheaton. I had no idea the Bible had that much to offer anyone.

I was ready to go now. Everything had been taken care of. My son Bill was due in late that night. He was driving straight through from the East Coast. I knew he would be tired when he got in. He still had his key, so I didn't have to stay up to wait for him. I heard him come in during the wee hours of the morning. He was so exhausted he went right to sleep.

The next morning I took the dogs out for a walk, and there, sitting on my front lawn, was a brand new Toyota Corolla FX-GTS. Wow! It was so sharp—and it was brand new! It was just what I needed. Bill knew I always wanted a Toyota because of the lack of repair they require on a good preventive maintenance program. I couldn't wait until Bill woke up, because he had the keys.

"Did you see the car?" he asked when he woke up.

"I sure did. Wow!"

"It's a limited edition, so it will keep its value up better. I knew you wanted a Toyota, so that was all I looked at. Mom, I am really sorry it's white, but that was the best deal I could find."

"Bill, three months ago I was walking in the park and asked the Lord, if I ever had another car, to let it be white. God made sure that was the best deal you could find. "

"Mom, I wanted to get something I wouldn't be ashamed to drive myself if I had to take it back." He paused. "What happened to all the furniture?"

"I auctioned it off."

"How long have you been living like this?"

"Four months. It hasn't been bad. I've gotten use to it. Bob had to know what it was like to go through a wipeout with me as you did. Now both of you have experienced it with me. I don't have room for it in Wheaton anyway, because my apartment is furnished."

Does God hear our prayers and fill our needs? Absolutely! As we delight ourselves in Him, He gives us the "desires of our heart." But what people often don't realize is that sometimes it is the Lord putting the desires on our hearts. One thing I learned, though, was that it was God's car, just at it was God's computer. I was the vessel He chose to bless with it, but everything I had was God's. True, He used my sons to provide the blessings, but I knew who set the stage for my blessings.

CHAPTER XVII

Introduction To Wheaton

This move to Wheaton was my twenty-fourth move in twenty-three years, and I had only enough material possessions left to set up house-keeping. I was leaving St. Louis where I had lived longer than any other place in my adult life. St. Louis represented, to me, some of the worst heartaches and greatest fears I had ever known. But it is also where I had come to know Jesus personally.

The saddest thing about moving was that I would be approximately 400 miles away from Gregory, and I wouldn't be able to visit him regularly. By this time, there was no question for either of us that God had called us together, and our friendship had grown and blossomed into the kind of love that lasts a lifetime. I knew this gentle giant of a man would be my husband as soon as he was free.

❖

Settling down in Illinois was easy. That was fortunate, because the equivalency testing was held the week after I moved in. I went through six hours of testing. The questions were foreign to me. After receiving the results of the equivalency test, I had to add New Testament and Old Testament Survey to my fall course work, which overloaded my schedule.

I went to the bookstore and came home with twenty-four, hard-reading theology books that were required reading, and I only had five classes. One of the books was 1200 pages using and ten-point font, ugh! I scanned a couple of the books to see what I was in for. With my reading skills, this was really going to be a challenge. I hoped the Lord knew what He was doing with me.

I had the same professor for four of the six Bible and Theology classes in my program. He was also my advisor. I started right away being the target of his "old" jokes, seeing I was the oldest student in the class. I was not offended because it was the only thing I could understand in his classes. I was lost! I would leave classes in a fog, having no idea what had been said. My listening skills were useless. The professors used words I never heard of before, and they kept running around in my head. Propitiation, autonomy, hermeneutics, atonement, apocalyptic, pseudepigrapha, Parousia, Pentateuch, Torah, Talmud, exegesis, and on and on they went.

Not only did I have to take basic Bible, but also I had to learn a whole new vocabulary for subjects in which I was illiterate—that was all of them. On top of that, God called me to be an intercessor during my school career. I spent between twenty and thirty hours in prayer each week. It seemed a spiritual decathlon was before me. I was in a school that no one can "skate" through. Even the brightest students complained about the volume of reading.

I found a church whose pastor was a Wheaton College graduate and a forty-year evangelical, who believed in the spiritual gifts for today. If it had not been for that church, I don't think I would ever have made it through school. Often I left class wondering who God was. The God they seemed to be talking about was not the God with whom I had a personal relationship with in my prayer time. I was confused with intellectual versus spiritual Christianity. It was as though I was bouncing between the Pharisees and the Zealots, back and forth from one view to another. I was almost afraid to say I was Charismatic, until I found out 50 percent of the graduate school had their roots in Pentecostalism (which surprised the staff, too).

I often felt spiritual warfare going on around me, so during those days I would usually fast. In one particular fast, I was into some heavy warfare. The first night God pulled back the spiritual curtain, and I saw the enemy throwing darts at me. I could literally feel pricks in my flesh. I prayed and prayed, and called intently upon the Lord. At one spell during the battle, I felt a heaviness coming from a dark area of the room to my right side. I spun around facing that section of the room. The Lord let me see the devil himself in the spirit. "Get out of here, you foul devil, in Jesus' name," I commanded, and he left. After more than an hour, I got a release in my spirit.

The next night it started again. The travail and groanings were intense again. After a spell, I started getting strong pains in my mid-section. I asked the Lord to show me what was going on. Again He rolled back the spiritual curtain, and I saw more demonic activity. This time there was a message with it. "You defeated my infantry; now I'm sending my artillery after you." I could feel hits to my spirit. It felt as though someone was kicking me in the stomach. I groaned and travailed for at least an hour. After a most difficult spiritual battle, release came.

"Lord," I prayed, "if this fast is going to be like this every night, I don't know that I want to go through with it. What else is the devil going to throw at me?" I wondered if all Christians go through the sort of spiritual battle I was going through. I later discovered that most don't, although by keeping my ears open I learned that many missionaries who serve in Third World countries have similar experiences, because of the prevalence of voodoo and witchcraft they must deal with on a regular basis.

On the last day of my fast I was walking down the prairie path praying. As I neared the park I normally turned into, I felt a spiritual heaviness build up around me. It was heavier than anything I had experienced so far. I asked God, "What is going on?" Again, He opened my spiritual eyes. All along the path were demons, huge ones this time. They were jeering at me, but not reaching out at me. Their presence, however, created a cold heaviness around me that made me feel claustrophobic, as if I was shut up in a room with them. I continued to walk and pray. As I turned to go into the park, suddenly Satan jumped up in front of me, saying, "You got my infantry and you got my artillery, but I'm sending the nukes after you now."

I was alone in the park, so I answered him softly, but firmly, "Satan, you can't defeat the blood of Christ." Then I saw something "in the Spirit" that set me to weeping. "Look behind you, Satan; you have had it," I said. Just then, I saw Jesus grab the devil by the nape of the neck and throw him down, saying, "She's mine. You can't have her anymore." I broke down in tears. Seeing Jesus come to *my* rescue was more than I could bear. He really did love *me*. Now I understood the reason for this fast. I needed to see His love in action.

❖

I didn't talk openly about my intercessory prayer experiences, for there are a lot of Christians who don't understand this part of spirituality. Perhaps some of you reading this book are not familiar with this type of demonic activity, which the Lord let me see on numerous occasions. But the Bible is filled with references to demons and their activities. Devils, Satan, Leviathan (a demon spirit), hell, outer darkness, angels and "principalities and powers" are mentioned at least 550 times in the Bible (KJV). Ephesians 6 tells us that our struggle is against the "principalities and powers of darkness." I trust other experiences I will share will be more clearly understood in light of the above.

❖

I had a couple extra dollars one week and decided to go visit Greg.

I figured I could drive to Potosi, the prison Gregory had been transferred to, which was closer. I could spend time with him then drive home the same night. That means I would have twelve hours of driving and six hours of visit. It would be difficult, but I knew I could do it for less than $50.00.

As I neared St. Louis, I sensed the Lord tugging at me to stop by the courthouse and check the status of Gregory's 29-15 motion. Obediently, I did so. I talked to the clerk at length and as soon as I mentioned brothers, she remembered the case. She pulled out the information and told me everything was on schedule. Then she commended me for what I was doing. From there I went to see Greg and we had a good visit.

Saturdays were the highlight of my week during my first semester at Wheaton. Gregory called every Saturday night. It was our weekly "date," and Saturdays just couldn't seem to get there fast enough for me. Our relationship stood up to a real test when my phone was disconnected because I couldn't manage the phone bill. We could only communicate by mail then. I waited anxiously for the mailman every day, just as I had during my ex-husband's two tours in Vietnam, but I learned as a military wife, that "no news is good news," and try not to worry.

❖

Towards the end of the semester, we had to write a paper on the Gospel of John, which was to be returned to us in the last class of the term. The instructor made few comments as he handed the papers back, until he got to mine, which was on the bottom of the stack. There were still a dozen students in the class when he gave me my paper. In a voice loud enough for everyone to hear, he said, "I don't know how far you plan on going in school, but you can't write for beans. I was shocked at your poor writing skills, seeing your oral communication is so good." He paused a moment and continued, "I have to admit I love the way your mind works, though."

His comments were uncalled for. If he had something to say to me, I felt he should have said it in private. I shook it off well outwardly, seeing the other students were there. What they didn't know was that I was doing poorly in everything. I held last place, grade-wise, in all of my classes. My test scores were horrible; now it was common knowledge that my writing skills were terrible, too. Under the circumstances, I don't know why anyone would want to stick it out through that first semester. If it had not been for the strength I gained by continual communication with the Lord, through prayer, I would have walked away from everything.

I was frustrated with school and sought out my advisor, Prof. Scott. He was a wonderful professor. He had studied under F. F. Bruce, one of the world's finest New Testament theologians. Prof. Scott was my "F. F. Bruce," and only he will truly understand my feelings when I say that. He told me something that touched me deeply. "I passed Dr. Phillips in the hall the other day. He said, 'Bonnie is having a hard time in my class.' 'She's having a hard time in mine too,' I told him, 'but I'll take 100 Bonnies over some of these other students.' Dr. Phillips agreed with me."

What a profound effect Prof. Scott's words had on me. I had been ready to crawl into the nearest hole. All the students seemed to have a scholastic ability that I did not possess. I was older, unskilled in the subject matter, and yet I knew I was called of God. I couldn't understand why God was doing this to me. I had had so many failures and disappointments in my life. I certainly didn't think I needed another one. Why did He put this on me too?

By the favor of the Lord, however, and with a lot of help from my professors, I passed all of my courses. Not having a 3.0 GPA, however, I was treading on thin ice as far as entering the Master's Program was concerned.

CHAPTER XVIII

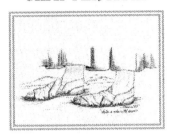

Springtime Struggles At Wheaton

In the spring, 1989, semester, I continued with advanced Bible and theology subjects; I also had to take undergraduate Basic Theology, because I had failed the equivalency test. I had taken a master's level theology class; now I was going to get the basics.

❖

One day, I walked out of one of Prof. Scott's tests really upset because I had done poorly again. A fellow student from Canada began asking me how I thought I did on the test. My disappointment showed. "Where's your Bible, Bonnie?" he asked.

"In my back pack." Seeing my backpack was on my back, I turned around and told him which pouch to get it from. As soon as he found it, he turned to the Scripture I needed. "I claimed this Scripture when I started here" he said. "I think you need it."

I took my Bible and read,

> *"I would have lost heart, unless I had believed that I would see the goodness of the LORD in the land of the living. Wait on the LORD: be of good courage and he shall strengthen your heart: Wait, I say, on the LORD"* (Psalm 27:13-14, NJKV).

Tears flooded my eyes as I wept, because I knew God was going to carry me through no matter what price I had to pay. Somehow that Scripture helped to deaden the pain of being the worst student, and not having the credentials needed for the academic environment I was in.

Around mid-semester, Dr. Scott called me up to his lectern after class to tell me Wheaton College had just waived its requirements for acceptable GPA's. They would now accept a 2.8 from incoming students. "I checked," he said, "and you're running about a 2.75." Tears

135

began to fill both of our eyes when he said, "Your prayers are getting answered, Bonnie."

❖

A visit from my parents came when I should have been studying for one of Dr. Scott's tests. I took the test without studying, and before he had a chance to grade it, I went into his office and began to unload. I told him that my parents' visit had upset me, causing me not to study. "I'm thinking of dropping out of school," I said.

Then he had his turn. "Bonnie, there is only one thing you said that concerns me, and that was when you said you were thinking about dropping out. God didn't put you here to be a quitter. I don't want to hear that kind of talk from you." He scolded me, and I knew he was right. I knew I had to hang in there and fight to the finish, regardless of what the world would think. Frankly, though, I wasn't eager to do that.

Dr. Scott graded my test. I got 50 percent. He told me to go study and come back, and he would give me an oral test, so I did. I got a passing grade on that test, and that was enough to satisfy him.

❖

During this spring semester, my phone was turned on again, and then disconnected again, mostly due to Gregory's collect calls. They really added up fast, and I couldn't keep up, so our correspondence would have to be through the mail again. Then the Lord started speaking to me about "putting Gregory on the altar," leaving our relationship in God's hands, because of some disobedience in his life and my life. It was the hardest thing I ever did, but I wrote Greg and told him I had to end the relationship, at the direction of the Lord. I still loved him as much as ever, but I had no choice but to obey. The months began to drag by, because I had no Gregory to share things with. There would be no letters to look forward to, no one to look to for encouragement and support. There seemed to be a big, empty hole in my life.

❖

At the end of one of my Church History classes, Dr. Scott called me up to the front of the class again. "Bonnie, do you recall I told you they waived the GPA requirements?"

"Yes."

"Well, they did, but it's not going to take effect until next fall, and you don't qualify." He paused, then continued. "This is what I want you to do. Write a letter requesting they waive the requirements for you this spring so you can enter the Master's Program. Let me read it to make sure it's okay, and then give it to Dr. Phillips. He's the head of the committee that will review it."

I wrote the letter and submitted it (after Prof. Scott's review), and two weeks later I received a notice that my requirements for GPA were waived. I would be allowed to enter the Master's Program if I could attain a 2.8 GPA. At the end of my first year of studies, my GPA was—you guessed it, exactly 2.8.

❖

One morning near the end of the semester, Dr. Scott came in before class and wrote the test breakdown on the board. There was only one other student, Dr. Scott and myself in the room. He wrote down the number of students who received 95-100%, how many received 90-94%, etc. Finally, he wrote the lowest grade: 1 - 64%. "That's me," I shouted. Dr. Scott turned around and said, "That's right."

"At least I'm consistent."

"You just can't take a test, can you?"

"Nope, never could."

Class went as usual, and we reached the end of the semester. It was as though all the months of studying were starting to pay off. The things I learned started to make sense to me, and I was able to put some of the puzzle pieces together. Once after class, I even had a question for Dr. Scott—and it was a challenging one, too. He gave me the answer, with a board illustration, then turned around and said, "That's why I don't worry about your tests anymore, because I know you're learning."

❖

Summer was drawing near, and I didn't know what God wanted me to do. I wanted to go to school to get ahead of schedule, to make it easier for me when I got ready to write my thesis. I checked in periodically with Chad Everett, the director of the college's Prison Ministries Program and was directly affiliated with Chuck Colson's ministry, *Prison Fellowship.* I was hoping for a summer project that would give me independent study credits. Chad finally came up with one, but it wasn't what I expected. I knew as soon as Chad told me about it that I was ordained to go, by the way the Holy Spirit witnessed with my spirit when he told me the assignment. I was to spend the summer in California working with children, with a satellite ministry in a ghetto housing area. The program would give me eight independent study credits towards my Master's degree in Interdisciplinary Studies.

I proceeded to make plans for the trip I couldn't afford. Through an advance on my pay and a love offering from my church, which was the greatest help and encouragement, God provided enough money for me to travel across the country and for purchasing the needed items for a two-month stay without substantial income. Through prayer, God gave me specific instructions for this mission. I was to remain on a partial fast throughout the program. Like the biblical Daniel, I was to eat vegetables, fruits and bread only. On my fast there would be no sweets, meats or carbonated beverages. All these things would affect my sensitivity to the leading of the Holy Spirit, which was absolutely necessary for my success. I was going into the front lines of a spiritual battle that would require much spiritual strength, and I had to be in top form.

❖

Then, with my summer all planned out for me, the Lord spoke to me one afternoon while I was praying. He said, "Take Gregory off the altar." I began to question, because I knew God was un-changeable and didn't change His mind. But when I heard the same thing a second time, I decided not to press the issue. God was giving Greg and me a second chance! I sat down immediately and wrote Greg, asking him to call the next Saturday. By the time the call came, I was so edgy I jumped a foot in the air when the phone rang. I began to cry as the operator connected the call; it was the first time we even had a chance to discuss why God had asked me to put him on the altar. But God had used it to wake Gregory up, and he had finally dealt with the stubbornness he'd been displaying.

I was able to stop and visit Greg on the way to my summer mission outreach in California, and we were able to catch up on the news of the past months. We stayed in touch throughout the summer, through letters, and an occasional phone call. He kept me updated on his appeal, which still seemed to be moving at a snail's pace because of the 29-15 motion, and his emotional and spiritual well being.

CHAPTER XIX

The Master's Program

On my drive back to Wheaton after my summer assignment in California, I stopped by St. Louis to visit with my son Bob, who was attending college in Columbia, Missouri, for his birthday and to see Gregory. Gregory hadn't heard anything about his 29-15 or appeal. So I stopped by the courthouse again and wound up talking to the same woman. The information I looked at showed me that Gregory's motion had been denied six months earlier, but nobody had bothered to let him know. So all this time, the appeal had actually been moving forward, and Greg had no idea what was happening! What really angered me was that I had to be the one to tell him six months after the fact what the public defender should have told him. All we could do now was wait on the appeal court. By this time Gregory had already spent over four years incarcerated for something he didn't do.

❖

Most of the time when I would visit Gregory, our conversations would either be about his case or the Lord. I would get so tired of talking about his case and the injustice that some of our visits were very draining on me and I left wanting to give up. But this "tug" from the Holy Spirit kept me going.

I often challenged Gregory on issues that were not clear in my mind. There were only two points about his case that I really questioned about his testimony. Time and time again he responded consistently and with determination. He never got angry with me for my doubting and he never showed any emotion other than sincerity and firmness about his actions on that fatal night.

Trying to have a personal relationship with Gregory was almost impossible and on those times that I needed a little personal attention like hearing Greg saying things like, "Gee you look nice…" or something that made me feel like a woman, all I had to do was let him know. Then we would change the focus of the conversation. He could be very romantic.

Not unlike me, Greg is a very focused personality and could be more stubborn than me. There were times when his stubbornness exasperated me, but also times when that was what I needed, especially when his stubbornness was actually steadfastness in the Lord.

Gregory was developing a faith during this season at Potosi that began to generate a lot of harassment from the other prisoners. He was vocal about his faith and what he believed the Lord was telling him. He kept telling the men that he would be delivered from Potosi and they would mock him, because Potosi had the reputation of being the prison that no one leaves. Most of the inmates there had either mandatory life sentences or were on death row.

Another thing I admired about Greg was his gentleness. He was the same way with everybody. Even to those who were disrespectful to him he was a gentleman sharing from his impoverished state.

❖

Back at Wheaton, I loaded my schedule during the fall semester so that the only work I would have left for the Spring Semester was my thesis. I took Philosophy of Ministry, Psychology for Ministers and Isaiah. I also audited the Prison Ministry course.

My philosophy class was frustrating. I usually remained quiet during class periods. Occasionally, I would make comments about my right brain not dealing with the subject well, and the class would laugh at it. Most of the other students seemed to fit in and were able to play the intellectual game. I hated that game. Every time I exploded on a philosophy, I never did it without using real experiences I had in dealing with my guys or my summer experience in California.

Class discussions were boring. The class was dominated with philosophies for the local Sunday school classes in middle class suburbia. I was exasperated because nothing related to dealing with someone on the street or the real issues this country is facing today. One young man from this class, Jim, actively ministered in the inner city of Chicago and was one of six Catholics attending Wheaton. Because we had a common interest, we had dinner one night and I was able to give him suggestions that helped him in his approach to ministering to the gay community. During one of our class breaks, I cornered Jim and shared with him my frustrations about the classroom discussions.

"Speak up, Bonnie, you're right." Jim said encouragingly.

"I'm not comfortable in this class because they are all so intelligent and don't understand where I'm coming from."

"Just speak up," he encouraged again.

The class resumed and went in the same direction. Nowhere! I couldn't take it any more, so I finally spoke up. "I haven't said much in this class because I really didn't think this left brain class could handle what this right brain crazy charismatic might say, but Jim suggested I do. So if you don't like what I say, blame him. All I do is sit here and listen to talk about middle class suburbia's Sunday School class, but what about that hurting person on the street who doesn't have the fine clothes or the fancy cars and income? They're uncomfortable going to stereotypical churches full of wimpish Christians who sit on the pew talking a talk, but who are too afraid to be a witness for the Lord. God didn't give us a spirit of fear, but of power to use against the enemy, who is bound to counterattack any effort to reach the lost."

"Preach it, sister," shouted the professor, "and finish it. "Give us a spirit of love and a sound mind."

"Yes, and I'm tired of all the philosophical stuff. I use the power God gave me. How many others do?"

"I'm glad Jim told you to speak up. It's about time." The professor addressed the next comment to the class. "You know what I do when I get bored reading all your papers? I look for Bonnie's. I know she is going to have something to say."

The discussion mushroomed, and finally some aggression came forth for the truth of the gospel. At the end of class, a young man from South America spoke up tearfully, "I can't believe what is happening in this class today. I have sat here all semester concerned because I was trying to figure out how any of this relates to the ministry I had to go back to. To see there is an awareness of the real problems and that there are people who are willing to stand up is such a blessing." He continued to choke back tears.

We were all touched by this young man's sincerity. He was discouraged over the attitude of the top rail philosophical intellects that think they can remain on the top rail and solve problems with logical processing and formality. To someone who has been down in the muck and mire, these intellectuals cause more harm than good, and all the bottom rail or experiential intellect can do is shake their heads in wonderment at the intellectuals who think they have all the answers but never get their hands dirty.

❖

During the school year, I tried to get down to see Gregory as often as possible, which wound up being once a semester. I had learned to make the trip on $35 and a full tank of gas. I would leave Wheaton about 5:00 A.M. and drive straight through to Potosi, arriving just before visiting hours, which began at 1:00 P.M. I would stay the entire visit, which lasted until 7:00 P.M., then I would leave and drive straight through to Wheaton arriving home at about 2:00 A.M. I had to make sure I was up for the drive when I tackled it since it made for a very long day.

The guards at Potosi were far more intimidating than the guards at Missouri State Prison (now Jefferson City Correctional Center). They would glare at the inmates and their visitors. I can remember one time when it was close to time for me to leave. There were only a couple of minutes left to visit and Gregory leaned over to kiss me. (An occasional small kiss was permitted.) The young guard broke it up instantly and the other couple in the room just looked at us and we looked at them in amazement because they had been giving each other little kisses throughout the entire visit. The difference was Greg was black and I was white. We ran into prejudice occasionally—that is, until the different guards became accustomed to Greg and me and realized that their disapproval wouldn't change things.

❖

The completion of my fall classes made my schedule wide open for a concentrated effort to focus on my thesis and on my prayer time. The first week of the spring 1990 semester I set up an appointment with my professor to discuss what would be required of me regarding my thesis. I informed him that I wanted to relate what I have learned about the criminal world in a paper and integrate my practical experiences into the thesis.

"All the research in the world," I told him, "can do nothing for the reality of the truth of experience, because research top rails the problems avoiding reality, while experience bottom rails the truth. By combining the two the paper will be more accurate."

"You can't do a thesis on that."

"Why not?"

"Because the thesis has to be proved through research. You can, however, write an integrative paper and incorporate real experiences."

"What exactly is that and how do I go about writing it?"

"You write it like a book."

"That's it?"

"Yes, that's it."

"Well then, that is what I'll do. How often do you need to see me?"

"Give me an outline as soon as possible and then check once a week or once every other week."

"Okay, I'll get you the outline next week."

"You also have to take comps."

"Comps! Oh no!" I exclaimed. "Comps, too? I thought I could get by without taking them if I wrote a thesis."

"Oh no, you have comps too."

"What do I study for?" I was upset.

"Because of the nature of your program, I want you to write a comprehensive question or two for each topic of study you have had. That is, write comprehensive questions for psychology, philosophy, theology, Bible, crime, Scripture, etc. Submit about ten questions. I will review them and pick the five I want you to thoroughly answer, which will include the necessary research."

"It is not a timed, multiple choice test?"

"No."

"Then it would be like writing five research papers along with the Integrative Paper?"

"Yes."

"When do you need the questions?"

"As soon as you can get them to me."

I was not excited about having to take comps, but at least I didn't have to take one of those so-called objective multiple-choice tests I viewed as being totally subjective.

What I discovered as I began to work the paper around my outline was that with effort I was able to work several of the term papers I had already written into the paper. I decided if I could write this like a book, then that was what I was going to do. I would write the book I needed my computer for. From that point on, *Cry Justice: The Criminal World in Light of God's Truth*, became a reality in my life. As I began to write it, I realized that this book was going to be controversial as a Christian work.

The English Department offered help with writing major projects. So two or three times a week I went to the Writing Lab with my work. It was like having my own personal English tutor to address my problems. I worked my schedule to stick with one person so that my tutoring and editing would maintain a consistency. Numerous times I sensed she was showing signs of frustration with my horrendous skills, but for the most part she was patient. I learned a lot through the editing process.

One of the students, a communication major, who looked at me like a spiritual mother, wanted to help me with editing, too. I was thrilled, knowing how gifted she was. One day she began to read what I had written so far. After only reading a couple paragraphs, she began to laugh hysterically at my writing.

"What is so funny?" I asked.

"This is terrible. I didn't know your writing was so bad."

"I told you I needed help, though I don't think it is a laughing matter. Actually, I think it is sad that I am working on my Master's Degree and can't write. At my age—with my education—I think that should tell you something about the system I went through."

Finally, my persistence paid off. In May, 1990, I graduated with a Masters of Arts Degree in Interdisciplinary Studies, holding a Certificate of Advanced Bible and Theology. God did it—He got me through—and I completed with a 3.25 GPA!

CHAPTER XX

Faith

During the two years I was at Wheaton, I had numerous things happen to me that I refer to as my "Holy Ghost Stories" or my "God Stories." I want to tell you only one of them, because it directly impacts my relationship with Gregory.

❖

The only thing of value after the auction that I had was a diamond sapphire ring that my ex-husband gave me as my graduation present from Kansas State University. I think the reason I didn't let it go was because it was my graduation ring and symbolized eight years of hard work. It was the most expensive gift he had ever given me. I wore it when I went to the California because I didn't know how I was going to get back. I thought, "If I need to hock it to get back, I will." God provided for me, so I still had my ring.

One day while in prayer I had my ring on. It was a three-quarter carat sapphire with a small diamond on either side of it. The ring slipped into a diamond jacket with eight smaller full-cut diamonds in it. Its value was probably $1,500-$2,000. I was saying to the Lord, "Lord, you know Gregory and I don't have any money and it would be nice if I had a ring. Couldn't we just take the stones from this ring and remount them in something more dramatic?" I began envisioning what would be nice. I wanted a more elongated mounting. A marquee cut sapphire would work better, but maybe we could pick up a couple small sapphires to give it the look of a marquee. I really liked the mounting I was seeing in my vision, but I knew that was out of the question. I knew, too, that whatever the Lord would have me do with my ring, there would come more healing from the pain of my past.

The day finally came when the Lord showed me the destiny of my ring. I was to give it to one of the women at church. I was a tad reluctant, because I was hoping to give it to my sister. I called one of my prayer partners over and we prayed. I asked her to pray to see if the Lord was sharing anything with her about my ring. We began to pray.

"You're not suppose to give it to me," she said disappointed.

"You're right."

We continued praying. Surprisingly, she said, "What does Jenny have to do with your ring?"

"Why?"

"I had a vision of Jenny jumping up and down with your ring on."

"That is who I believe the Lord wants me to give it to. That's all I needed to know."

I planned on giving it to her the following Sunday at church.

The next Saturday, September 22, 1990, my parents came to town unexpectedly. Gregory called while they were there, so I asked him to call back the next day. During the course of our brief conversation, I thought Gregory was off on a point of theology, so I was seeking God, in my mind, as to how to correct him. I will never forget the response as long as I live. I heard God's voice in my spirit as loud and clear as I have ever heard His voice saying, "He's your head."

"What, Lord?" I questioned in my mind, and again the voice came clearly.

"He's your head," the Lord said as I was hearing Gregory's voice, but not listening to what he was saying.

Okay, Lord, then you're going to have to correct him, I thought. I couldn't get over what I just heard. I didn't say anything to Gregory. I just cut the phone conversation short and went back to visiting my parents.

The next day I went to church and gave my ring to Jenny. She was so blessed. It's not often someone walks up to you and gives you something of that value and says, "God told me to give this to you." I was blessed, too, because of her reaction.

Praise and worship began, and I had my hands up praising the Lord, when suddenly my pew partner grabbed my hand, pulled it down, put something in it, and said, "God just told me to give this to you."

I looked down and in my hand was a three-quarter carat marquee' cut sapphire surrounded by twelve full cut diamonds with a considerably greater weight than the ones I had just given away. The ring in my hand was the ring I saw in my vision during that prayer time earlier. I exploded in tears and asked, "God, what is this?"

"That's your engagement ring." Sweetly came that still voice. Needless to say, I was blessed and could hardly wait to tell Gregory that afternoon.

When he called, I asked, "Do you remember my diamond and sapphire ring?"

"Yeah, you had to give it away, didn't you?" he said without hesitation.

"Yes, how did you know?" He snickered as I continued.

Midway through my telling Gregory he interrupted me and said, "When you get finished I have something to tell you."

I told him the whole story, including the Lord telling me he was my head. Then it was Greg's turn.

"I was looking through a catalog a couple months ago and was looking at rings and things. I cut out the information and stuck it to the wall of my cell, then I went to the Lord and said, 'Lord, I want Bonnie to have a ring and I can't afford to give her one. Will you give her a ring?' What does it look like?"

I described it to him as clearly as I could. I don't think there was any question about what the Lord had in store for Gregory and myself. The Lord saw that Gregory and I became engaged on September 23, 1990, just five days after my 46th birthday. The proof is in my supernatural, Holy Ghost engagement ring, which was identical to my vision.

CHAPTER XXI

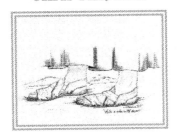

Behind County Bars

During the first week in February 1990, I was researching Martin Luther King Jr. for my Integrative Paper. In his book *I Have a Dream*, I saw a picture of Dr. King being arrested in Birmingham, Alabama, and being roughed up by white police officers. That picture drew my spirit toward it again and again. The editors quoted Dr. King as saying, "If you don't have something you would die for, you don't have anything." Those words kept ringing in my mind, and I knew that we as Christians must have that same commitment toward God. We have to be willing to lay our lives on the line for God and His righteousness, justice and mercy. We can only do that if we have a relationship with Him as our personal God. As these insights developed within my spirit, I felt the Holy Spirit was telling me I, too, would be called upon to suffer arrest and would spend time in jail for the sake of God's justice.

That same night my neighbors upstairs asked me to come up to see a video. The movie was the story of Stephen (Tseombo) Beco, the South African civil rights leader who was arrested and beaten to death for his stand against injustice. When I got home, my spirit was very heavy and upset. I knew beyond any shadow of doubt that God was confirming what I knew in my heart—that He had been speaking to me.

I had known for a time (in sketchy detail) that God was calling me to minister to ex-convicts and "an oppressed people." I wrestled with this and shed many tears because of the faith and strength I knew would be required of me. But I kept coming back to the same conclusion: God had called me to the front lines, and He was going to use me in setting the captives free spiritually. I knew life was not going to be easy on the front lines, but I also knew God would equip me for whatever battles lay ahead. And I "knew that I knew" this was from

God, because I received one confirmation after another.

About three weeks after I became aware of the larger scope of my calling and that I was going to be put in jail, I received a personal word from our church prophet in front of the whole congregation. I can't remember exactly how the message went, but the focus of it was that there were three people who were going to come against me, but that the Lord would give me the strength I needed and put the right words in my mouth for the situation. He said He would be with me and that I was to trust Him. As he spoke, I had a vision of the three appeal court judges who would come against me. I didn't like what I was seeing, but I knew that God was in control.

At the end of February, a couple of weeks before Gregory's appeal hearing, his lawyer sent me a copy of her original brief, the State Attorney's rebuttal, and her counter-brief to his rebuttal. I was angered by the State Attorney's brief, but didn't feel at liberty to write anything to the court at that time. In my opinion, the State Attorney's brief was a joke, seeing he did not address any of the pertinent information proving or disproving Gregory's guilt. He, instead, nit-picked at technicalities that had been the fault of Gregory's previous Public Defender, a man that Greg had never met.

I had already written three letters to the Appeals court on Gregory's behalf in reference to his case and the injustices I had witnessed first-hand. After the first letter, I received an answer back from the head judge of the Court of Appeals. He acknowledged the receipt of the letter and placed it in the file per the Supreme Court Rule 84.20, pertaining to extra correspondence relating to a case. He responded to the second letter in the same fashion. Because of the responses, I had no reason to believe I was doing anything wrong. I was just responding to how the Holy Spirit was leading me. Each time I had the peace of the Lord with me, so I wasn't worried.

As I went about my research for my book, I uncovered information that was pertinent to Gregory's case. I prayed about it, then pulled out the briefs and began to pick them apart, based on the Federal "Speedy Trial Act." By the time I got finished, I had built a strong case on Greg's behalf. I wrote a letter to the Appeals Court addressing the issues of timeliness in Gregory's case—the same things the State Attorney had addressed, only my arguments were against the State. I prayed hard about it and sent the letter to the head judge. I believed God directed me to have it to the court by Wednesday, March 8, 1990—one week prior to Gregory's hearing. That would give the letter time to circulate.

As I finished the letter and mailed it, I still had this nagging feeling that I was about to experience the discomfort of being put in jail for justice's sake. I called two friends over to pray about the situation. As we prayed for each Appeals Court judge, our spirits bore witness to the spiritual condition of each of them. When we got to the third judge, it was a tremendously troubling prayer time. We all knew in our spirits that the judge in the number three position was the one to watch.

The morning I left to attend Gregory's appeal hearing, I received a phone call from a friend of mine who has a prophetic call in her life. She asked me how much fasting I had done, and I told her which days and which meals that week I had fasted. She told me she thought I had some more coming, so I prayed about it, and I received confirmation. This last fast before the appeal hearing was to be no water or food. Then she gave me several short words from the Lord; the first one being that God had anointed me for the warfare. I was to walk a straight line; God's Spirit was on every man; I was not to lean on my own understanding; I was to praise and pray; I was to anoint the courtroom with oil; I was to heed God's words; God called me out to set the captives free; God was warning me to keep myself pure for the power that was needed. She also gave me some Scripture references, including Hebrews 6:10 and 10:17.

On the drive to the hearing, I prayed hard and fasted until 4:00 P.M. as directed. I had also felt directed by God to call a girlfriend of mine to see if I could stay with her while I was in town. After 4:00 P.M., I ate, then drove to meet my girlfriend. I had to go without food and water until after the hearing the next day.

The next morning, March 15, 1990, I arrived at the Court of Appeals at 8:00 A.M. and was shown into the hearing room.

The Lord had instructed me to anoint the courtroom with oil, but there was only a short period of time in which I was alone in the room. I quickly anointed my hands with oil and walked around the room anointing the bench where the judges would be, the seats that the public defender and the State Attorney would sit in and the lectern where the attorneys would stand while presenting their arguments. Right after I finished doing that, people began filing into the room; there would not be another time in which I would be in the room alone.

I was reading my Bible when Ms. Lindsey, Gregory's lawyer, came into the room and sat right in front of me. She sat there for a few minutes; then, suddenly, she turned and asked, "Are you Bonnie Stuck?" We talked a little, and she shared with me what she was going to argue that day. Our conversation was cut short when the judges entered the room and the hearing began. State of Missouri v. Oliver was the last case heard.

Ms. Lindsey approached the lectern and began her appeal. During this time, Judge Frankfort, judge number three on the list my friends and I had prayed for, acknowledged that Gregory did not shoot anyone, and he agreed with Ms. Lindsay's assessment that the acceptance of the jury's guilty verdict needed to be re-evaluated.

At the end of Ms. Lindsay's argument, Judge Frankfort asked abruptly, "Who is Bonnie Lou Stuck?" Ms. Lindsey—surprised, pointed me out to him as I raised my hand in the back of the courtroom. "What is she doing writing the court?" he asked gruffly. Ms. Lindsey appeared shocked and uncomfortable at his tone. He questioned, "Did you put her up to this?"

"No, your honor." She replied in a concerned voice.

"Is she a lawyer?"

"No, your honor," Ms. Lindsey answered. "She's a divinity student."

He explained that the last letter I wrote had been sent down to the court. "Doesn't she know she can't write letters to the court?" he asked, still very gruff.

I was shocked, because there had been nothing to indicate that I was not allowed, as an interested citizen, to write letters to the court. If I were not allowed to do so, then why hadn't the Chief Appeals Court Justice told me in one of his letters? That would have been the end of it.

Ms. Lindsey and I had words after the hearing. She was concerned that she was going to get written up because of my letters. I tried to console her, but I'm afraid I wasn't very successful.

After Ms. Lindsay's and my brief discussion, I drove down to the penitentiary, about 65 miles away, to see Gregory. As I entered the building, the guard acted as though she recognized me from my last visit, six months before.

"Oh, yes—who is it you want to visit again?"

"Gregory Oliver."

She handed me an information card and asked me to fill it out for file updating, so I did. Gregory had been transferred to this new "super-max" facility in Potosi because of the length of his sentence. It was from that card that a new computer check was done on my record.

Six hours after the court adjourned, while I was visiting with Greg, I was asked by one of the guards to go up to the front desk. I knew, in my spirit, this was it. I was in trouble. Judge Frankfort had appeared angry with me at the hearing. I was expecting to get arrested for the letters I had written.

When I saw the Sheriff's Deputy I wasn't sure the extent of my trouble. The guard at the desk abruptly told me to sign out. I did so without arguing. The Sheriff's Deputy went through his procedure asking my name, etc.

Then he said, "I have a warrant for your arrest."

"For what?" I asked.

"For a dog running at large in 1986."

"You've got to be kidding," I laughed.

"No, ma'am, I'm not. The O'Fallon Police are on their way here to get you."

I couldn't figure out how in the world there could be a warrant for my arrest that was supposedly issued on April 1, 1986, when I had been cleared to visit the Missouri State Penitentiary twice in 1987, and again in 1988. Also in 1988, I was cleared to visit another State Penitentiary. Then in July, 1988, I was stopped and ticketed for expired tags on a rental car I was driving while my car was in the shop. And in early 1989, I was stopped (not ticketed) in Illinois for wearing earphones while driving. Because I had a Missouri driver's license, the officer had to run a check on the Joint States' list of warrants. None of these computer checks had shown any warrant for my arrest. Suddenly, four years later the very same day a judge gets indignant about my writing letters to the court, I was being arrested on a trumped up charge for something I had no knowledge of until that day.

After I was arrested, the officer took me to the local jail. I was booked and mug shots were taken. The sign I held up in front of my mug shot read,

Bonnie Lou Stuck

Dog at Large

March 15, 1990

I was now one of the bad guys.

I was put in a holding area that had a one-piece unit lavatory and stool. There was a brick wall divider that had a shower behind it, and the entire room was 14'10" long and 6' wide. There was a wooden slat bench about 8' long. The door was heavy metal with one 8" by 8" window, which was covered with paper. The room was cold, and I was wearing a lightweight summer dress. At least the guard let me take my Bible and a pen in the cell area.

I felt the peace of the Lord through the whole ordeal and was not upset or panicky. I was to wait for the O'Fallon Police to come take me back to O'Fallon, over 100 miles away. It was my understanding that the police do not drive over 25 miles from their base to pick anyone up unless it is a wanted felon. I don't think I fell into that category!

After a couple of hours, the guard moved me to another cell, which was much smaller and had no facilities. It was the "drunk tank," and it was stripped of everything. The floor was the only place to sit. The guard did, however, give me a chair to sit on, which I appreciated. I continued to read my Bible, and God showed me a couple of Scriptures. I found myself reading the Psalms, which I seldom read. The Spirit began to minister to me as I began to read Psalms 105:13-15:

> *When they went from one nation [State] to another*
> *From one kingdom [freedom] to another people [prisoner],*
> *He permitted no one to do them wrong;*
> *Yes, He rebuked kings [judges] for their sakes,*
> *Saying, "Do not touch My anointed ones,*
> *And do My prophets no harm."* (NKJV)

Those verses ministered to me and I was reminded of another time when I was anointed for the Lord's work, and people who came out against me were punished severely.

The second verse of Scripture that quickened my spirit was 1 Peter 2:13:

> *Therefore submit yourselves to every ordinance of man for the Lord's sake, whether to the king as supreme, or to governors, as to those who are sent by him for the punishment of evildoers and for the praise of those who do good. For this is the will of God that by doing good you may put to silence the ignorance of foolish men—as free, yet not using liberty as a cloak for vice, but as bondservants of God.* (NKJV)

I knew that the peace I was feeling was giving me the strength not to get angry at the stupidity of the whole situation. I knew, too, that my behavior commanded the respect of the guards because they treated me like a lady. You could tell the sheriff's deputy refrained from laughing at the whole situation. He stated under his breath as he shook his head, "We have all kinds of dogs running around this county." The police had a job to do; I didn't fault them for it.

I had spent a couple of hours in the small drunk tank and was uncomfortable because I had to relieve myself. In my mind, I let God know my discomfort and, all of a sudden, the guard opened the cell and took me back to the other cell, which was larger, warmer and had facilities. During this time I began singing praise to the Lord, and He gave me some beautiful words that I sang out loud. I knew that God was in control and that He would find Himself glorified by this experience—somehow.

It was getting late and I had not even been allowed to make a phone call. I wasn't sure what was going to happen when I got to O'Fallon, but whatever happened, I had no transportation there. My car was still at the penitentiary, nobody knew where I was, and I didn't have enough money to post bail if it was necessary. I was hoping for the guard to come back, and he did. He asked me if I wanted a blanket and pillow. I asked if I could make a phone call. "You have to call collect," he said.

"That's fine. Can I use the phone directory?"

"No, we're not allowed to let you use it."

"Well, can I call information?"

"No, ma'am, you can't."

"All my numbers are in my car back at the penitentiary."

"I can't help you," he responded.

Then I remembered that the deputy had allowed me get my purse from the car when I was arrested, and I had my sister's new phone number with me. She could contact the friends I'd stayed with the night before, and perhaps they would be able to help. The guard said he would be right back after he locked some people up, but he never showed up.

The O'Fallon Police finally arrived, and I was let out. I still hadn't made my phone call, so I asked if I could call before we left. I knew we had a two-hour drive ahead of us. I was allowed to call my sister and then I was ready to go. The sergeant who was driving pulled out his handcuffs and just sort of looked at me, bewildered and almost embarrassed at the situation.

"I'm going to cuff you in front."

"Aren't you required to cuff women in front?" I asked.

"No, we aren't."

I held my hands out, and he gently placed the cuffs on me. He took extra precaution not to cut off the circulation to my hands.

They placed me in the back of the police car and strapped me in. I showed them a shorter and faster way to get back and, believe it or not, we had a delightful conversation. I felt they knew I was being harassed, just like the Washington County Sheriff's Department knew I was being harassed. We arrived at O'Fallon, and my girlfriend's husband, Jack, was already waiting there to bail me out. If God had not led me to stay with them while I was in town for the hearing, I would not have had access to money to pay my bail and still get home, not to mention trying to get back down to the penitentiary to get my car.

Jack could not believe they had me in handcuffs. He said that when he called to get information about my situation, the officers at the police station were laughing at the predicament I was in.

Once at the O'Fallon Police Station, I had to go through another booking process, this time including fingerprinting. When everything was done and they were getting the paperwork together, the police officer on inside duty said, "Bonnie, there's no paperwork here to indicate you were ever notified of the complaint with a summons."

"You're right," I said. "I had no idea. If I had, I would have taken care of it four years ago."

That was sufficient proof to me that this was a clear case of harassment to try to scare me off whatever God was leading me to do in regard to Gregory's case. My letters would not threaten any person with integrity.

I could not legally be prevented from helping Gregory, so something from the past had to be used against me, no matter how stupid or insignificant. The "dog-at-large" complaint was the only thing that could have caused this incident to occur. It must have laid dormant all this time because the police knew the reputation of the neighbor who made the complaint. He called the police for everything, including me watering the grass, in his opinion, too much. This warrant materialized because somebody wanted to find a way to interfere with what I was doing in Gregory's case.

❖

I arrived in Wheaton shortly after midnight, Friday, March 17, 1990. The phone was ringing while I was unlocking the door. It was Gregory. He had been calling every time he could get to the phone that day, and his frustration level was up wondering what had happened to me.

"Hello."

"Boy, am I glad you're home. What happened?"

"I was arrested."

"You were what?" He said totally shocked.

"Arrested. I'm one of you guys now."

"For what?"

"A dog off a leash."

"You're kidding?"

"No, I'm not. They didn't tell you?"

"No, as soon as you left the visiting room, they told me the visit was over. I asked them what the problem was, but they wouldn't tell me anything. They just wanted me out of the visiting room."

"I told you the judge was mad. Let me tell you I was never so glad to get out of a state in my life. I was ecstatic when I crossed the Illinois border. What did you do after they took me?"

"I knew something was wrong, so I grabbed a couple of Christian brothers and told them, 'Bonnie's in trouble.' And we all began to pray for you."

"Thanks, I needed it."

❖

I forfeited the $50 bail, using it to pay the fine so I wouldn't have to drive three hundred miles for the court appearance. The drive would be more expensive than trying to salvage the fine, and I didn't have the money to fight it.

On March 22, 1990, I received, in the mail, a summons dated March 16, 1990 from the City of O'Fallon. The summons was for a "dog-at-large," for which I was arrested on March 15, 1990. This was evidence proving I had never been served a summons four years prior and that I was arrested unjustly.

On April 26, 1990, I received a notice in the mail from the O'Fallon Municipal Circuit Court stating, "failure to pay or appear on the above date would result in a warrant for my arrest." I was assured on this date that the court clerk would transfer the bond money, and my case would be clear.

CHAPTER XXII

Evil Invitation

The event of my arrest had severe repercussions in my heart. I even doubted whether or not I should continue with this relationship with Gregory. I was even afraid to visit him now seeing I was arrested at the prison and the system would see me as a bad guy now. There was also a suicide spirit around me that would rear his ugly head every once in a while. The one thing that I could count on was Gregory's encouragement. No matter what he was going through himself, he always had a word of encouragement for me that lifted my spirits. Such a blessing he was.

❖

I thought school was finished for me when I graduated from Wheaton, but God had other plans. While taking Philosophy of Ministries I had a chance to talk to my professor on a one-to-one basis. He encouraged me to go on towards my Doctorate degree.

"You're kidding?"

"No, people like you have the tenacity to do it."

"I'm not Doctorate material."

"You weren't Master's material either," he reminded me.

"You're right about that. What do you recommend I do?"

He gave me some names and told me about a curriculum in Adult Education that I might be interested in at Northern Illinois University.

"Have you taken the GRE (Graduate Record Exam)?"

"No."

"You'll have to. They offer them here."

I prayed about it and even wrestled with the thought of more education. I got the answer from the Lord to pursue more education at a higher level. I checked on taking the GRE and got their schedule. I did all the preparatory work I could to enter the program without formal acceptance. I even started taking courses the summer of 1990.

After Wheaton, a secular school was like shock therapy to me. I was so bold in my faith that I did not miss many chances to let it be known. I carried my Bible like any other textbook to class. I couldn't get into what the other students did, so I stayed to myself. I thought philosophy was boring and ridiculous. Sometimes we spent almost the entire class period (2.5-3 hours) debating about the implied gender of an expression that generated bad feelings. The intellectual community would spend so many hours discussing something so trivial at that high a level that it really upset me. What was amazing was the professors who led those classes were getting paid more than the professors at Wheaton but put in what appeared to be less effort.

In the meantime, I received the results of my GRE. My scores were so low that "when they looked up they saw bottom." According to the test, I definitely was not graduate school material. It was a little late to find that out, seeing I already had my Master's Degree. I should never have been allowed to enter Wheaton College with GRE scores so low. Again, however, my strength was in math. It was my only score above minimums, but it was not strong enough to make my combined score acceptable. I continued on, however, to finish the course work that I had already started on seeing this time I couldn't be put on academic probation.

❖

In late July, 1991, I received an upsetting letter from Greg. To my shock, his brother Ronald had just died. Throughout his imprisonment Ronald had to be kept on drugs to keep him under control. Ron and Greg were cellmates when Ron was in the penitentiary. I can remember when Greg and I were on the phone that I could hear the guards in the background ringing the bell and hollering for the inmates who needed to go and get their medication. This was a daily routine so they could monitor those taking medications. For some unknown reason, they gave Ron several days worth of medication for him to administer himself. Ron didn't like taking his medication because it made him lethargic, consequently, he didn't take it properly. When the authorities found out that Ron wasn't taking his medication as prescribed, they confronted Greg about it. It was as though they were expecting Greg to be Ron's nursemaid.

During a time when Ron was sporadically taking his medication, he had a spell where his mind snapped completely. On the last night Greg and Ron celled together, they were saying their normal evening prayers before going to bed. Greg said that Ron's prayer really bothered him because it was as though Ron was inviting the devil in. About 2:00

A.M., Greg awoke abruptly and looked over at Ron just in time to see him standing on his cot rigid like a board and non-responsive. Immediately, Greg called for the guards and Greg helped the guards carry Ron to the infirmary.

Greg was not able to see Ron until two weeks later. They had a good visit and Ron seemed to be doing well, except for his eye. Greg later found out that Ron tried to scratch out his own eye. Another week or so passed, and Greg received a visit from the chaplain telling him that Ron had passed away suddenly.

Rumors began to surface throughout the prison. Upon Ron's death, the authorities were planning on putting Greg in solitary confinement, not knowing how he would respond to his brother's death. But the chaplain and caseworker intervened and told the authorities that Greg was not a problem and wouldn't create any so they agreed to let him stay up in general population.

Ron's death brought talk of riot. Two inmates, who saw the circumstances around Ron's death, were blaming two correctional officers for choking Ron to death. Supposedly they were preparing to transport Ron to Fulton Psychiatric Hospital when his death occurred. Greg stopped the talk of a riot by telling the inmates, "The Lord will vindicate my brother and I will not hear of riot!" The chaplain and caseworker were right; Greg wasn't the problem when the rumors spread.

CHAPTER XXIII

Deliverance

I had thought that I had put my past behind me after I got rid of everything, including the sapphire ring that reminded me of Bill, but such was not the case. I realized later that I still needed to get rid of the demonic influences in my life that were affecting me emotionally, my relationship with Greg and my walk with the Lord.

I began praying, in faith that the Lord would deliver me from the pain in my life that was brought about through my relationship and ultimate divorce with my husband. No sooner did I get that prayer out of my mouth, than I felt something coming up from inside me. I felt like I needed to choke, cough and possibly throw up. I grabbed a wastebasket and went into my spare bedroom, which was the most isolated room in my apartment against sound. I knew my deliverance was beginning. I was delivered from one demonic stronghold after another that had been brought on by Bill's adulterous affairs. I wrestled prayerfully with the strongholds until each one was brought down and defeated.

Through faith, I kept attacking the demons that were affecting my life and future without a husband. One by one they fled as I was delivered. After about half an hour, I asked God to show me what was going on. He rolled back the spiritual curtain, and there beside me was Jesus helping me through my deliverance. His hand was on my back. He was getting those demons off my physical and emotional self. I was so blessed! I knew we had the victory, so I pressed on until I received a release in my spirit.

Next I prayed that the empty places in my emotions and heart be filled with the Holy Spirit of God so that the demons could not take up residency again. The demons controlled my flesh and my mind with thoughts of doubt, fear, insecurity, rejection, rebellion, humiliation, loneliness, hurt, heartache, humanism, worry, introversion, jealousy, envy, distrust, confrontation, pride, control, withdrawal, depression, etc. In some cases, I had multiple strongholds in one area. The total deliverance took about two hours. I used my own faith in the process, which had been built up strong for the occasion.

The next day I began to feel different, but I knew I had a lot of hurt from my youth left along with insecurity and fears I acquired through generational curses. There were numerous things I needed to get rid of. I made a list and went after them one at a time. The list even included behavioral weaknesses I knew I had. I prayed down one stronghold after another. I drove those foul demons out of my life one at a time, coughing, choking and gagging all the way. Some of the strongholds were weak and some were stronger than I thought. Sometimes there would be pain associated with a stronghold because the grip on me was so powerful as a result of the years of torment. I pushed through the pain until I got release. This second session took another two hours or so. I saw two angels helping me through this second session in the name of Jesus.

I wasn't satisfied that my deliverance was complete, so that evening I went at it again. I hit areas of occultism and witchcraft, etc., that had been operating in my life through my associations with such things as psychics, palm readers, tarot cards, ouija boards, yoga, etc. Again I attacked the devil one stronghold at a time, with success following every attack. This deliverance was not as long, but it was long enough. When I was finished, I felt as though I had been through a total spiritual purification process. I had such peace. I could not believe what I was experiencing. My insides felt like the razor sharp instrument had reamed out the piston in me completely. I was left with no emotions, I could not laugh, I could not cry, I could not feel anger, I could not feel emotional hurt, I could not feel anything. I covered myself with the blood of Christ again and prayed that every nook and cranny be filled with the Holy Spirit where the devil had been.

It was not until days later that I could feel anything again. If I were to say how many strongholds I attacked in those two days, many would think I was crazy, but I reaped the benefits and my hurt and anger for my ex-husband left. I felt compassion for him, even though he had tried to destroy me.

The night after my last deliverance I went through a demonic attack like I have never gone through before. The worst one to date had been the battle with the Devil's artillery, but this one lasted several hours and it threw everything at me at one time, which according to

Scripture is exactly what he does. He brings back seven worse than himself (Matt. 12:45; Luke 11:26). The battle was on. Thank God I had the Holy Spirit praying and showing me what to do, or I would have lost the battle. If I did not have the ability to edify myself and submit myself totally to the Holy Spirit, activated through the speaking in other tongues, I would not have made it through the spiritual battle that was waged against me.

One does not tear down as many strongholds as I did at one time and not expect a fierce counterattack. The battle lasted at least three hours, during which time there was no let up. Thank God, my prayer gave the strength needed to ward off the spiritual enemy.

God wants us clean spiritually so that we can be clean physically and mentally. Deliverance is not exorcism because a Christian's spirit belongs to the Lord completely. Our mind and body, however, can be attacked and influenced by demonic forces like Paul's thorn in the flesh, and like Job's trials and sicknesses.

Alcohol and cocaine, for example, are mind-altering drugs, but they do not change the spirit of a person. Often when people are under the influence of these substances, they do not know what they are doing. They were tempted and submitted to that temptation, which did not come from God or His Spirit. The more you rely on God's Spirit through everything in your life, the stronger your spirit, filled with the Holy Spirit gets, and it becomes easier to discern and cast down the imagination and temptations that come from the evil one.

When it comes to God and His work in your life, you always know what you are doing and you can will to turn your mind over at any time to God; you never forget when God is doing something.

The use of the spiritual gifts is the same. If your will does not want to use your gift you will not receive it. For example, the Spirit can and will well up inside me to intercede for someone or something, but I can opt not to respond. The Spirit might nudge me a little harder, but if I choose not to open my mouth and pray, the Spirit will eventually leave my stubborn will to itself. I will, however, be held accountable for that act of stubbornness. The Holy Spirit is gentle, and if you do not want what God has for you, through His Spirit, He will leave you to your idolatrous self. But do not blame God for situations in your life that you actually created. God renews our mind to function better through the washing of the Word (Romans 12:1ff; Ephesians. 5:26) which is there to purify the Church, His bride (Matt 6:33, 12:32; Colossians 2:23; 1 Timothy 4:7,8; 6:3,4; 2 Timothy 3:5).

I have been through minor deliverance since because the flesh is weak and some of the old strongholds get a toehold, but they go down easier the second and even easier the third time. Paul says that we have to "fight the good fight of faith," and we have to do it continually trying to keep the vessels God gave us pure for the battles that lie ahead.

CHAPTER XXIV

On The Shelf

My spring semester was the last one at the secular university. My financial situation became so bad that I was forced to drop out of school about the time I was rejected for the Doctoral Program. Earlier in the semester I had a vision of my next move; so I was not too upset. My vision was of Calvin College and Seminary, in Grand Rapids, Michigan. I didn't know what it meant, but because I was in an academic environment, I thought the Lord was telling me to enter seminary at Calvin. Hence, I began the information gathering process.

I made arrangements to move again and did the necessary preparatory work for enrolling in Calvin Seminary. I had left Michigan 26 years earlier after I married a career soldier. Now I was going back to the state of my roots.

I had planned to have my sister's house as home base until I knew whether or not I was going to seminary. My car would be my closet for the next six months until I got settled. The rest of my possessions, which consisted of books, two bookcases, odds and ends, linens and kitchen equipment, enough to set up housekeeping, were in storage.

My presence at my sister's was not popular with my brother-in-law. Our spirits clashed big time.

One day I felt the Lord was telling me to move out, but I didn't know where to go and I didn't have a job. I decided I would stop eating at my sister's, trusting God for my provisions. In the meantime, I made contact with a prison ministry. After trusting God for my food a couple weeks, the Lord put it on my heart again to trust Him for everything and to move out of my sister's home.

I washed all my clothes and loaded the car. That night I slept on the floor of the prison ministry. There was a sink there, so I was able to wash up before the day began. I let a few people know I moved out of my sister's. I told the truth when people at the ministry asked where I had slept the night before, but I could not continue because they were not zoned for overnight guests.

I drifted from parking lot to parking lot. I'd catch a few winks here and there. I showered at Calvin College as soon as the doors opened in the morning. Then I would go about my business, whatever it was for that day. I lived one day at a time. On Sunday mornings, I would get ready for church in the bathroom of a local restaurant.

I kept crying out to the Lord and asked, "Why, God? What did I do wrong? Where did I miss you?" Even though my lifestyle was not the norm for a faith filled Christian, as I had been taught, I never stopped tithing and giving offerings. I knew and understood the principle of sowing, reaping, and laying up my treasures in heaven.

Then one day when I was crying out I received an answer very clearly. *"Foxes have holes, birds have nests, but the Son of Man has no place to lay His head."*

I exploded in tears, because I knew I was right where God wanted me. Knowing that made the fire I was going through much easier to walk through peacefully. The Lord went on to tell me with that soft voice of His, "Right now you are where many ex-convicts are when released from prison. Many of them cannot contact their family, they have no money, they have no job, they have no place to go, and all the education in the world does not help them. I'm going to walk you through this, as a woman, and you are not going to fall prey to drugs, drinking, prostitution or any other vice. Then no man (male) will be able to give you an excuse for failure."

"But Lord, right now I'm a total failure."

"Only in the eyes of humanity."

I was frustrated over my situation. I could not figure out why God had me on a spiritual whirlwind in the previous years, but then let me hang without clear direction. During one of those days of frustration, I stopped to get something to eat. I took my favorite devotional book *God Calling* with me. I opened the book to May 1, and began to read.

DELAY IS NOT DENIAL[1]

Nature is but the expression of Eternal Thought in Time.
Study the outward form-grasp the Eternal Thought, and if you
can read the thoughts of the Father, then indeed you know Him.

---

[1]Russell, A.J. editor, *God Calling*, A Jove Book/published by Dodd, Mead & Co., June 1987.

Leave Me out of nothing. Love all My ways with you. Know indeed that "All is well." Delay is but the wonderful and all-loving restraint of your Father-not reluctance, not desire to deny-but the Divine control of a Father who can scarcely brook the delay.

Delay has to be-sometimes. Your lives are so linked up with others, so bound by circumstances that to let your desire have instant fulfillment might in many cases cause another, as earnest prayer, to go unanswered.

But think for a moment of the Love and thoughtful care that seeks to harmonize and reconcile all your desires and longings and prayers.

Delay is not denial-not even withholding. It is the opportunity for God to work out your problems and accomplish your desires in the most wonderful way possible for you.

Oh! children, trust Me. Remember that your Maker is also your Servant, quick to fulfill, quick to achieve, faithful in accomplishment. Yes. All is well through however long or whatever this season was.

Reading this was rhema to my heart. I began crying, knowing I was not in error. I needed to know I was in God's perfect will for my life. I knew now I was going into a holding pattern for a season. I did not know how long the season was going to be—I just knew I would walk and trust God as I followed that familiar "tug."

CHAPTER XXV

The Working Woman?

A few days after I had moved out of my sister's house, I received a phone call from my sister at the ministry. She had been talking to Woody, one of the maintenance men at Calvin College about my situation. He responded by saying, "Tell your sister I need a tentmaker. Do you know if your sister might want to help me do a tuck-pointing job on my house?"

"I need to make a tent," was my response.

I contacted Woody and started right away. He would not let me climb above the first floor because of insurance. Therefore, my job was the whole first floor, weather permitting. I was to seal with silicone every mortar joint to preserve the existing joints. My hands could not take weather less than 50 degrees Fahrenheit; because of the exceptionally cold and wet fall there were few days I could work. With this work, however, I was able to keep gas in my car and food in my stomach.

One day when I stopped by the ministry, I was told one of the tenants in the building needed a delivery driver. "It doesn't pay much, but it is a real job." I made the necessary contact and I was hired on the spot—no questions asked.

Now I could look for a place to live, but having no credit made it difficult. By this time my sons, Bill and Bob, were concerned about me, especially Bill. He did not know how to get in touch with me. He and his brother sent me flowers for my 47th birthday. They sent them to my parents' house in the Lansing area, because they had no idea where I was. I never saw the flowers except in the picture my mother took.

I found an affordable apartment. I called my son to see if he would co-sign for me. We started the process, but when they realized he was from another state, I was denied. Then someone else tried to co-sign for me. I was denied again. Then Woody and his wife came to my rescue to co-sign and I was finally accepted. I now had an address and could look for another job.

I still had another week in my car before I moved into my apartment. Some of the nights were long and I got little or no sleep. I bounced from one parking lot to another—large motel parking lots or 24-hour restaurants. I went everywhere and anywhere, testing the waters.

My favorite story happened during that last week in my car. I thought I would be safe for awhile in a restaurant parking lot, parking in the employee's section. I crawled into my snug sack to keep warm and rest for awhile. I was thankful for my down jacket and snug sack during the cold fall weather.

After putting up my window shades up, I settled in for a couple hours sleep. Suddenly, from the depths of my spirit came the message, "Go to the store now." Each time I received the message it seemed to get more and more urgent.

"Go to the store *now!*"

"Okay, Lord, okay, I'm going, I'm going." I wrestled out of my snug sack, got my shoes on and started the car. In my rear view mirror, I saw a car coming towards me from across the parking lot. I backed out and began to drive off. As I drove off, the car I saw in my rear view mirror pulled up and stopped right across the parking space I had just left. It was the police!

"Wow! Thank you, Lord—the police car would have pinned me in and my out-of-state tags would have made me a sure hit for vagrancy with no avenue of escape. Thank you, Jesus!" I exclaimed as I drove off safely.

❖

I can remember being thankful during those nights that I had been married to my ex-husband. He was a driven man himself and drove me into suppressing many of my fears; consequently, I was able to draw upon the strength that developed during those years to survive this test. Bill taught me how to survive in difficult circumstances. I am not taking away from God in saying this, because it was God who reminded me of the things Bill taught me. A career soldier learns survival, as does his family.

I never regretted any of those nights in my car, because of the close relationship I had with the Lord. During that season of my walk with the Lord, I was like Elijah by the brook and Elijah with the widow woman. God had me go through this experience to teach me some things, including His provisions. Then He had me go there for a season and provided for me there. Then He had me go to another place, each time making provisions and putting people in my path.

Sometimes the only way I could look forward in faith was to look back to see where God had brought me; then I could look forward to the vision He had given me years before. As I did that, I could see the wonders of God as He broke the pride, stubbornness, fear, intellectualism, insecurity, rejection, rebellion and self-righteousness of this open and willing vessel. During this breaking process, He also did some healing of my emotions from past pain. Through all of this, my greatest lesson was forgiveness. Forgiveness is *the most* powerful tool available for healing one's mental health.

❖

The night I finally moved into my apartment I did not bother to unpack. I sat in the middle of the floor crying out to God. "Lord," I sobbed, "I don't even know that I want to get back into the rat race again. I don't want these bills or these responsibilities—in the car it was just You and me. It was difficult, but I knew You would take care of me." I cried remembering the excitement of sleeping in the car. Then I cried, "O God, do I want this? Help me Lord, Help me to understand the Whys?" After crying and praying for a long time, I fell off to sleep right there in the middle of my living room floor.

The next month I wrestled two jobs. I was excited when I received my first paycheck from my delivery job. The excitement waned quickly when the check bounced. No wonder the boss didn't ask me any questions.

Then the Lord told me to go apply for a job at the superstore down the street. I was reluctant, but did it anyway. It was as though my application was hand-carried through. The boss promised me more hours if I would work the Service Desk. So I agreed. After I was hired, I discovered one of my responsibilities was to work the lottery booth. A moment of truth was here. I mentioned my displeasure to the trainer who said, "It is no different than the sale of liquor."

"Oh, but it is different."

"Then you'll have to talk to the boss."

I knew talking would not work for me because of the fear of confrontation that always gripped me. Confrontation this time meant my paycheck and I was unsure about compromising that. Instead I decided to put my argument in writing. If they did not like it, they could fire me. I was not going to compromise my integrity by appearing to support idolatry with all of its greed.

In my letter I wrote, "I am studying to be a minister of the Gospel of Jesus Christ and though you may feel the lottery and the sale of

Faithwalk

alcohol are in the same class, I disagree. By making me work the booth, I am being forced into the sin of hypocrisy over the idolatry of chance through the sale of lottery tickets. Not only do I understand the sin, but I also understand authority and will submit or evaluate the position if I am forced into participation with the sale of lottery tickets. I cannot submit, however, without stating my position in writing for the record."

I placed the letter in the boss's mail slot and went to check my schedule. I was scheduled for lottery the next week. That night I wound up in the Med Center having an EKG because of the spiritual battle that waged against me over working the booth and the possible confrontation with my boss. The EKG tested out fine.

The next day I went in to see my boss. She had received and read my note. "There is something I have to add." I said. "I spent last night in the Med Center having an EKG. I don't think you realize the spiritual battle I have in being forced to supporting this sin."

She took me to a private room to talk. What a blessing that turned out to be. I was taken off the lottery booth permanently and asked not to say anything. Then she shared some about her faith. I was able to minister to her a little and the bond between us grew. I was able to make a stand for my faith and have someone receive it without insult, arguing or rebuttal.

❖

During this entire time of uncertainty, again Gregory's letters were the only encouraging things I had to look forward to. He had an incredible ability to lift me up in the midst of his own problems. Encouragement came especially from the songs that the Lord gave him, as he worked. Gregory's witnessing to the other inmates, keeping his mind stayed upon the Lord, his prayer life and his singing were his stress relievers in the midst of the hellhole he was living in. I kept wishing the delays would end with Gregory's case. His case was in the Federal Appeal court by now and we believed that the Lord would move on the Federal court to see the travesties in his case and overturn the decision.

174

CHAPTER XXVI

Servants Everywhere!

The next year (1992) was a time of strengthening. It was difficult for me to answer people when they found out how much education I had. "What are you doing working at a service desk?" they would ask in a condescending way.

My response was usually, "The Lord has me here, and I'm in a holding pattern right now until He puts me into full time ministry."

I often felt ashamed to let people know where I was working. Thus, I didn't talk about it much. I just did my job as efficiently and faithfully as I could. I did my work as unto the Lord. I cannot say I didn't like the job or the people, because I did. It was the status symbol I had to get over.

Even my sons would fuss at me. "Mom, what are you doing working in a grocery store?" they would say it in a way that at times came across as arrogant.

"It's a clean living and honest work. Besides, there aren't a lot of jobs you can get when you are over-educated, under-qualified and nearly fifty years old. Besides trying to get a job when you don't have an address is almost impossible. A time will come when you boys will understand why I have to go through this and you will say, 'That's my MOM' with pride." I knew God was teaching me something through all this, but my sons had a difficult time with it. Their mother looked like a failure and it was difficult for them to tell people about my activities when asked. It was harder for Bill than for Bob. Bob took pleasure in telling my stories. On the other hand their father was successful, had all of his ducks in a row and all of his cards punched from a worldly perspective. So, naturally it was easy to talk about him.

"Yeah, but your job doesn't even pay the bills," they kept saying.

"I know, but just wait; there will be a day."

I sowed seeds of faith every once in a while, but because my sons were not "born again" and I had changed so much through my walk with the Lord, they didn't quite know how to deal with it. I used caution so I wouldn't antagonize them. In the meantime, I prayed that they would someday understand why I had to go through the trials I went through alone. I prayed, too, that their communication with their father would improve, and I never stopped praying for their father and that he would quit hating me for standing up to him. At that point in time, the boys didn't want their father and I to be in the same room for fear of what might happen and of the negative effects it would have on me.

I soon began to realize I did have a purpose at the service desk during that season of testing. It did not take long for everyone in the store to tag me as the religious one at the desk. I sort of liked it because it gave me a special identity.

Sometimes when I came in to count my drawer before going on duty, there was a whole group of cashiers and service desk people in the countdown room. If I discerned a bad spirit, I spoke loud enough for the devil to hear, "Boy, the spirit is bad in here. In Jesus' name, devil, get out of here." The room would clear out and the spirit would get sweet. One of my best supporters on the desk was usually in the countdown room whenever I did something like that. She never failed to comment about the change of spirit whenever I came to work. In the other room I'm sure the comments were different.

❖

Shortly after I started working at the superstore, God began encouraging me to take "prayer walks" around the store. At times, He would wake me up early in the morning and put it on my heart to "pray walk" the store. It was open twenty-four hours, so that was not hard to do. One Saturday He had me go on a prayer walk mid-morning just before I was to start my shift. He wanted me to walk the store twice. This store needed upper management change, so I prayed over each department and top management.

As I completed my first round, I was walking by the exit lanes and I touched my fingers to the ends of the lanes. I looked up and saw the lottery booth. In my mind I said, "Lord, if I knew I wouldn't be playing with charismatic witchcraft, I would curse the lottery booth for the way it plays on the poor."

I just thought it and headed in that direction to use the restroom before making my second run of the store. Suddenly, Shane, who was running the lottery booth, looked up and saw me. His eyes opened wide as he said, "I might have known you were here."

"Why?"

"The lottery machine just broke down."

I had all I could do to control myself as I broke into hysterical laughter.

"You would think it funny," he said.

"If you only knew why God brought me here, you would know why it is so funny. God is just letting me know my prayers are being heard."

They got the machine up and running again as I was on my second go-around in the store. I finished with the lanes again, and when Shane saw me the second time, he said in exasperation, "Oh, no! She's here again. It just broke down again." He threw his hands up saying, "I believe, Bonnie, I believe."

"Good. Praise the Lord!"

They eventually wound up replacing that machine.

❖

I was in the countdown room one day when an employee from another part of the store that I had no dealings with came in. I was talking to Susan and was being my outspoken self for the Lord. My speech must have contained vernacular that let it be know that I was Charismatic because the woman who entered asked, "Where do you go to church?"

"I'm sort of at a stalemate right now. I have been praying that God lead me to a supernatural church."

"I go to one."

"Really."

"Yes, it is in the inner city, but because we have grown so much they hold their Sunday services on Calvin's campus in the Fine Arts Center."

"No kidding! On Calvin's Campus, huh?"

"Yes. The pastor is black and so is the congregation."

"I don't care. I just have one question, will the pastor toss away his sermon if there is a move of the Holy Spirit?"

"Yes."

"Then that is where I want to go."

That Sunday I went to Calvin's campus to attend church. I realized after the first Sunday that the reason I had the vision of Calvin College was not to go to seminary. No, instead God had called me there to sit under this pastor for a season. And did they know how to have church!

❖

It was payday, and as usual we were busy. A man came up to get his check cashed. I asked him for two pieces of ID because I was not familiar with him or his check. He got huffy with me and I just kept quiet. But I insisted on the two pieces of ID and he mumbled something, then said, "I've had a bad day."

I reached across the counter, grabbed his forearm and said, "In Jesus name, I pray that your day changes at this moment."

As he looked up at me, I could see he was fighting tears as he said, "Thank you."

"Thank Him. He is the One."

❖

Not all my customers were that open. I was busy taking care of my customer when I heard one of the girls having a hard time with a customer. The customer's volume was loud, and the words coming out of his mouth would make a sailor blush. I could not take it anymore, so I stepped back to get the customer in full view and shouted, "Praise the Lord, Jesus gets equal time!"

Everyone stopped and looked at me. Then the man decided to say a few more choice words. "@!#!% %#%$ $% #@$"

Again I stepped back and shouted, "Praise the Lord, Jesus gets equal time!" No one said another foul word. As a matter of fact it was very peaceful.

Later, one of the girls said to me, "What did you do that for?"

"God didn't make him cuss at Sandra. So why do we have to shut up and listen to the devil? Jesus gets equal time as long as I'm on this desk." I don't think the other employees really understood where I was coming from. But who cares? It shut the devil up.

CHAPTER XXVII

The Honeymoon Cottage

In March of 1993, the Lord impressed upon me very strongly that I was to be faithful with His money and other people's money. The message came with urgency. I knew I was in for a big test so I heeded the message. Within a month, my drawer at the service desk came up about $100 short. As soon as that happened I knew what my test was going to be. During the next months, I went through several shortages, and the disciplinary action that went along with it. My two bosses believed in my innocence but could not do anything while security was on me like a hawk. I held strong and faithful, but the inevitable happened. The night came when my boss called me in to let me go, He kept saying, "Why you Bonnie, why you?"

"Kevin, what you don't understand is that this is a spiritual matter and the Lord warned me of it. I will tell you something now and I want you to remember I told you. Within the month you will catch two people stealing." That night I walked out to my car saying, "Lord, well it is just you and me again. I am totally and completely in your hands. What do you want me to do?"

"Write your book now."

"Lord, I was fired! I can't go to unemployment. How in the world am I going to be able to write?"

"It's time to tell your story," came that familiar still small voice.

"Lord, if that is what you want. You're on the throne."

I stopped by the store to hand in my smocks a couple days later and ran into one of the managers that I talked to once in a while. "Where have you been?" he said.

"Didn't you hear? I was fired!"

"No you weren't. You are supposed to be working in the Hallmark shop—part time." He said.

"You mean they took away my full time status, demoted me and took my benefits away?"

"Yes, go check with Kevin."

"Well, no one called me about it." I was even scheduled to handle money. I worked one night, but it wasn't right so I refused the demotion. With that maneuver I went over to the Unemployment Office and applied. I was approved and my unemployment was almost what I cleared per week working full time. While I was waiting for the checks to start coming, I made contact with my son, Bill, which ultimately resulted in contact with his father. My reason for doing that was because just months before Bill and I had our first decent conversation in many years on the occasion of Bob's graduation from college. He told me that if I needed anything to contact Lil' Bill and that he would be our conduit and he would give me the message. Well, believe it or not Bill supplemented my income with the exact amount that military retirement was several years earlier when he was paying it faithfully. I was now making more money than I had in years and was able to write my book while looking for a job. Only God could have managed that. By the way, they caught three people stealing in that month after I left.

I was now nearing the end of my unemployment benefits. Consequently, I had to think about moving, since I could not afford my apartment and I still hadn't found a full time job that would support me.

One day while I was on one of my prayer drives, I brought up my living conditions to the Lord. I was telling Him that I needed to cut my cost of living expenses, because I was not going to be able to hang on much longer.

As I was driving along, I kept envisioning a mobile home, not knowing exactly what that meant. I was trying to make ends meet and there was no way I could afford to buy anything, since I wasn't working.

Then it dawned on me. My sister, Barb, had a friend who had a mobile home in the same park as she lived in. I rushed to a phone and called her.

"What is the status of Myrna's mobile home? Is there anyone living in it? I need to get my cost of living expenses down and I was thinking of her home."

"Gee, I don't know. Her boyfriend's daughter was living in it, but I don't think she is anymore. I'll call and find out."

"I had a vision of living in a mobile home, so if this is truly God then it will be vacant."

About one hour later I was at home and Barb called.

"Myrna said, 'If Bonnie wants to move in, she can do it tomorrow, provided the management approves.' Myrna will sign the title over to you, because that is a requirement for the park. Then if you decide to buy it, you can give her $50 per month."

"You've got to be kidding?"

"No, that's what she said."

"What is this place like."

"It's older, but it has been taken good care of and you know how clean Myrna is. The original owners took excellent care of it. The interior style is dated, but a little paint and imagination will help. I know Myrna wouldn't mind if you spruced it up. If you decide not to buy it, then sign the title back over to her when you leave."

"This is God."

"You have to get through management first, and she is tough."

"Tough" wasn't the right word for management. She literally ran me through the ringer because of my former bankruptcy that I filed while attending Wheaton College. I have never had such a difficult time trying to get in anywhere. It took over a month to get approved even after paying rent faithfully for one and a half years at my apartment.

I would not have continued the pursuit, but something happened that let me know God wanted me there. One day I took my friend Mary over to the mobile home to see it. As we entered the park, we had to cross a stream. When my wheels touched the bridge over the creek that flowed through the park, a flock of birds flew right across my path. I remembered one time the Lord used three flocks of geese to give me a message confirming I was right where He wanted me to be.

"What kind of birds are those, Mary?"

"They're geese, Bonnie!"

"Are you sure?"

"Yes! Look, there is the evergreen tree! This is it, Bonnie. Greg is coming home."

I thought the combination of the three things the geese, the water and the trees confirmed a vision that I had that Greg was getting out during the season when the geese were flying, the trees were green and I saw water running at a higher level as though it was a season that had more rain.

I moved in April 15, 1994. I was only able to get the living room and the office painted and papered before I moved my possessions in. The more I did to the place, the more I realized that the home I was living in had to have been the Cadillac of the industry when it was built. My home was a two-bedroom expando. My living room was 14' by 18,' which is big by any standard. On top of it she gave me the dining room table and chairs, a double bed (I didn't have a bed, I had been sleeping on an air mattress on the floor), a single bed I used as a day bed and a chest of drawers. The stove and refrigerator were nicer than I have ever had. There was also a washer-dryer combination that I was able to use, a nice size deck and storage shed, and it had central air and piped in speakers. This was all so grand and now I had room for Greg.

It took a full year, but I got every room finished and updated. To look at it you would never guess it was 25 years old. It hardly cost anything to fix it up either. My sister is a super garage sale shopper. My whole place was done in garage sale merchandise, and anyone coming in would never guess that. My adorable little "Honeymoon Cottage" was ready for the groom.

CHAPTER XXVIII

I Walk By Faith

Seven years had past since I met Gregory and began my advocacy on his behalf. His case had been at the Federal Court level for two of those years. Mr. Michael Dodger, the Chairman of the Board of Parole and Probation, had told me at a meeting we had the preceding fall that he wouldn't do anything in relation to clemency until the Federal Court had taken it thru due process of law. "If they do not turn Gregory loose," he said, "Then I will get involved, but not before."

On June 2, 1994, Gregory got word of the judgment on his writ of habeas corpus from the Federal Court. On that same day I kept getting in my spirit an old song by Peter, Paul and Mary and I kept singing, "It's the hammer of justice. It's the bell of fr-ee-dom. It's a song about love between my brothers and my sisters a-all-l over this land." I must have sung the song for an hour straight with such passion that I knew everything was okay. I knew justice was near and Gregory would be a free man before too long.

The next day the song "Amazing Grace" took the place of Peter, Paul and Mary's song. All day long I sang it. I don't think anything could have cut through the joy I was feeling.

I was expecting a call from Gregory the following Saturday. When the call came and the operator connected us I began singing, "It's the hammer of justice—it's the bell of fr-ee-dom."

"Oh, you think so, huh?" Gregory said when I finished.

"I know so." I said determined.

"I prayed that God would prepare your heart to receive the news," came Greg's gentle thankful reply.

"What news?"

"The Federal Court denied my writ."

I was disappointed, but something inside me kept saying, "It's okay." So we just continued not letting the news ruin our phone visit.

I knew my next step was to contact Mr. Dodger. I knew, too, that it had to be in person, not through a letter. I called his office the following Monday to set up an appointment. I was able to get a confirmed appointment two weeks later on June 23, 1994. I had a three-day trip planned and no money to make the trip.

It was important that I be prepared. I got the transcripts out and began studying, but I didn't know where to begin. "Do I go back to my original arguments or do I approach it from another direction?" I finally decided just to address the errors in the Federal Review and Recommendations (FR&R). But the more I studied and prepared for my meeting with Mr. Dodger, the more I wanted to get to the truth about what happened that fatal night.

I still had some questions and I wanted answers to those questions. In my spirit, I kept getting a riddle, "The truth is in error in the mouth of two or three witnesses." I kept pondering that in relation to what I had learned about studying the Bible and searching for the truth in scriptures. In light of that, I began looking for the threads of consistency that would open up the truth in Gregory's case. I kept being drawn to the rebuttal witnesses, two of whom were psychiatrists that the state brought in. Both of them had examined Gregory's brother Ronald and the third and last rebuttal witness was a young man of 15 that the prosecutor used to try to impeach Gregory's testimony. Even up until the last of 28 witnesses, Gregory's testimony held strong. Evidence of this is in the out-of-jury-range discussion prior to the last testimony. The prosecutor said in defense of his last rebuttal witness, "The credibility of Gregory Oliver is at issue also." Further in this conversation the prosecution continued, "I think Gregory Oliver's testimony can be impeached by this."

I began thinking about the witnesses who had testified. Fourteen of the witnesses were related to the kidnapping case against Ronald. The last witness on the stand was used in hopes of impeaching Gregory's testimony. It didn't work! Moreover he was related to the kidnapping charge, not the murder charge. If Gregory had been the focal point of his own trial, I'm sure he would have been a free man. The kidnapping witnesses might not have testified because Gregory was ***not charged with kidnapping,*** even though the jury found him guilty of kidnapping. The trial judge brushed the erroneous verdict aside. That maneuvering went unnoticed by everyone except Greg and I, and is recorded in the transcripts.

In light of this new view of the testimony, I began looking harder for consistencies and answers to my own questions. Obviously, Gregory was one link to that consistency, but was there some other link I could sink my teeth into? My other questions about the case were answered through continued study of the transcripts, but another thread of consistency was yet to be found.

In reviewing the state's witnesses' testimonies, I discovered the numerous times the defense objected to the prosecution impeaching its own witnesses. On several occasions, I thought, *How sad it is when the prosecution can't even present a consistent case.*

What was I to do now? I was drawn to the two rebuttal psychiatrist's testimonies again. In the past, I had just glanced over their testimony. I began to notice a consistency in the report about Ronald's testimony to them about the happenings of that fatal night. The interesting thing was that only the opinions of the psychiatrists about Ronald's mental condition were allowed for the jury to evaluate. Any comment made by Ronald to the psychiatrist about the night of the shootings was to be disregarded because it was hearsay testimony. Yet the entire case was tried on a statute of Inconsistent Statement and the testimony, was *all hearsay.*

Each psychiatrist that testified acknowledged that Ronald was borderline retarded with serious mental problems. That was consistent. Where they disagreed, however, was in Ronald's mental condition during the actual crime. In every case, they could only speculate. Yet that speculation was accepted as evidence and Ron's testimony to them was hearsay and not accepted.

Seeing I wasn't bound by the jury instructions, I began to consider Ronald's comments to the doctors. In all three cases (2 State, 1 Defense), when Ronald told the doctors of the knife threat he saw on his brother Gregory's life, he was consistent with the story but inconsistent with the evidence. Gregory had testified that there was no threat on his life and there was no knife found at the scene. Ronald said he saw a knife that wasn't there. That was hallucinatory.

There was a consistency in Ronald's testimony that drew my attention. Ronald *never* stopped saying he saw Sandy Nicholas with a shotgun. Each psychiatrist reported the same thing. My thoughts sought the logic in this to make it presentable. Then it dawned on me—someone who hallucinates *would be inconsistent* with the lack of evidence found at the scene—the knife. Someone, however, who was not hallucinating *would be consistent* and the evidence would support the testimony—the shotgun. This fact was the second consistency, but it was one that the jury was *not allowed to even consider* during the trial because of its hearsay nature. Yet they allowed the professionals to speculate about Ron's mental status without really knowing his condition at the scene of the crime.

I kept wrestling with the facts of this case and these consistencies. Then I remembered that the defense council managed to get the subject of the shotgun out briefly in cross-examination of the state's star witness. I turned quickly to that section of the transcripts and began to read.

Q. [By Mr. Neustead, Gregory's lawyer] Was there a gun in that kitchen, a loaded shotgun with the serial number not discernible, was there a gun in your kitchen that evening?

A. [Sandy Nicholas] No, there was not.

Q. So if there was one found by the Evidence officers, you don't know how it got there?

A. No, I do not.

Q. And in particular, in the southeast corner of the kitchen, you wouldn't have any idea how a gun would get all the way into your kitchen in the southwest corner?[2]

NOTE: There seems to be confusion here in the direction, but the key direction is south.

A gun was found at the scene in the kitchen of a vacant apartment across the hall behind the door in the Southeast corner. According to transcripts, no one else had entered the room that the gun was found in, not even Ronald. How could Ronald have seen the shotgun in Sandy's hand when no one else saw it? This question bothered me because I didn't know what the floor plan of the apartment was like. My theory was building as to the truth of the events that night. Ronald hallucinated the threat to Gregory, but he didn't hallucinate the shotgun in Ms. Nicholas' hand.

The truth was concealed in the psychiatrist's report because it was not to be considered as testimony, while the half a dozen lines in the cross-examination revealed an element of the truth that is supported by evidence found at the scene. Thank God the defense council, Mr. Neustead, managed to get that in.

My conclusion was that although the psychiatrist's reports were contradictory, they were *all right* about Ronald's condition. Ronald was both insane and sane at the scene of the crime. He *hallucinated the knife threat* to Gregory when he shot and killed Bruce Campbell, because there was no knife at the scene. Then Ronald *was not hallucinating* the shotgun he saw in victim Sandy Nicholas' hand, because a shotgun was

---

[2] State of Missouri v. Gregory Oliver trial transcripts.

I Walk By Faith

found at the crime scene.

The other thing was that the police were *not* the first people at the scene, as I had to be able to prove some how. Sandy Nicholas' sister, Susan Miller, testified that she sat outside with her friends in a car and waited for the police to come and that neither she nor any of her friends went up to the apartment. That too was difficult to believe because her children were up in the bedroom of the apartment from where she heard the gunshots and saw the men running, but I couldn't prove that she or anyone else went up into the apartment and possibly moved the shotgun.

Theory was all I had to work with, but that was not my only concern at this time about going to Missouri. I had to travel across the country for a three-day trip to present my case, but I didn't have the money to travel. A friend from church told me that the Lord put it on his heart to give me $100 for the trip. He had two weeks to get it to me, but he didn't.

The Tuesday night before I left, I was at work. I was ready to go, except I had no money. I had an opportunity to leave work an hour early that evening, so I took it. I kept seeking God as to what I should do. I still needed money to get there. The Lord put it on my heart to call my girlfriend Liz, because she had $50 for gas to get me to my first destination. I called Liz as soon as I got home. I asked her for help without telling her what the Lord had put on my heart. Her first question was, "Did you get the money together for the trip yet?"

"No. Do you think you could possibly give me enough gas money to get down there? Then I'll have to see what happens once I'm there."

"Do you think $50 will cover it?" She asked.

"It sure will. Thanks!" I said, "Can I come get it now?"

"Sure, come on over."

The next morning I made a reservation at my favorite motel in Jefferson City and called my sister to let her know I was going. I had three copies of what I was to present. My sister was to receive one and Gregory's mother would get one. I was covering my bases, because *in my mind* I was exposing something that *could* cause a major investigation of some people in positions of authority. I also knew what it was like to be arrested on a trumped-up charge because of my investigation and stand on Gregory's behalf.

❖

On my way to visit Gregory, I kept looking at my gas gauge because it didn't seem to be going down. I knew how many miles per gallon my car was using, and what I was seeing couldn't possibly be correct. I thought, "My gas gauge is broken," so I stopped to top it off. To my surprise I was getting 42 MPG. That was a first! I have never gotten more than 32 MPG in the 130,000 miles I had driven my car. This was a sign from God to let me know I was right where He wanted me, and that He would provide. For the rest of the trip I got my normal 30-32 MPG.

I knew I had to go to Gregory's mother's house. I believed that the Lord was telling me she had $50 to take care of my motel bill. Sure enough, that is exactly what she had. I shared with her what I was going to present to Mr. Dodger. Her only comment was, "What would a lawyer do with all this?"

"Nothing, because they don't care and lawyers are what created this!"

❖

I was restless that night knowing that the next day I would make a presentation that could possibly expose some courtroom manipulation and cover-up and ultimately a case of involuntary manslaughter at the hands of the state, but it was still just theory. I had to find out from Gregory what that apartment looked like.

Gregory was glad to see me. We had a good visit, though we focused on the meeting for the most part. I began asking him questions about the apartment and its layout. He kept taking me to what the outside of the building looked like.

Angrily, I said, "I don't care about the building. I want to know what the apartment looks like."

So Gregory started in again. "This is the entrance," he said as he began to draw a diagram with his finger.

"The entrance to what?"

"The building."

"Gregory!" I said firmly. "The devil apparently does not want me to know what the apartment looks like and he is using you to anger me. Let's start all over again. What is the layout of Sandy's apartment?"

"You mean a diagram?"

"Yes, the architectural floor plan."

"I'm not an architect."

"I know, just tell me what it looks like, please!"

Finally I got through, and my theory was turning into reality as Gregory moved Coke cans and candy wrappers around to illustrate the crime scene. Once I saw where everything was, including the location of evidence and victims, I knew God had opened the window of truth up to me.

I ran through the diagram myself just to make sure I knew where everything was. Once I had it down, I exposed my theory to Gregory as to what actually happened and why no one else saw the shotgun. He was dumbstruck. You could see his thoughts going back and replaying the night of the shooting. Then he, too, realized the truth that had been hidden so long. "You're right! That's what happened. I couldn't have seen her with the shotgun, because no one was paying attention to her; we were too afraid of what Ron would do next."

Gregory signed over some of his property to me that day so I would have some legal information that I was lacking. I left early enough so I could go through the legal work I had picked up on the way out of the prison. I only had one hour to go over it before the meeting. In it was the affidavit signed by the alleged kidnap victim, stating that Gregory had not participated "in any kidnapping." I needed that because the FR&R stated, "The court found that Oliver had participated in a kidnapping earlier that evening." Gregory *had not been* charged with kidnapping, yet *the jury had him convicted of it, and the judge was picking up on the erroneous conviction.*

There was no more time to waste; I had to get over to the probation office for my meeting. When Mr. Dodger came out to meet with me, I asked him if he remembered me. He had. I began by giving him the pile of paperwork I had prepared. I had it organized so he wouldn't have to look twice nor shuffle through transcripts to find what I was talking about. I began by bringing the focus to the "Plain Error" rule from the Black's Law Dictionary, which states:

> The doctrine of "Plain error" *encompasses those errors which are obvious, which affect the substantial rights of the accused, and which, if uncorrected, would be **an affront to the integrity and reputation of the judicial proceedings**.* The principle, that an appeals court can reverse a judgment because of an error in the proceedings even if the error was not objected to at the time. "Plain error" doctrine applies where evidence is extremely damaging, the need for a limiting instruction is obvious and failure to give it is so prejudicial that it affects the substantial rights.
>
> "Plain error," requiring an award of a new trial although no objection was made at time of error occurred, is error possessing a clear capacity to bring about an unjust result and which substantially prejudiced defendant's fundamental rights to have jury fairly evaluate merits of defendant's defense. (Italics/accents added)

I wanted my focus to be on the integrity of the court, not on Gregory, because politics often times lacks integrity and the need to get

integrity back into the state of Missouri v. Oliver case was absolutely
necessary.

That established, I proceeded with my arguments one at a time. I
began with the statement that "the court found Oliver had participated in a kidnapping earlier that evening," and went from there
showing my affidavit, etc. He was more abrupt with me then he had
ever been when he said, "That's the law, the State can prosecute even
if the victim isn't prosecuting. They have that right."

"But he wasn't even charged with kidnapping." I responded. I was
taken aback as he continued to explain the State's right. I felt as if he
had slapped me across the face verbally. Not knowing what else to do,
I went to the line in the FR&R that stated, "Petitioner and his brother
went to the home of [Sandy Nicholas] who, at that time, was watching several small children, *two of whom were* Robert Franklin, [victim
#3] and Bruce Campbell, [the murder victim] (italics added).

That sentence is saying that the victims are children." I said. "The
judge thinks the victims are children. That will affect his whole perspective of the case."

I could see Mr. Dodger's displeasure with me at that comment.
Curtly he said, "That doesn't say that. He doesn't think they are children." Smack, blow number two. By this time, I wanted to leave and
I really didn't know what to say next. I knew I didn't want to argue
with him because I wanted and needed his help.

In my mind, I prayed, "Holy Spirit, you didn't bring me down here
to lose the battle. You've got to take over!" Then I remembered how
the Lord had begun to show me my theory step by step. So I began to
share that theory with Mr. Dodger.

"You know, I have studied this case for seven years and I know it
better than anyone except Gregory. I kept getting the message as I
studied for this meeting, *'The truth is in the error in the mouth of two
or three witnesses.'* I didn't know how to go about finding that truth so
I started looking for consistencies."

I spoke for the next fifteen minutes, having his undivided attention.
When I finished I said, "I have a theory based upon evidence, on what
really happened that night. Can I show you?" He quietly nodded,
"Yes." I went through the same scenario as I did with Gregory. I had
drawn a sketch of the inside of the apartment and labeled the position
of the evidence and victims. "When the first shot was fired, this is
where everyone was. Ronald and Bruce Campbell were arguing. What
people do not know is that Ronald had gotten cut with a knife a couple months earlier in that same apartment complex over an argument.
The argument is what I believe caused his mind to snap and that is

when he hallucinated the knife threat on Gregory's life. Per one of the psychiatrist's testimony, Ron 'was insane' at that point, but *I believe* he snapped back to sanity after the victim fell."

"At the point of the first shot, all eyes were on Ron and the corpse of Bruce Campbell. Sandy, who was in the kitchen here (I point out the location on my drawing), heard the shot, grabbed the shotgun and started into the living room yelling at Ronald. He saw the shotgun in her hand and shot her in the shoulder or arm where she took the first rounds (according to trial transcripts). The shotgun was thrown back into the kitchen unseen by anyone else in the room. She continued to yell at Ronald and he kept firing at her until she shut up. Sandy was shot four times from that 38 caliber gun."

"Then Ronald turned to shoot the other man in the room in the leg. All the while Gregory was jumping up and down yelling at Ronald, 'You can't go shooting people! What are you doing?'" Proof that the third victim was shot inside the apartment and not in the hall as the prosecution was trying to lead the jury to believe is the fact that blood was found on the threshold and it was never revealed whose blood it was. It was only assumed to be Sandy's. If this information had come out, the prosecution's case *could* have been damaged. They tried to hide the shotgun from the jury too, but Gregory's lawyer managed to get a couple of lines in about it. Because they were not to accept anything Ronald said to the psychiatrist, it was overlooked as key to what actually happened that fatal night."

"There is something else—the issue of smoking marijuana in the apartment before the Oliver's showed up. It is my understanding that they were actually smoking PCP, which is hallucinogenic. Prosecution, in the Andrew Franklin deposition, inferred marijuana, and because it is more acceptable than PCP, it was the drug acknowledged and no one questioned it. Do you know what burning PCP smells like?"

"No."

"Formaldehyde! That is what I understand it to smell like. The lab report said, 'There was no unusual odor on the body.' A smell like formaldehyde would go undetected in a lab."

"That's right. It would," he said as though a light went off in his head.

There was no doubt that Mr. Dodger received everything I said when he responded with, "So the truth is in Ron and Ron is dead?"

"Yes."

"How did Ron die?"

"The autopsies report I read in layman's terms says, 'He drowned in his own blood after being restrained to a bed.'"

"Where was he?"

"There is contradiction there. I have heard that he died at J.C.C.C. while they were getting ready to transport him to Fulton Psychiatric Hospital. There are two inmates that testify that they witnessed it and say his death involved the two guards who were transporting him. There is something else. Several of the inmates wanted to take the guard out that was accused of actually killing Ron, but Gregory would not hear of it. Every so often the guard in question would walk by Gregory's cell. He would stop and stare in at Greg. On one of those occasions, Gregory let the guard know that there were no hard feelings in spite of the rumors. That is the kind of man Gregory is."

"Okay, what is this pile here?"

"When Gregory filed the 29-15, we continued to wait for an answer. The delay was so long I personally went to the courthouse to find out the status of Greg's case. That is when I discovered that the decision had been made six months prior. I was angry at the inefficiency because I had to be the one to tell Gregory that the 29-15 was denied. I then sat down and wrote a letter to his lawyer for the 29-15, trying to find out why the delay in notification. That top letter was her response. She was horrified to discover Gregory hadn't been notified and retrieved his file. She relayed the information to the lawyer for the appeal and let her know that she was to keep me informed.

"The next letter is from Ms. Lindsay—this letter accompanied the briefs for the appeal hearing. That is why I knew what the State was going to argue ahead of time. I was angry when I read the State's argument. I prayed about it, then just set it down and went about studying for my Master's Degree integrative paper. During my study, I discovered the 'Speedy Trial Act,' which was a complete rebuttal to the State's argument on timing. I prayed about it and then wrote the letter that is referenced in the following letter from Ms. Lindsay. That was the letter that caused the judge to strike out at me in open court for exercising my First Amendment rights. That same judge stated in open court, 'Gregory Oliver did not murder anyone.'"

"I remember you telling me that."

"That comment should be in the transcripts of the actual appeal hearing."

Six hours after that judge struck out at me, I was at the penitentiary visiting Gregory. When I entered the prison, the guard recognized me. She was real smooth when she asked, "Who is it you visit again?"

"Oliver," I replied. Then she went on to tell me that they were updating their records and asked if I would mind filling out a new information card? I wasn't concerned because I knew my records had been transferred from J.C.C.C. That card generated a new computer check, and five hours later I was arrested on a trumped up charge. Two days later I received in the mail, the summons for my arrest dated the day after my arrest, proving it was trumped up."

"There was no warrant for my arrest. They said the warrant was from April 1, 1986. Between the years 1987 and 1989 I had passed four prison security clearances and was stopped for expired tags on a rental car I was driving. The authorities then told me it was on the joint state warrant's list. That too was a lie because I was stopped in Illinois for wearing earphones while driving. I still had a Missouri driver's license so that officer would have had to check the joint state's list. There was no warrant for my arrest. I spent six hours in jail, three of them in a drunk tank and was transported over 100 miles on a 'dog off a leash' charge."

"Needless to say, I have been low profile for the past couple of years because of the fear that raged inside me after being thrown in jail on a trumped up charge—fear of the Missouri good guys, fear of the police and fear of anybody in authority. Well, I've come out of hiding now and I'm not running any more."

"What have you done about it?"

"Nothing, I couldn't afford to do anything at the time. *The poor do not get due process*. I did pray about it, and I do know I will be vindicated."

"The first time this case came before me, it didn't set right with me," Mr. Dodger said. He then went on to say, "The second time it came before me it didn't set right with me again. Now where is his request for clemency? I'm going to the governor."

"Right here," I said as I handed him Gregory's new request for clemency.

He instructed me about the procedure he had to follow and reminded me that it was a political issue.

I spoke up, "I have to say something—no, maybe I'd better not. Yes—I'm going to! When is it 'politically right,' and when is it 'morally right'?"

"We want to do what is just," he replied.

I left it there, because I knew he knew what was just. "Thank you again, Mr. Dodger, for your time and attention."

"You'll hear from me before the end of the year."

"Thank you."

I walked outside elated. Before I got to the car I felt a raindrop hit my face. By the time I was a quarter of a mile down the road there was a tremendous downpour with thunder, lightning and strong winds. I viewed it as a sign from God that He was washing all the trash away from Gregory's case.

The next day when I visited Gregory to update him, he told me he knew the results already. "When I saw the thunderstorm, I started jumping up and down praising the Lord because I knew the meeting was over and that we won—that my case was going to the governor. The Lord gave me Psalms 81:1-7, along with other Scriptures!"

> *Sing for joy to God our strength;*
> *Shout joyfully to the God of Jacob.*
> *Raise a song, strike the timbrel,*
> *The sweet sounding lyre with the harp.*
> *Blow the trumpet at the new moon,*
> *At the full moon, on our feast day.*
> *For it is a statute for Israel,*
> *An ordinance of the God of Jacob.*
> *He established it for a testimony in Joseph,*
> *When he went throughout the land of Egypt.*
> *I heard a language that I did not know:*
> *I relieved his shoulder of the burden,*
> *His hands were freed from the basket.*
> ***You called in trouble, and I rescued you;***
> *I answered you in the hiding place of **thunder**;*
> *I proved you at the **waters** of Meribah. Selah.*
> (accents added) NASB

It was God's timing and God's place, and it was for God's purpose.

I left the prison after only an hour and a half visit. I had no money at all to get home and only enough gas to get to St. Louis. The Lord had showed me a vision of a crisp new $100 bill if I would get to Wentzville, Missouri by noon. I arrived in the nick of time and I saw an old friend of my son's there.

"Hello, Sweetheart," he said as I walked into the store.

"Hi, can we talk a minute?"

"Sure."

"I need your help getting back home."

"Will $100 be enough?"

"That's more than enough." He pulled his checkbook out of his pocket and went to the cash office. Shortly he came back with a crisp, new $100 bill.

"Here you go. Have a safe trip," he said as he walked away.

"Aren't you going to ask questions?"

"Nope! I have to go to a meeting—I'm already late. Have a safe trip."

That was it! I sat there dumbfounded with a $100 dollar bill in my hand, thanking God, because by following that "tug"—He did it again.

CHAPTER XXIX

Walk A Mile In MY Shoes

One night shortly after I knew that Gregory's case was going to the governor's office, I was secure at home in my comfortable little Honeymoon Cottage, but there was something lacking. I was miserable in spite of all of the signs that the Lord was really working. I was discouraged about my low-income status and feelings of failure, so in prayer that night I was crying out to God to please give me some direction.

The next morning I got up and began my morning prayer time. I began singing in the Spirit. Words kept coming up out of my spirit as I continued to press in, singing in the Spirit. "Walk a mile in my shoes, walk a mile in my sho-oes-oes, walk a mile in my shoes-oes, walk a mile in my shoes-oes-oes. Though the way is rugged and the road is long. Walk a mile in my shoes-oes I will carry you along...."

As I continued to sing, I began seeing a vision of Christ's feet and He was walking through the desert. I knew that I was suppose to draw what I was seeing in the Spirit so I grabbed my drawing supplies and began to draw as I continued to sing. In a couple of hours I had finished the drawing. I was so excited with what I had just drawn.

Since the time I was born again, the Lord would not let me use any of my artistic abilities for anything. He had stripped me of everything. I was to rely totally upon Him in my prayer life, in my walk and in my rest and relaxation. Every time I tried to draw on my own, it looked like an amateur with no talent at all. Now after this anointed morning of praise and worship I was drawing again, only this time the results brought tears to my eyes.

I excitedly took the drawing over to my sister's house. I told her about my morning and then I showed her my drawing. I loved the expression on her face and wished I had a camera. The drawing affected her as it did me.

Later that afternoon as I was home alone, and I was singing and worshiping the Lord, I saw another vision to draw. It too had a song. "If I could but touch just the hem of your garment, Lord, If I could just reach out and touch just the corner of your robe. I know vir-tue would flow...." As I was singing this, I saw another vision with Christ's feet and the widow with the issue of blood. So again I sat down and begin to draw. Again I was excited about the drawing.

Then another song came into my spirit and I began to sing, "I want to sit at your feet Lord. I want to sit in the very best place. I want to sit at your feet, Lord. I want to know-ow you-r heart. I want to know-ow, I want to know-ow, I want to know-ow your-r hea-a-a-rt." Then another vision and another drawing was given to me. During the next week I drew several drawings.

The following Sunday I was looking at my drawings. There were nine of them I was trying to make sense out of why the Lord gave them to me the way He did. Finally, I got the answer. The nine drawings could be broken down into three categories, which represented the body, soul and spirit of Jesus, and within each category there were three drawings and each of the drawings represented the body, soul and spirit of each of Christ's tri-part being. So what I had was the beginning of the "Walk A Mile in MY Shoes" note card series, and it depicts every aspect of our relationship with the Lord.

The Lord was giving me my drawing ability back and I loved the result. Why? Because of the "tug." But there was a message too that came with all of the drawings, that as Christians we ought to strive to walk even a mile in Christ's shoes. Then and only then will we begin to know Him and understand that "Tug."

Walk A Mile In *MY* Shoes

The Body of Christ

Walk a Mile in MY Shoes
Body of the Body

The Very Best Place
Soul of the Body

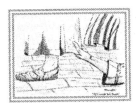

If I Could But Touch
pirit of the Body

The Soul of Christ

Faith
Body of the Soul

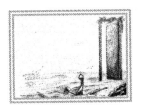

Hope
Soul of the Body

Love
Spirit of the Soul

The Spirit of Christ

Come Unto Me
Body of the Spirit

The New Covenant
Soul of the Spirit

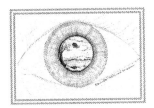

Eye On The Sparrow
Spirit of the Spirit

CHAPTER XXX

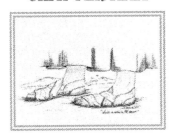

Preparation For Marriage

After my successful trip to Missouri, I began to feel another "tug" in my spirit from the Lord. I spent a season, 40 days, praying and fasting. During that time, Lake Michigan became my church. I went there on Sunday and walked the beach or went out on the pier, seeking the Lord. I continued to ask God to explain what He was doing with me. He then took me to the Scripture where Elijah had called down fire on the prophets of Baal. Right after doing so, Jezebel, being angry, tried to kill him. So fearfully, he ran into hiding. God got his attention and sent him into the wilderness to fast and seek Him. I believe this is what God was doing with me. I had just exposed some things that political people do not want to hear about, and now the spiritual battle I was about to wage would require all my spiritual strength.

Not only was I being made aware that I was to go through a major spiritual battle, but I was getting a second message that troubled me greatly. I sensed in my spirit that I was to marry Greg while he was still in prison. The thought of marrying Greg was not the problem; the problem was that he was still in prison.

Late spring, 1994, I received a quickening in my spirit that I was to ask Greg to seek God on when he and I were to get married. I kept sensing September. Since Greg's case was now going to the governor, I figured that could be a possibility. The next time Greg called, I asked him to pray about it. On his next phone call he brought the subject up. "Do you remember when you asked me to pray about us getting married?"

"Yes."

"Well I did, and I came up with the month."

"When?"

"September."

"Really?"

"Yes. I believe that is what the Lord was saying to me."

"That is the same thing I have been coming up with."

Not much more was said other than wishful thinking about Gregory's release. I was told I wouldn't hear anything on his pardon until the end of the year; therefore, Gregory would still be in prison in September.

I didn't want to marry a man while he was in prison. It didn't make sense, and I couldn't understand why God would even think of me doing anything like that. I prayed as hard as I had ever prayed. I even tried to get a "no" answer, but it didn't come. "God, what are you doing to me?" I cried out.

I really needed to know God's will for my life, so I tried to think of all sorts of ways to seek it, but God's answer was the same, "Marry him."

Then it dawned on me that I needed to sit down and write down two lists, which would examine the pros and cons of marrying Gregory. I just knew that the cons would outweigh the pros and would tell me I was *not* to marry Greg while he was in prison. So I began my list. (Figure 1)

When I finished the list, I was amazed at what I discovered. The pros outweighed the cons three to one. Then I noticed something else about my list. On the con side, the reasons not to marry him were temporal, while many of the reasons to marry him were eternal.

Now I really sensed the pressure on me to marry him even though I resisted it. I kept thinking, "How am I going to tell my family? What are they going to think? They will think that I have really lost it now."

I was reminded, "You've never hid Gregory from your family. Why are you hiding him now?"

PROS	**_CONS_**
1. God brought us together.	1. He's black, I'm white.
2. He's gentle.	2. I'm more educated.
3. We're equally yoked, spiritually.	3. He's in prison, I'm not.
4. He sees Jesus in me.	4. His families background vs. mine
5. Our relationship is God-centered.	5. He's twelve years younger
6. We pray together.	6. His past.
7. He knows how to handle me gently.	
8. He's not an angry, bitter man.	
9. I see potential in him.	
10. It is not good for man to be alone.	
11. "_A man who findeth a wife, findeth a good thing and obtaineth favor from the Lord._"	
12. We take disagreements to the Lord.	
13. We communicate.	
14. We find each other physically attractive.	
15. We share secrets.	
16. We trust each other.	
17. We understand each other.	
18. We laugh together.	
19. We cry together.	

Figure 1

"Oh, Lord!" I cried out, "what do you want me to do about marrying Gregory?"

I always received the same answer, "Marry him."

"But give me a sign, God."

"You will discern this by My Word. There will be no sign, because of the emotionalism involved," came the answer. I believe part of the emotionalism around my marrying Greg was because of the high profile murder trial of O. J. Simpson, which was going on at the time.

"Okay, Lord, by your Word." Then I thought, "What would Jesus do?" (Figure 2) So again I made a list, only this time I could back it up with Scripture. Before writing the list I wanted to see what the Bible said about faith. I discovered that the word, "faith" is used 245 times in the New Testament and only 2 times in the Old Testament. Then I continued with the study and asked myself what Jesus would do.

I realized after this that I had no other choice. I had known for years, since before I even received my Holy Ghost engagement ring, that God was calling Gregory and me to be together. I just didn't know when.

What Would Jesus Do?

1. Jesus *believed* God. (Hebrews 11; Matthew 8; 9; 15; 17:20)
2. Jesus *did only those things He saw His Father do.* (Matthew 3:9), Abraham is our father and we need to use his example. (John 5:19; 5:30; 8:39; Luke 1:72; 3:18; Romans 4:16; James 2:21) A problem I had was God's sending me to another state to marry. I wanted Scripture to back that up. (Genesis 25 – Isaac and Rebecca)
3. Jesus *didn't compromise the Word of God.* He didn't listen to the world. (John 5:19)
4. Jesus obeyed God. Even death did not stop Him from obeying God. (Matthew 27; Mark 15; Luke 23; John 19)
5. Jesus *agonized over God's purpose for His life,* in the Garden of Gethsemane. (Matthew 26:36; Mark 14:32)
6. Jesus *ultimately did God's will*—not His own. (Matthew 26)

Figure 2

"But—while he's in prison, Lord?" I questioned.

"Yes!" I kept getting the message, "While he's in prison!"

I shared with Greg what I was wrestling with as far as us getting married. There was no doubt in his mind that we were both hearing from God.

Greg found out, after the reality of what God was asking of us, that there was only one month in the next six months that the prison would allow inmates to get married. That month was just around the corner—the month of September.

In order to get married while in prison, Gregory had to make certain arrangements with the authorities and I had to take a trip to Missouri to obtain the license. It couldn't be done via the mail.

Gregory went to the head chaplain to see if he would marry us. To Greg's surprise, the chaplain refused because he didn't think Greg and I were equally yoked spiritually—Greg being black and me being white was his reason behind determining spiritual yoking.

So Gregory went to another chaplain to see what he would say. After hearing our testimony, his response was, "Of course!" He had no problem with our yoking. Actually, he too believed we should be together.

I knew my Christian friends wouldn't think I was nuts, but what would my family and the legalistic Christians think? I set up an appointment with a United Methodist minister that I knew. He shared my concern for ministering to inmates; therefore, we had a common interest. I asked him if both he and his wife could meet with me the morning I was to make my first trip for the wedding preparations to obtain a marriage license. That was August 30, 1994.

I shared with them for two and a half hours so they would have a solid foundation of what God had done in my life and what God had called me to do in ministry. I felt they needed to know also what process I had gone through to confirm what I believed God was calling me to do. I was concerned about being deceived, and I made sure I let him know that. I couldn't expect them to council or advise me about anything without knowing the facts. Finally I popped the question, "What do I do?"

His answer was without hesitation and surprised me. "You don't have a choice. You have to do what you believe God is calling you to do." That is not what I was expecting him to say. I was expecting him to tell me I missed God.

I felt relief after receiving conformation that I was hearing God's voice, and I left to visit Gregory and take care of business. The physically closer I got to J.C.C.C. the happier I was feeling in my spirit. I began singing songs of marriage and feeling good about it. I was so thankful to God for putting the people in my path that He did. If He hadn't, I wouldn't be driving down to prepare the way for marrying Greg. Among these people were Rick and Dottie, friends in the Chicago area, whom the Lord moved to call me shortly before I was firm on my decision to marry Gregory. I told Rick my situation. He, too, believed God was leading me to marry Gregory in September. He was so sure that he and his wife prayed to see how much money they were able to send me to take care of the expenses for my first trip.

I visited Gregory before I went to the county clerk's office to get the license. I wanted to make sure he really wanted to marry this older woman. On that issue I had done much wrestling, and I needed the reassurance.

I felt uncomfortable when I went to get the license because of the circumstances surrounding the marriage. I believed our wedding present would be Gregory's freedom.

The reality of my getting married again was taking form. There weren't a lot of plans to make because nothing could be fancy. My sister, Barb volunteered to come with me to give me moral support. We were able to split the expenses on the trip, which helped tremendously.

We arrived the night before the wedding and received approval from the motel to dress for the wedding after the check-out time without being charged for it.

Our plan was to visit Greg in the morning so Barb could meet him personally. She had only talked to him on the phone and received letters from him through the years. Then we would leave, come back to the motel to get ready and return to the prison at 3:00 P.M. for the ceremony. There were three weddings that day.

All went well on the visit. Just as I expected. Greg sang a couple songs and we had a good time.

Back at the motel, however, Things were different. That is when we had the problem with the ring, and what started out being a leisurely amount of time to get things done wound up in a frantic race to get back to the prison in time to get married.

Gregory was on cloud nine after the wedding. He was so much fun to watch. We were allowed five minutes to visit after the ceremony with family, then we had to leave.

On the drive back, the first thing Barb said to me was, "How do you feel?"

"I know that I did what God wanted me to do. I just wish I could take him with me."

"You can really tell that you two love each other."

I don't think she will ever realize what her saying that meant to me. We had hours of driving ahead of us to get home. We entertained ourselves by listening to an audio taped version of "To Kill a Mockingbird." I was wishing Gregory had an attorney like Addicus Finch—one who took a strong stand for justice and would not back down to adversity.

The marriage of my youth started with geographical separation also. One month after I was married to my high school sweetheart, we were separated because of Vietnam. The adjustment period of our relationship was given to Uncle Sam. During the first four years of our marriage, we were separated for two tours to Vietnam. At the end of each tour when I was anxiously awaiting his return, I received a phone call saying he extended his time in Vietnam for career reasons. One was to receive his direct commission and the other was an inspection of the headquarters' company under his command. I had to get used to it—delays, separations, the proverbial "definite maybes." This past conditioning had prepared me for what was now taking place, though I cannot say that I liked it.

Gregory began to get some understanding as to why we had to marry when we did, and it was beginning to make sense. When a Christian becomes born again, they become the "Bride of Christ."

There is no consummation, there is no honeymoon per se. There is only faith and trust in knowing that someday the Bride will be able to attend the "Wedding Feast" that has been prepared for her. Oh, how I wrestled with all of this, because I felt I was being told that I was not able to have a normal relationship with anyone. I was to walk in faith, as Christians do, believing that someday we would be the guests of honor in the Bridegroom's arms. That seemed to be the reason for the onset of our marriage, beginning as it did. It was a sign of our relationship with Christ. I can't say I was thrilled when the revelation hit me, but I could understand it. Now I await my bridegroom with loving patience, knowing God has a plan for us. This extended tour is due to career advancement in fulfilling God's purpose, not man's.

By February, 1995, we still had received no word from the governor's office. How long must we wait, Lord, how long? I decided to try and set up another appointment with Mr. Dodger. I called and left a message on his secretary's voice mail. Two days later as I was arriving home from work the phone rang. It was Mr. Dodger himself. I told him I was calling to set up a follow-up appointment, seeing it had been nine months since we had met. He assured me the clemency paperwork was on the governor's desk and that nothing else could be done at that point. It didn't dawn on me until later, but the fact that the paperwork was on the governor's desk meant that Mr. Dodger did indeed get the board to agree with his decision to recommend Gregory for clemency. Two hurdles in agreement were complete; only one to go before Gregory is a free man.

CHAPTER XXXI

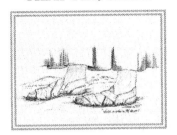

More Tests And Delays

I continued to plod along at my part time job at the supermarket, barely making ends meet. I don't know why but the Lord kept me at poverty level even though I was capable of so much more if I had done it "my" way. Then one day I prayed to the Lord for direction in getting a job that would cover my cost of living. The very next day a couple came through my checkout line at the grocery store. They were having a good time teasing each other about her new job and all the overtime hours she was working. I asked her a couple of questions while making conversation, and before I finished ringing up their order she had written down the information about her job and whom I should contact.

The next morning, I sought the Lord about applying for this job. Peace permeated my spirit about applying, so I pursued it. I believed that if the Lord wanted me to work there, I would be hired right away. I went down to the factory, filled out an application and went home. I didn't see anyone but the receptionist. By the time I got back home, I had a phone message asking me to call and set up an appointment for an interview.

Because of the personnel director's busy schedule I had to wait a couple of days for the interview. "Why are you applying for a factory job?" He asked me.

The only response I had was, "I'm over educated, under qualified, over 50 years old, I need a job and I'm not too proud to ask."

I was hired on the spot. My job was polishing brass parts before they received their final coating. I had to stand on my feet for ten hours a day. They gave me a break the first couple of days and I left after eight hours, until I could get used to working ten hours a day. Jokingly on that first day my team leader told me she was the "Gestapo" there. I thought she was kidding, but I knew right away that she was no one I wanted to get ruffled.

I could tell the people I worked with had been prompted that I was very religious and educated; consequently, they were all on their best behavior. I made my objection known to the team leader the first day about the language I was hearing from people who were stopping by to give the line instructions or who were just "shooting the breeze." I tried to be diplomatic, and gentle by putting my objection in the form of a question. She handled my comment quite nicely. Later that day the supervisor pulled me over to the side to ask me how my first day was going. My first comment to him was about the crude language I was hearing all too frequently. Word got around fast. Some people didn't like working with me because they had to behave themselves. Then there were those who were considerate and even apologized if they slipped and used foul language.

It was a tough adjustment to make for me. I discovered during that season just how hard factory workers work and how unappreciated they are. It seemed as though the harder a person worked, the less money they made. You could tell what level people were or how long they had been around by how much time they wasted. Some people were very skillful at taking extra breaks while others were skillful at getting unnecessary overtime. The thing I had the hardest time with was the way that the team leaders and supervisors just stood around jeering at the line employees as they worked. They were making sure no one was sloughing off for even one minute. In the meantime, they wasted a lot of time trying to catch others wasting time.

"The strong shall survive" is the bottom line in our society. But who really were the strong? Today's society thinks it is the one with the biggest mouth that practices the "squeaky wheel" syndrome, but I disagree. I'm so glad that the Lord doesn't operate that way either. As long as I had the Lord on my side and knew in my heart that He put me there for a reason, I knew too that I would make it through another difficult season of delay.

I had the opportunity for eighteen grueling months to let the Lord's rules of submission take precedence in my life. The Lord also showed me weaknesses in myself. Time and time again I made my stands and bit my tongue when I got mocked. I would just press into my job and tell the Lord, "I would only do this for you, Lord." Then I would add, "Whatever the reason you have me here, show me, convict my spirit and get me out of here!"

At night I would go home and I could hardly move from the pain from standing all day. I only had two steps to climb to get up to the Honeymoon Cottage and I would just about crawl up those steps, because my knees and my feet hurt so badly. Ninety days passed before I finally received medical insurance. When that time came, I rushed to the doctor to have my legs and feet checked. Arthritis was the diagnosis for my knees and heal spurs for my feet, which didn't make me happy, and I knew that my job was just aggravating it. So I had to start praying for healing and strength to endure the pain during the healing process.

One very difficult day the Lord showed me something about myself that I didn't like seeing, but I was thankful He showed me how difficult I could be if something wasn't done to my liking. For example, wrapping the brass parts and packing them is what the Lord used to teach me. I would wrap a nice neat tight wrap on most things while others would just slop them together. One was just as fast as the other, but the neat one was easier to handle and pack, saving the packer time. Often when I was packing only, I would rewrap the other girls' work. Usually, I was fast enough to keep up. Then one day the Lord got my attention and showed me a bit of myself. I had snapped at the sloppiest wrapper because her final product was so much harder to pack. "Does it really matter?" The Holy Spirit chimed in loud and clear. "Do you both get the job done? " He asked.

"Yes, Lord."

"Then who are you to say your way is the only way?" That cut like a knife, but of course He was right. My whole family is that way. We are all talented. We all did things well and had a certain way of doing things. We are good, efficient, make steps work for us workers, but our way is not the only way. That was a valuable lesson for me because I knew I didn't have to be concerned about pleasing anyone but God. I knew if I pleased God, He would be sure I found favor with others.

Many days I would just laugh under my breath at the antics that people would go through to try to get the best of me, get me fired or kicked out of an area. In eighteen months, I made three lateral moves. I was scorned, mocked, harassed, lied about, laughed at and pushed on some days to almost the limit of my ability, but I never gave in or up. God had placed me there for another season of refining.

Financially, I was almost beginning to make ends meet outside of trying to pay back my student loan, which I had been able to defer. I was nearing the limit of my deferments and the **BIG** monthly payment was looming over my head.

❖

Gregory called every other week in the beginning, but then he started calling every week. My phone bill was high. Trying to limit him to one hour was hard, because Greg is indeed a very talkative man. On one of our phone calls he played a tape of his song "What's Wrong With The Family Today." He had finally been able to get some time in the recording area. He had full instrumental and back-up singers. They were only allowed one take, so they had to take what they got. The song was great. The men recorded four gospel songs. Two were Greg's songs and two belonged to another inmate. I was so proud of him and his music. I made copies once I got my own copy of the tape and started sharing his music with others.

❖

Mr. Dodger had told me that Gregory's paperwork was going to the governor's office on June 23, 1994. We were married on September 14, 1994 and I started my factory job in October 1994. We were both eager for the end of the year to come because Mr. Dodger had promised me that we would hear something by then. In my free time, I worked on editing my book with my friend Cheryl. But 1994 ended and still no word on Gregory's clemency. I tried to remain patient, though, believing that the Lord was in control and that we would hear some good news any day. Then in the fall of 1995 while I was at Cheryl's house, she showed me an article in the paper about the pardon of Johnny Lee Wilson. I was so excited because it confirmed that the governor had some sensitivity and would pardon someone, in special cases.

Shortly after that Gregory asked me to write to a ministry in Missouri that was getting very active in helping the families of the incarcerated. Months passed before I received an answer, but it was favorable. On my next trip to Missouri, I was invited to attend one of the meetings of the "Friends and Family of the Incarcerated" and tell Gregory's story on television to start exposing some of the travesties in his case. I told Greg's family about it; eleven of his family members showed up. That was hard to believe. For eleven years, Gregory had not heard from or seen most of his family. Now with the thought of public exposure, they showed up in droves! I was angry and didn't hesitate to tell Gregory so, because none of them bothered to drive another eight miles to Jefferson City to visit Greg. They could have visited two at a time or I could have left and they could have visited three at a time—but they didn't.

It was the end of 1995—and still no word. In February, 1996, I contacted Jeramy Shriver, the governor's chief legal council. He was the man who was reviewing all requests for pardons. I asked to see him as soon as possible. My timing was definitely the Lord's because I was able to get an appointment the following Friday afternoon. The study time I had was only one weekend, which proved to be fruitful and gave me more insight into the mishandling of Gregory's case.

As soon as I found out that I was going to have a meeting with the legal council to the governor, I contacted New Life Evangelistic Center (NLEC), which is a Missouri based ministry that defends the poor and homeless in the community. They also sponsored the "Friends and Family of the Incarcerated" gatherings. I let them know I was coming down to meet with the governor's council and I wanted to know if they wanted someone to join me for the meeting. One week later I was sitting at the governor's office, waiting to see Mr. Shriver. Larry Rice, the head of NLEC, was with me. As we were sitting there waiting, he offered me a job in Missouri working for the center in St. Louis. The pay, of course, was less than I was making, and there were no benefits other than an opportunity to work for the Lord full time. There was no way I could possibly do that with my debt structure the way it was. Before the meeting, Larry and I decided that it would be better if I remain Bonnie Stuck for my advocacy, seeing I started it under that name. It would avoid confusion and maintain my credibility by not coming across as the wife of an inmate.

At the meeting with Mr. Shriver, I began the conversation in a challenging way by saying: "I'm here to follow up on the Oliver case, which you already know. I don't have formal notes from this last study of mine, but that shouldn't matter. I'm here to field any questions of doubt that you might have about Gregory's case that might be holding it up. I will field your questions, rebut them and tell you where to find the answer in transcripts, and I will do it without notes."

Mr. Shriver's first challenge was to say, "Greg said, 'Ron did it,' and Ron said that 'Greg did it.'"

I know my jaw had to have dropped down to my chest in shock that he even suggested such a thing. "What?" I exclaimed.

"Maybe I had better look at it again," he said moving on to the next question. "Well, there is the issue of the 'inconsistent statement' of Mary Thomas."

I had him and I knew it. That is what I just studied. For the next half-hour I had his attention. After fifteen minutes of those thirty, he asked me the same question that everyone asks me. "How did you get involved in this?" he said with an air of disbelief.

I answered him briefly as I did everyone else who asked me that, and went on to discuss not only Greg's case but the atrocities that I discovered in the system while I was studying the case. I broke down crying twice during the meeting, but at those times I was appealing to his integrity in light of the abundance of injustices that are continuing to happen at an increasing rate in this country and in our courts.

I have to admit he was more knowledgeable about Gregory's case than I thought he would be, which pleased me. He told me, "If Gregory's case did not have merit, we would have kicked it back a long time ago." He informed me that he was the only one who was working on the cases and that he had 150 cases to review. The normal procedure was to stop everything else when there is a scheduled execution so he could concentrate on that case. I could understand that and was satisfied for a season.

At the end of the meeting, I told him I wanted to end on a light note, because there had been tension in the meeting. I reached down in my bag and pulled out a small fish bowl full of postcards requesting Gregory's pardon. I set the bowl on the table and said, "In this bowl are several cards requesting Gregory's freedom. The reason for the fish bowl is to say that the sign of a Christian is a fish, and the requests are saying that Gregory is one fish that is worth pulling out of the muck and mire." He just smiled and took the bowl.

Two weeks later I was back in Missouri after a follow up letter to Mr. Shriver. It just so happened that New Life Evangelistic Center was having Mr. Dodger speak to the "Friends and Families of the Incarcerated." Before the meeting started, Mr. Dodger nodded "Hello" to me. It had been almost two years since I had seen him, and he seemed to recognize me. He addressed issues about parole and probation only. A couple of times I raised my hand, but the opportunity never presented itself for him to call on me or else he avoided it. At the end of the meeting, a group of people rushed up to him to continue questioning him about their cases. I hung back thinking, *Lord, "If you want me to talk to him you'll provide the opportunity."*

Within minutes, Mr. Dodger was able to get away from the others and began to walk away. He saw me and came right over to me. I shook his hand and asked him, "Do you remember me?" He acknowledged that he did. "The Oliver Case."

"When I had seen you in June 1994, you indicated that we would hear something by the end of the year. Now here it is almost two years later and still no answer."

His response is what continued to keep me going as I rehearsed it over and over in my mind each time I wanted to give up. "Mr. Shriver called me last week," he said, "and asked me to get some information on Gregory's case." He paused and said in a very personal way, "Don't give up." He shook my hand while looking directly into my eyes and left the meeting.

I was dumbfounded, a man like that in that sort of position telling me, "Don't give up!" Wow! What a boost that was for both Gregory and me.

❖

After I got back to Michigan, I received word that the alleged kidnap victim was ready for me to interview her. So I made another trip to Missouri, and on March 31, 1996, I interviewed Mary Thomas in front of a video camera. There were times while I was waiting to make contact with her that I wanted to leave. The spiritual climate around that whole trip was horrendous, but I kept hearing Mr. Dodger's voice saying over again, "Don't give up. Don't give up."

My videotaped meeting with Mary was incredible, and well worth the wait and frustration. I discovered:

1. Mary witnessed Ronald reloading the gun when Gregory was not present, which disproved the theory inferred by the prosecutor that Gregory reloaded the gun instead of unloaded it. Physical evidence supported Gregory and Mary's testimony to his unloading of the gun, but I discovered in this case that the prosecutor's inferences, which often times were outright lies, took precedence over evidence and "the truth." Now we had "newly discovered evidence" to prove that Gregory was telling the truth when he said, "I was shocked and was trying to figure out how the gun got reloaded."

2. That there was a relationship between the *ringer hearsay witness*, Edward Dean, and the victim, which never came out in the trial. They were brothers-in-law. The only thing that Edward Dean said at the trial that supported that relationship was how he found out about the shooting. His sister-in-law, who would have been the wife of the deceased, Bruce Campbell, told him.

3. That Edward Dean went around and talked to all of the state's witnesses trying to get them to nail Greg and Ron and he was asking for the death penalty for them. That appeared to be "tampering with the state's witnesses" to me. Mary was the only one who stood up for the truth and never changed her story.

4. That the jury was stacked with two members of Edward Dean's family. His uncle, who was the jury foreman, and one of his aunts sat on the jury. In the transcripts, I discovered how they artfully stacked the jury. While reading the list of prospective witnesses to the jury, Edward Dean's name was conveniently omitted. He was then endorsed two days after the jury was sworn in. Conformation of this manipulation is in the transcripts where the prospective jury members were questioned,

and a second piece of evidence is in the court record—the endorsed witness list. There were names, including a couple of police officers, that were endorsed the same day as Dean. Their names appeared on the list of possible witnesses for the perspective jurors in the transcript. Only Dean's name was omitted.

I was so excited over these discoveries. I made several copies of the video with the help of my son and was ready to send them to the governor's Office and the Here's Help TV station to air it and expose everything in a documentary of the case. I received a check in the spirit from the Holy Spirit to "Stop!" Instead, as soon as I got home I faxed both Mr. Dodger and Mr. Shriver a letter dated April 1, 1996, informing them of the stacked jury against Greg and Ron.

There was something else that came out during my interview with Mary that angered me to no end, and it took me years to get over it and to see God's hand in it. I had asked Mary why she hadn't told anybody at the time that the jury was stacked and she said, "I did! I told her!" She pointed to Greg's mother who was present at the interview "But she got angry, started hollering at me and hung up the phone on me." Mrs. Oliver told me the day after this came out that she remembered Mary saying something to her. I was enraged with the whole thing. I couldn't understand why any mother would keep quiet as both of her sons went to prison knowing there was a stacked jury.

Both lawyers had questioned and objected to Edward Dean testifying and wondered where he came from because his name hadn't shown up prior to the trial. Dean's testimony lacked credibility with all its inconsistencies. The judge, however, used it as his main testimony to defend his option to uphold the jury decision on the statute of "inconsistent statement," and to defend the jury selection process in a nineteen-page memorandum.

Now I realize that in order for the Lord to stretch me, He had to use things like this to do it. Unfortunately, it cost Ron his life through improper care and it has cost Gregory years out of his life—paying for his mentally impaired brother's actions.[3]

❖

When serving the Lord, I have discovered that there is no coincidence when it comes to spiritual battles. On this last trip to interview Mary, I had four road hazard accidents, which I know were meant to scare me off. The last one happened after the interview as I was on my

---

[3] NOTE: If the reader wants to learn more about the actual crime and the injustice of the trial, please read the Appendix.

way home. I had just gassed up at the last exit before entering Illinois. While entering the highway this very dark night I hit a large chuck-hole—hard! It scared me because I knew that I had done some serious damage and I didn't have the money to take care of it. I couldn't turn around because the bridge over the Mississippi was right there and the closest exit was three miles into Illinois. The car seemed to be doing fine as I neared the first Illinois exit. So I continued and as I neared each exit for the next few exits, I noticed that the car continued running smoothly so I just kept driving and drove all night, arriving in Grand Rapids about 2:30 A.M. I glanced at the car before I locked up for the remainder of the night—everything looked fine in the dark.

The next morning I went to go out and found my tire flat and my rim badly bent. I drove all night, from St. Louis to Grand Rapids, Michigan, on a bent front rim, never lost any air pressure and didn't do any damage to my new tire either!

❖

Even though the process was slow for getting the attention of the right people for Gregory's case, Greg continued to declare his freedom to all of those around him. He spoke with boldness when he would say; "I'm out of here!" He even had a slogan hanging on the wall that he used to speak all the time in 1994 after Mr. Dodger said we would hear something by the end of the year. The slogan was "OUT THE DOOR IN '94". Through the years that followed he continued to display his slogan, confessing that the work had already been done in the spirit and then he would say, "I'm Gone!" "It's a Done Deal!" The harassment that he took never altered his faith. As soon as he would make one of his bold comments, he would suffer harassment; then would seek the Lord, and the Lord never failed to minister something to him that confirmed that he was right to stand in the midst of the persecution. He never faltered. He even rebuked me at times when I would say anything that was contrary to his faith.

❖

Back at my job, some of the people I worked with had taken an interest in the case and what was going on. Others thought I was nuts. I had to do whatever I believed the Lord was leading me to do regardless of the mocking.

It was fortunate that I was able to make so many trips during the winter of 1995-96, and the Lord had the right players in place at the right time for me. One of those players happened to be my son who had moved back to Missouri. I stayed with him when taking care of business. So all I had to come up with was the gas money to run back and forth.

A couple months had passed and I was offered the job with the ministry again. This time, however, it was in the Central Missouri area, which was close to the prison that Gregory was in and 80 miles from my son's home. I really couldn't see myself taking less money, losing my benefits and moving across the country at my own expense again. Then one day my son Bob called from the Czech Republic, where he had been living for several years, and said he was coming to the States, but that if I wanted to see him I would have to come to Missouri, because he wasn't going to Michigan. Then my son Bill called and asked if I was serious about accepting Larry's offer. When I asked him why, he told me his father wanted him to move to Florida and help him with his invention. Bill needed me to live in his house and take care of his dogs until he could get settled, but he didn't know how long that would be. Then if, and when, he sold his property he would see what happened. In other words I would be able to live rent-free and not have to disrupt my household in Michigan, plus I would be in Missouri when Bob got there. In addition, of course, my husband Gregory lived there and I could see him every week.

CHAPTER XXXII

Back To Where It All Began

The reasons for moving back to Missouri were increasing no matter how much I disliked the thought of living there again. Missouri meant oppression that plagued me continually whenever I was there. I had my little "Honeymoon Cottage" in Michigan and I was happy there, plus I was finally buying something I could call mine.

I thought about how every time I crossed the Missouri border it felt like the demonic militia was attacking me. I operated in fear whenever I was there, especially since I refused to back off Gregory's case. I had discovered so much about Greg's case and I learned through my struggles that you couldn't trust anyone, no matter what his or her position was. Michael Dodger was the only person I had contact with at this time who seemed to care. But I knew even though I was beginning to trust him that he had to deal with all of the people I feared and who had as much if not more authority than he did. I didn't have a feel for Jeramy Shriver yet; all I knew was that he had a prosecutor's frame of reference, which troubled me.

With all of the things pulling on me to go to Missouri, I finally took the plunge. That summer I moved to Missouri on what I considered a sabbatical. Once down there, however, I realized I was trapped. I thought I was choking and was under such an oppressive cloud that my prayers were short and seemed to bounce off of that cloud. "Lord, do what you're going to do with me and get me out of here!" I cried—again.

I lived in fear my whole stay there. I was low key and avoided contacting friends back in Michigan because I didn't want anything to be traced back to them or to anything I was associated with in Michigan. I communicated with my sister via the fax machine only at work. No one knew my phone number or address. As I did when I was being terrorized years before, I drove out of the rear view mirror of car. If anyone was behind me too long I went off the road to test the waters or did some other maneuver to find out if my mind was playing games with me. My son's home was secluded, which was good and bad for my fear—down two dirt roads. There were times at night when I turned into the first road surrounded by trees and would turn my lights off immediately to make sure the turn went undetected. Then I would creep along until I felt comfortable enough to put my lights on again and I knew I wasn't being followed.

After being in Missouri one month, my son called and said that he ran an ad in the paper to sell the property. The property was beautiful and I knew it would sell fast, but what was I going to do? I was still paying for the "Honeymoon Cottage" in Grand Rapids and I couldn't go back. I was committed and felt like I was strangling. The ministry put me up in a little round house they owned. The house was brand new and just perfect for me. It was about the distance of two city blocks away from the TV station.

My rent and electric bill took half of my paycheck. Now the problem was twofold: I had rent and utilities to pay in both Michigan and Missouri and I was making less money—a little more than minimum wage. Plus my faithful car was feeling the pain of 10 years of faithful service on my trips back and forth to Missouri.

After about a month in Missouri, I had car trouble for the first time. My car had 190,000 miles on it and had performed like a champ all that time. I felt hopeless at this time. I had no money, my cost of living doubled my income, I couldn't defer my student loan anymore, and to top it off my son called and told me he was selling his land. I was trapped, but not defeated—yet.

Sure, I got to see Gregory every week, but I was miserable. It was taking everything in me to stay there, but then—I couldn't leave—my car couldn't make the trip and I didn't have the money.

I fought fear daily, moreover, the ministry I was involved with was getting more and more active and vocal about the injustices in the courts of Missouri. They also began to step on some toes as hard as they could—on precisely the toes I was trying to win favor with. I was quiet, though, and wanted to remain that way. The Lord put it on Greg's and my heart to be quiet, while the ministry fought relentlessly day and night for Gayle Boone's pardon and the lives of those whose names were coming up for execution.

❖

A brief story of one of the decisions I had to make at the ministry will give an example of some of the tension that could develop. Larry and Penny were gone so I was the one who had to respond to situations. A young couple came in and wanted Larry's help. The husband told his story to the receptionist, and she didn't know what to do. So she called me. He had just gotten out of prison at Potosi and wanted Larry to help him. I knew Potosi's reputation of housing the "worst of the worst" because Greg had spent years there. Not knowing what his crime was, I proceeded with caution.

Mark, Larry's assistant was also in the front office when the man repeated the story to me. He was telling about police harassment he had just experienced and described the incident. I have to admit I believed him. But then he said something that caused me to turn him away without consulting Larry. "What do you want Larry to do about this?' I asked.

"They have a warrant out for my arrest."

"For what?"

"Vehicular assault on a police officer."

I couldn't allow this man to go any further and I couldn't give him any help with that confession. So I jumped in with both feet very boldly. "Because you have told me this, I have a moral obligation to call the police."

The man knew I was right and didn't give me any problem; he just left and I indeed called the police. They couldn't do anything about it, but I was covering the ministry.

Larry questioned me about what happened and why I contacted the police when he called in. So I told him, "Because the reputation of the ministry was at stake. If I had tried to help him knowing there was a warrant out for his arrest, the ministry could have been considered as 'aiding and abetting.' So I called it as I saw it." I think he was ultimately glad I had the courage to handle it the way I did. That didn't mean that I wasn't attacked at times by fear though, for some of the things that the ministry was getting into.

Working for Larry one could live in fear every day of his or her life. It takes courage to minister to the poor, homeless and ex-convicts, and Larry seemed to handle it well. I think his ability to intimidate the intimidator threw people off most of the time. He kept the upper hand and didn't allow for idleness, and he never stopped directing people to Jesus. Under that aggressive exterior he is a very generous man, who has a heart to help those who can't help themselves. As thousands will attest to, he does it well—and he is noisy about it, which angers a lot of people.

❖

With the phone calls being so inexpensive while I was in Missouri, I was able to keep up better with Greg's daily routine. I noticed how much he had grown emotionally and spiritually. One day he and his cellmate were just sitting in their cell, minding their own business, when a young man came in and slugged Greg in the face. As Greg was rising up to his feet to address the issue, he sought the Lord for the best way to handle this attacker. He looked his assailant right in the face and said as he turned the other side of his face to him, "Do you want to hit the other side too?" The inmate ran out of the cell and back to his own walk (tier). Later he came back and Gregory was able to minister to him about how the Lord can change his life. Greg was being tested to see if he walked his talk. He passed with flying colors.

On another occasion, Greg was busy working when another inmate came in, harassing Greg about his Christian faith, weakness, and meekness. Greg is a large man about 258 pounds and 6'3" tall so just his size alone can be intimidating. But this particular inmate, being aware of Greg's gentleness, decided to push him as far as he could. Fed up with the verbal harassment, Greg began to take off his coat as if ready to go a few rounds. While he was doing so he said, "Let me tell you something about us Christians, man. Don't you ever mistake meekness for weakness. Do you want to try it?" The man backed down, knowing he bit off more than he could chew. Greg did have a reputation of strength and speed from his city jail days.

❖

Behind the scenes at home, I wrote an entire newspaper about the Oliver case, entitled "Freedom Express." (Parts of this newspaper are reprinted in the Appendix.) I did all of the artwork, paste up and writing. Then I took it into work one day and Larry had 5,000 copies made, just like he did for the Gayle Boone case. I passed them out to all of the legislators, hoping someone would pay attention—but to no avail. I even sent copies to Mr. Dodger and Mr. Shriver, but again I didn't hear back from them. Included in the newspaper was the story of my arrest.

❖

One day Gayle Boone's case was on national television—the main case Larry was working on. The ministry gave out its 800 number for anyone to call who wanted to show support and receive literature about the case. I fielded over 500 of the 1,000 calls we received that day, and I have to admit there was a spell where inside I was angry. I was so tired of hearing how "innocent" she was for shooting and killing a man "in self-defense." Her situation was hard, and I wanted her to get released just as they did, but I couldn't say she was innocent.

Her lawyer advised her to plead guilty to second-degree murder. Being scared, she compromised her integrity, bore false witness against herself and pleaded guilty to something she wasn't guilty of. Now they were trying to get the governor to sign a pardon for her.

Self-defense doesn't make one innocent, however, and I struggled with that every time I heard someone calling her "innocent." Gregory, by contrast, didn't kill anyone, didn't know what his brother was going to do, didn't compromise his integrity because of threats and he wouldn't plea bargain for something he wasn't guilty of. Consequently, he didn't bear false witness against himself—that's "innocence." I sought the Lord hard in the seconds between phone calls to help me get through the day. Finally the Lord spoke to my spirit and said, "Every call you answer is a seed for Gregory's freedom." With that, my whole attitude changed, and I handled the calls with all of the professionalism I could muster up.

During the season when everyone was working feverishly on Gayle Boone's case, I would drive up to the capital building every morning on my prayer drive before work. I would circle the building in prayer or pull off the road on the other side of the river where I had a clear view of the Capital. Some mornings I would stop on the riverside of the Capital between the governor's office and the historical monuments and pray or read and focus on the governor while praying for him to have courage, wisdom and integrity. On two of those mornings I had a vision.

First Vision: As I looked at the Capital Building from across the river, I could see a hand coming down from heaven. The hand was pointing its finger and the tip of the finger touched the very top of the Capital Building that was adorned with a statue of a Greek goddess. It was as if the Lord was letting me know that He had everything under control.

Second Vision: I could see demonic activity around the capital building, when suddenly that still small voice spoke to me and said, "The demons know who you are."

Praise the Lord, I thought. *Now I wouldn't have to battle so hard anymore.* It took months of testing, however, before the territorial demons were convinced that I indeed knew who I was in the Lord and was aware of my anointing. That didn't mean, however, that I would never have to battle the devil again in my life. There are always new devils at every level of faith that we obtain as we move up the spiritual ladder, growing in sanctification.

Behind the scenes and the activity of Gayle Boone's fight for freedom, I was continually working for Gregory. After every contact I made with the governor's people, I came back to work and was questioned about what the governor's people said about Gayle's case, because they were as intense about her case as I was about Gregory's. I would tell them curtly, "I wasn't there for Gayle; I was there for Gregory!"

CHAPTER XXXIII

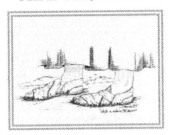

More Truth

One of the greatest discoveries I made in Gregory's case happened by accident. Larry Rice handed me a resource book that was published by the state, which listed "Who's Who" in state politics and the state judicial system. I glanced through it and saw a picture of Gregory's trial judge. I showed it to Larry. We made a couple of remarks. Then I gave it back.

Not too long after that I had this urge to look in the state's "Who's Who" book again. This time I read the information listed about the trial judge. I was astonished at what I learned. In the brief description, I discovered why the appeal judge gave the appeal lawyer such a difficult time over my letter writing. The appeal judge had mentored the trial judge during two of the summers that he was in law school. *No wonder,* I thought, *the appeal judge was angry with me and struck out at me during court as he did. I was challenging the integrity of his protégé's court.* By moral law, he should have recused[4] himself from the case because there was something that could show his bias in ruling on the case.

This new discovery answered more of my questions and exposed even further manipulation and cover-up of the truth of the Oliver case. As soon as I discovered this, I wrote another one of my infamous letters to Michael Dodger and Jeramy Shriver and included a copy of the judge's picture with the write-up naming the appeal judge as his men-

---

[4]re-cuse a: to challenge or except to (a judge) as interested or otherwise incompetent, b: to disqualify (oneself) as judge in a particular case. *Webster's Dictionary New International Dictionary.* 1959, p.1900.

tor. I also sent a copy of the first and last page of the appeal decision with the signature of the appeal judge on the same case as his protégé's, which confirmed with real evidence the relationship and probable bias on the part of the court.

❖

In October, 1996, on one of my appointments with Mr. Dodger, I received a surprise that wound up being the biggest blessing and break through to date. As I waited in the lobby for Mr. Dodger to call me into his office, I was going over in my head what I was going to present that day. He was his gracious self when he came up to meet me.

"It's good to see you again," he said as he shook my hand. Then he turned and escorted me saying, "We're going to meet in the conference room today. I've invited someone to sit in on the meeting."

"Is that good or bad?' I questioned.

"It's good." Inside the conference room was an attractive young woman. "I'd like for you to meet Jessica Kage. She is the lawyer who has been assigned to work on Gregory's case. His case is one of the key cases up for the governor's review."

I couldn't do or say anything; I just exploded into sobbing tears at the thought of Gregory's case making it to this level without a lawyer. Mr. Dodger rushed out of the room to get me some Kleenex. All I could do was apologize for my reaction.

At this meeting I presented the video of Mary Thomas revealing the jury stacking, along with the copy of her police report that I had with me, confirming Mary's credibility to identify the jurors. In the video, Mary said that her baby was Edward Dean's niece. As further proof, in the police report, all of Mary Thomas's children's names were listed and the youngest child's name was Tiffany Dean.

I was armed with both pieces of information, proving why the prosecutor had to discredit Mary Thomas with hearsay testimony as he tried to support the statute of "inconsistent statement" on which he insisted in trying Greg's case on. Mary Thomas, the alleged kidnap victim and the only witness who did not budge from her story, was the only person who could point a finger of guilt to the prosecutor and the jury stacking.

After I finished this presentation and overview to Jessica, Mr. Dodger asked me, while holding a copy of the "Freedom Express" in his hand, "What do you want?"

I felt like Esther, being asked by the king;

> "... What [is] thy petition, Queen Esther? and it shall be granted thee: and what [is] thy request? and it shall be performed, [even] to the half of the kingdom." (Esther 5:6, 7:2)

This was my chance to tell them exactly what Greg and I were asking for. I couldn't get up to half the kingdom like Esther, but at least I was in a position to ask. My response even surprised me. "I am not asking for heads to roll. Gregory has forgiven everyone who has wronged him. I am asking and believing that there is still integrity in high levels of authority, therefore I am asking for that integrity to right this wrong."

Mr. Dodger injected, "You have made that quite clear."

"And I want retribution for eleven and a half years of wrongful incarceration." To that again Mr. Dodger shook his head in a slight affirmative fashion.

I was on cloud nine when I left the office. They were listening to me, and I believed that I was making headway even though the wheels of justice turned slow—very slow. I couldn't wait until I told Gregory.

❖

Gregory called that night to find out about the meeting. As I expected, he was elated. His tears came like a gush after a pipe bursts when under pressure for a long period of time. He had to remember where he was, though, and get himself back under control.

❖

Four months after my meeting with Mr. Dodger and Ms. Kage I felt led to call her to see if any progress had been made on Gregory's case. She told me that she hadn't even started looking at his case and that she could only work on one case at a time, and I knew whose case that was—Gayle Boone's. I flew out of my office livid with anger.

"Did they say anything about Gayle's case?" my coworkers asked me. I said little, but I left the office, telling the receptionist that I was going to lunch and I didn't know when I was coming back. She knew I was more than just a little upset.

What was the most upsetting to me was that Gayle Boone was eligible for parole and probation and Gregory wasn't. So why would someone who had other avenues have such a privilege seeing her parole hearing was just weeks away. I was wondering if the politicians lied and all the noise that Larry and the media were making in behalf of Gayle Boone had made a difference. Yet the Lord wanted Gregory and me to be quiet to grow our patience and maintain our integrity.

I started driving to vent my anger and seek the Lord for comfort, only this time I couldn't get any rest. I was like an angry bull with his nostrils spread wide open, ready to charge.

A couple of months earlier I had a vision of going to Mr. Dodger's office and waiting until he saw me, because I wanted some answers. That vision kept coming back to me as I drove. I was almost out of control, and when I realized that I yelled out to the Lord, "You are sovereign, Lord—not the state! This doesn't have to happen! You are sovereign!" I was so much out of control that I could hardly drive, and I was on a road I had never been on before. I sought the Lord again. But I kept seeing myself going to the Parole and Probation office and sitting on Mr. Dodger's doorstep until I saw him. Believing I was hearing from the Lord, I headed that way.

The first thing I noticed at the Parole and Probation office was the in-and-out board at the front desk—*Ah, good Mr. Dodger was in.* I tried to exercise as much self-control as I could as I introduced myself and asked to see Mr. Dodger. The receptionist told me he was out. I knew better, so I told her that I wanted to talk to him about a case that he has been working on for three years.

"He's not out of the building, she replied, "he is just out of his office. Let me see if I can find him." In the meantime, Mr. Dodger had returned, and I could see him from my vantage point. She approached him and he came right over to me, shook my hand and greeted me graciously as usual.

Still very upset I said, "Can I talk to you for a minute?"

"I'm getting ready to go into a meeting," he said as he looked at me right in the eye. Seeing how distraught I was, he escorted me into his office. We stood there just inside the door.

I began by telling him that I had just talked to Jessica Kage, the woman he had introduced me to four months earlier. "She told me that she has not even begun working on Gregory's case. I have a hard time with that." I paused to catch my thoughts and breath. "Prosecutors and lawyers work on more than one case at a time. There is no reason why Greg's case can't be worked on also, especially seeing there are over one hundred and fifty cases on the governor's desk. At that rate, they will never get through them." I paused, then blurted out trying to control my anger, " And right now you are the only person that can say anything to me that will calm me down!"

Sensing how upset I was, he asked me to sit down as he went around his desk to sit down. We discussed what I had presented to him. In essence he said, "We are not prosecutors and defense lawyers the way you think of it. I assure you we will get to Gregory's case." In the next few minutes, he said what I needed him to say to settle me down, and I was satisfied for the time being.

In reviewing what had just happened, I saw it as a victory. A man as important as Mr. Dodger actually took the time to see me, delaying his meeting even further. He saw me without an appointment, knowing I was upset and angry. His actions told me he was sincere and wasn't just putting me off. I had earned his respect or he would never have agreed to see me right away. I also had another Michael Dodger promise. In all my dealings with Mr. Dodger, he always performed what he said he was going to do within an acceptable time frame. He had once told me that I was Greg's best advocate and he would talk to no one else but me about Greg's case. The only problem was that he was not in control of everyone else, though he might be able to influence them.

❖

My Toyota was making a lot of noise and smoke was coming from the engine. Gregory realized a lot of what I was going through when one of the guards told him that he had seen me with smoke barreling out of my car. He began praying for my car and me.

One morning when I was driving to the prison, I began weeping and praying over my car. I told the Lord all about how sad I was that my car was showing the signs of aging. It had over 200,000 miles on it and still looked good. I asked the Lord to take care of it. Not two weeks later I went to the mailbox and found an envelope from my ex-husband. To my surprise there was a check in the envelope with enough money to fix my car. So I put it in the shop right away and they gave me a loaner. While I was driving the loaner, the supplier of the materials for the remodeling job being done at NLEC asked me what was wrong with my car.

"I have just the car for you," he said.

"I can't afford to buy a new car."

"This is perfect and has only had 50,000 miles on it. It's an '89 Silver Chrysler New Yorker and it is loaded. It is in perfect condition."

"Those are sharp-looking cars. My parents have one."

"Next time you're in Columbia stop by and I'll show it to you."

"I can't buy a car."

"Have your ex buy it for you," was his reply. "After all, he owes you for the pension he terrorized you out of."

❖

When Bob had graduated from college in Connecticut a year earlier, Bill and I had our first face-to-face conversation in years. While the boys were showing me around the manufacturing plant that all three of them worked in, Bill came up to me and gave me a quick kiss. The boys and I were shocked. He said his, "hello" then went back to work, but asked us to stop by before we left. He politely walked us to the exit. Then, just as we were about to leave Bill pulled me over to the side to talk to me.

"I don't know why life has dealt you the blows it has, because you don't deserve it." I started crying as he continued. "If I had it to do all over again, I would have just walked away instead of terrorizing you for those years."

I couldn't believe what I was hearing. He used the words I had never said before. He "terrorized" me and he knew it. Then he went on to say, "If there is anything you need, Lil' Bill will be our conduit. Let him know and he will tell me and if I am able I will do it for you."

❖

I couldn't shake the idea of a car big enough for Gregory to ride in comfortably. So I checked out the car when I went to Columbia. It was beautiful indeed. I called my ex-husband and told him the situation and gave him the price of the car. Then I asked if he would buy it for me. He didn't even hesitate with his response. "Yes, but it will take me a couple of days. Get me your account number and I will have the funds wired to you. I'll send a little extra for taxes and the extras you like to get with new cars. You'll have it Wednesday. Isn't a New Yorker a pretty big car?"

"Yes it is, but it is in mint condition. Thank you."

I had the money by the following Wednesday and I closed the deal on the car!

❖

It was nearing July and my son Bill was about to be married in Connecticut. I had no idea how I was going to get to the wedding, much less try to buy a wedding gift. I asked Bill what he wanted as a wedding present to which he responded, "All I want is a couple of your paintings. I want a lighthouse and a ship." I was honored, but I hadn't painted in years. I still had my oils and brushes but didn't know what condition they were in. After I checked, all I needed was to pick up a couple of canvases. As the Lord does things, I was able to find 16"X20" pre-stretched canvas for $5 each—what a deal!

About a month before the wedding, I took a weekend and tried my hand at painting for Bill and Sarah's wedding gift. They were not the best paintings I have ever done, but they were passable. Bill grew up with my paintings good and bad—all around him—and he always liked my work. He used to get mad at me for giving so many away—especially the ones he liked.

It was the Friday before I was to leave to go to the wedding and I couldn't go. Larry called me into his office for something and he happened to mention that I would be gone the next week.

"No, I'm not going."

"Your son is getting married, isn't he?"

"Yes, but I can't go."

"Why not?"

"Because you don't pay me enough to pay my bills—much less go to my son's wedding," I said haughtily.

"I want to put an addition on the dorm in the woods with two bed-rooms. Can you draw me a plan by Sunday? If you do, I'll give you $200. Will that get you to Connecticut?"

"It will help."

He gave me the check before I drew the plan, which allowed me to get a couple of things before I left. I delivered the plans for the dorm Sunday morning before I went to the prison to visit Gregory.

I took one of my cotton dresses with me, hoping it would work for the mother-of-the-groom dress. I figured that I could stay in the background and no one would have to look at me. I was going to stop in Michigan on the way, then drive to Connecticut.

When I got to Michigan, my sister asked about the dress I was going to wear. It was not to either hers or my mother's liking as mother of the groom. My mother had picked up a two-piece dress at the Goodwill store, which I thought would work out better, although it might be a little hot because it was black. The dress fit as well as any I had, so I decided to wear that.

Because I was so low on money, I couldn't stop at a motel. Therefore, I drove straight through, stopping periodically to take short naps. I was hoping to get in about 5:00 P.M. on the 24th but didn't arrive until 7:00 P.M. Bob had already checked us into the room. He left me a note that told me the plans. He was getting his tuxedo for the wedding with the guys and would check in later. I just went ahead and started unloading the car. I had no idea how I was going to get home because I only had $18 in my pocket.

As I was entering my room with my second load, I looked up and walking toward me was my ex-husband, Bill. He helped me bring some more things in from the car. Once we were both in the room he opened his wallet and handed me $100 without my prompting. He was planning on taking me to dinner if I had gotten there earlier, but seeing it was so late, he had to get back to his wife. He said some nice things to me, and of course I wound up crying (he did too) from all of the pain of the past and the destruction of our family.

My son's wedding was difficult for me. Later I discovered why. The Lord began to show me how I had been dishonored time and again in the past, that I had been lied to and stolen from. None of these things had healed, and they were festering wounds. Every time I had to see my ex-husband I went through the pain of the horrifying memories all over again, which would throw me into depression.

The highlight of Bill's wedding was when the groom danced the special dance with his Mom. The music that played was Kenny Roger's song "Through the Years." During some of the most difficult years when his father was stalking and terrorizing us, Bill was my rock. He never let me down. I looked to him for everything at his tender age, beginning when he was thirteen years old. I began crying when I heard the song and remembering. "Bill," I said, "did you pick this song?"

"No." Bill opened the lapel of his coat and said, "Mom, there is a napkin in there." So I reached up into his pocket and took it to wipe my eyes. Then Bill said, "Are you going to share it?"

I looked up at him and he was crying too. So I gave him the napkin back. When the song was over he leaned down and kissed me on the lips and he escorted me back to the table, the people at the table were also wiping tears. God honored me so beautifully during our dance.

Looking back, in spite of the good things that had happened, that week was perhaps the most difficult week of my life. I cried all the way to Connecticut because of the past rejection and I cried all the way home because of a different form of rejection and the honor the Lord bestowed upon me through my dance with Lil' Bill.

I was able to make it home with the $100 Bill gave me. I left the wedding reception at about 5:00 P.M. and drove straight home. It took 29 hours, catnapping along the way.

❖

After Gayle Boone had her hearing for parole, I called Jessica Kage to remind her that she promised that Greg's case was next and to set up an appointment. She was so receptive that I was able to set an appointment for that following Thursday to share some new information I had.

One night during one of Greg's and my evening phone calls we discovered something that proved there was someone in the apartment before the police came. This person could have moved the gun Ron swore he saw in Sandy's hand. As Greg was reading the police report, he read about a man named Andy Hill.

I stopped him, "Who is Andy Hill?"

"I don't know."

"You've never heard of him before?"

"No."

"It says he was in the apartment before the police came and that he ran away from there—fast. Read it again." Greg read it again.

We scrutinized the police report and transcripts for the next two hours. It turned out that in the police report, Susan Miller described Andy Hill as the man running from the building—not Robert Franklin. At the trial Susan insisted that Robert Franklin wore his hair in a long Afro style. But the third man she identified running from the building was wearing a medium Afro and was running fast. If Robert Franklin had just gotten shot in the leg, how could he run fast without at least a limp? During the trial, the prosecutor had insisted that Robert Franklin was shot on the steps as he was trying to escape.

Then there was the description of the clothing being worn by the victims recorded in the police report by Andy Hill. His description supported Gregory's testimony and refuted the inference that the prosecutor was trying to impose on the jury that Ron shot Franklin as he was escaping. Gregory testified that Ron shot Franklin while he was in the apartment during the shooting spree. Four witnesses testified to only hearing three shots yet there were six shots fired. Ron was shooting so fast and furious that no one could have stopped him. None of the witnesses were able to distinguish how many shots were even fired. Even a trained off-duty police officer that was in the neighborhood that night testified to hearing only three shots.

❖

The meeting with Jessica went very well. I presented the new information we discovered about the case to her. Then I proposed a meeting to review the entire case with her. "Would you be willing to allow me that time?" I asked.

Without hesitation she said, "Yes." Then she went on to say, "When you called me I ordered the transcripts and the paperwork from the trial. It should take a week to get it. Then I have to make a copy of everything and once I have read it I will call you and we can sit down and go over the case. I have already read everything that you have written about the case." That last statement certainly impressed me, and I left there excited, hoping for a fair review of Greg's case—finally.

The following days turned into weeks. Finally a month passed, and I hadn't heard anything from Jessica. In the meantime, the Lord impressed upon me that change was coming in my life, which He usually started telling me when it was time to make *another* move. Then one morning on one of my prayer drives, the Lord spoke to my spirit and told me I was going back to Michigan. He impressed on me that my father would be dying soon and I had to go back to Michigan.

Greg called that next night, and I told him what I believed the Lord was impressing upon me. Without hesitation, he concurred with me. The first thing the next morning I left a voice mail message on Jessica's machine telling her that my sabbatical was over and I was going back to Michigan. I asked if I could have an appointment with her before I left. She called me back within the hour, and we scheduled it for October 2, 1997.

I also had to tell Penny, Larry Rice's wife, that I was leaving. She was shocked, because the people at the ministry were making all sorts of plans that included me. I have to admit it wasn't easy for me to think of leaving either. I liked my job because everything I had been schooled and trained for, I was doing at the TV station. I even had an opportunity to get my drawing board out and work on a couple of design jobs. I played general contractor on the biggest design project I had worked on for the ministry—the remodeling of NLEC base operation in central Missouri. This project would maximize unused space and would provide a large kitchen that would accommodate food preparation for large groups, which often met in the facility. The pay, however, for using all that I had been trained for, was not in keeping with what I would have received in the secular world.

❖

Now that the decision was made, I was ready to go. Several months earlier it had become clear to me I could not keep up on the expenses of the "Honeymoon Cottage" plus my place in Missouri, so I had been forced to sell the Michigan home and move all my things to Missouri. All I needed to do was to repack and make everything more compact. I was ready to move in two weeks. I wanted to get rid of everything because I couldn't afford the move, but my family was resistant to me selling everything as I had given up so much in the past. So plans were made for me to rent a truck.

❖

Before I moved, one other thing happened that ended up bringing Greg and me closer together. As I was walking along the country road on my way to work, I noticed a pretty blonde Brittany spaniel on the opposite side of the street. I knew the dog did not belong to anyone in the area, as I was quite familiar with the homes around there. She spotted me and came across the street. She acted very friendly.

"Go home, dog," I said over and over again, but she just kept walking with me all the way to work. She hung around the station and everyone who came in mentioned what a nice dog she was and wondered where she came from. Then Larry came in, saying, "Whose dog is that?" When I told him she was a stray, he told me, "You need to take that dog home, Bonnie."

"I don't want a dog, Larry."

"I'm telling you, Bonnie, you need to take that dog home."

"I don't want a dog, Larry."

"Bonnie, you really need to take that dog home. I know strays and that is a good one. Go get her something to eat." So I went and fed her.

Later that day I discovered the dog was not only housebroken but also spayed. Knowing she belonged to someone we tried through various ways to find out who she belonged to—all to no avail.

Greg called and I told him about the dog. He sounded so excited I almost wished he wasn't so thrilled, for that would give me an excuse to get rid of her. He wanted to talk to her right away on the phone so she could get use to his voice before he was released. He then mentioned that his family had had a collie when he was growing up—so did I. We finally had something in common—our childhood pets.

While Greg and I were praying, I knelt down at the foot of the bed on my prayer pillow. Brittany (that's what I called her) sat down right next to me and put her paws on the bed, one paw over the other and rested her head on her paws. It was as though she was praying, "Oh Lord, let this one keep me." During the night she slept in the far corner of the bedroom watching over me. When I moved to Michigan, Brittany moved with me.

❖

My meeting day with Jessica finally arrived. I gathered all my paperwork together and headed for the Parole and Probation Office. Jessica was right on time—her arms loaded with legal paperwork. We met in a large conference room that looked like a boardroom so I could really spread out if I needed to. My plan was to get her attention right away and then walk her through how the rest of the travesties happened. I knew Greg was praying for me, so I was covered in the spiritual arena.

I started the meeting by showing Jessica one of the paragraphs in the Federal Review and Recommendation. It was the paragraph that proved that the federal judge had not done his homework on the case. I read, "...[Sandy Nicholas] was at home with several small children, *two of whom* were [Robert Franklin] and [Bruce Campbell]." Then I asked Jessica, "How old was Bruce Campbell?" (italics added)

"Thirty six." She replied quickly.

"You know that because you did your homework. How old does this judge think he is?" I read it again out loud. "'...*Two of whom were...*' He thought the victims were children—further biasing the case. That also would account for his seeming anger in the R&R."

"Oh," she said. " I didn't see that before." She grabbed her pen and began to make a note of that.

For the next four hours we went over the case while I asked questions and pointed things out. She clarified how the state would view things. At one point, I became frustrated. She had to tell me, "Bonnie, I'm not trying to argue with you."

"I realize that and I don't want to argue either," I said, "and I want to know how the state will view it because it will help any further study that I might have, and it will stretch me. It's just that it's so frustrating.

"Bonnie, when someone studies a case as long as you have, everything begins to look like something other than what it is. Besides, no one has ever said that Gregory murdered anyone."

"Then why is he in prison for Premeditated First-Degree Murder?"

"Because the jury found him guilty."

"Yes, but the jury was stacked, and it was Sandy's word against his, and he was a far more credible witness than she was," I said.

"What was the relationship again?" So I went through the relationships of the jury members to the ringer hearsay witness.

We then talked about Ronald's mental condition, Jessica explained about how the law views "mental disease and defect" and how it will not hold a person accountable for a crime if he or she is truly suffering from a "mental disease and defect."

"If that is the case," I asked, "then wouldn't it also follow that another cannot be found guilty of the perpetrator's crime and receive an equal or greater sentence?"

"I don't know. I'll have to check how the law reads on that." Then she took more notes.

Although I did not get to go through all that I wanted to go through in the four hours, I believed a lot was accomplished. Jessica went on to say different things that gave me clues that she was indeed evaluating the case from an unbiased standpoint, which delighted me to no end. She had definitely done her homework too. Finally, someone was *really* looking at Greg's case!

After the meeting, I had two hours left in which I could visit Greg. I hurried over to the prison. I reviewed the meeting with him—high point by high point. He became very emotional and cried more than once—someone was really seeing the case for what it was—a miscarriage of justice.

❖

My sister made provisions for the truck and the trailer for the Toyota to get back to Michigan. My son Bill had his friends come and help me pack. That was the real blessing. The truck was too small to take everything so I had to make some choices as to what I was going to leave. Plus, I had to leave room in the cab for Brittany.

The night I left Missouri, my feelings of discomfort as though I was being watched were confirmed. The roundhouse I lived in was exposed from all sides, though you could only access it by vehicle from one side. I had always kept the shades drawn and the lights out. I moved in the dark with night-lights glowing. Where the road was to my house there was no outlet and I was at the end so no one would just happen to wind up on my street near my house—it had to be deliberate.

I woke up from my nap at about 2:30 A.M. and got the last things together to make one last trip to the truck to take off. There were no streetlights, and since I was in the country it was very dark by the house. There was a vacant house to the east of mine, which the road to my house wound around to exit. With the dog's leash in one hand and my other arm filled with last minute things, I headed for the truck. I opened the back of the truck and put the last minute things in, then I had to walk around to the passenger side to let the dog in because I had a barricade between the seats.

Something made me look up at the moment I was getting ready to open the cab door and let the dog in. From out in front of the vacant house I could see the dark silhouette of a car against the reflected headlights of the cars on the highway. It crept forward with its lights off and then moved backward slowly. I froze for a moment and watched for any more activity that might be coming from in front of the house or around it for that matter. The passenger side of the truck was not visible to the car creeping around the house. I was so thankful that Brittany was quiet, because I didn't want any attention drawn to me.

As soon as I thought I was out of view of the car, I put the dog in the cab as fast as possible because the cab light would come on and we would be obvious. Then I rushed to the back of the truck on the driver's side so I could peek around to make sure I couldn't see any movement. When I felt all was clear, I dashed to the driver's entrance to climb in locking the door as I did so it would lock instantly when I closed the door. After jumping in, I sat motionless for a few moments, watching the road. When I felt more comfortable, I started the truck and inched foreword without headlights, trying to be as inconspicuous as a 15-foot truck with a car trailer could be. I was towing my Toyota, because my New Yorker's transmission died and was towed to Columbia to eventually get repaired.

Neighbors around the corner and down the road had mercury lights so I could see the road ahead once I rounded the bend. It looked like clear sailing, but I left my lights off until I got to the highway. A sigh of relief came, as I was able to hit the road. I only had one fuel stop to make, to top off the gas tank before I crossed the Missouri border. The closer I got to Illinois, the happier I was to be leaving Missouri. In Missouri I had lost my marriage, custody of one of my sons, I had been stalked and terrorized, I was arrested on a trumped up charge, and suffered a horrendous amount of fear and oppression, because of the so-called good guys of our society. But Missouri is also where I learned to follow the "tug." (Gayle Boone never received a pardon. She was eligible for parole and the governor chose to let the Parole and Probation Office decide her case. Gayle Boone was paroled in February, 1998.)

CHAPTER XXXIV

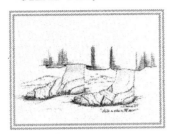

Back Home Again In Michigan

I began to realize as I was driving back to Michigan that if I had not married Greg when I did, then I would have thrown in the towel and given up. I would not have continued to pursue his case and ultimately discover the critical information I gathered while back in Missouri. I would have never heard Michael Dodger's words that permeated my soul—"Don't give up!"

My first stop in Michigan was Grand Rapids to unload my belongings in storage. My sister, bless her heart, helped me unload the first day. We were so exhausted. Then the second day my brother-in-law helped us with the remainder and the heavy things. I had to get two storage units to hold everything to the tune of $75/month—which I didn't have, because I was without income again!

My next stop was my parent's house in the Lansing area, ninety miles away. I wasn't sure if my Toyota would make it. I figured that this would probably be the last trip of any distance that I could make with my faithful friend of 10 years.

Once at my parent's house there was no where I could go, because I had neither money nor a trustworthy vehicle. I felt trapped—literally. It seemed like I moved from one situation or season of entrapment to another, and I couldn't figure out why the Lord had me going through all of this time and time again.

My father was definitely showing the signs of his 80 years. His heart was functioning at 25 percent of capacity, but he was still driving and did little jobs on the property, such as mowing the lawn.

My parents provided a way for me to have my New Yorker fixed in Missouri and bought me a Greyhound Bus ticket to get down there to pick it up. I traveled all night without much sleep. The bus driver dropped me off right in front of the Aamco Dealership, saving me cab fare. I drove down to the prison to surprise Greg with a visit, then hit the road, stopping in Illinois to get some rest before the last stretch back to Michigan.

Once back, I had a car, but no money to drive it. I started sending out resumes, but only to ads listed in the paper. While waiting for responses, I applied weekly for jobs at Michigan State University and Lansing Community College. I even called a couple of employment agencies. In all that, I never got one interview.

It was early November, so while the weather wasn't too cold we needed to get the snowplow blade on the tractor. What a job that was for my dad and me. My father had beginning stages of dementia. At first, he couldn't remember how to change the blades. But he finally figured it out. The plow blade was heavy, but the 5' wide deck with the lawn mower blades was even heavier and much harder to take off than the snow blade was to put on. That project of my father's and mine was a two-nitroglycerine job for him. I tried to encourage him to stop and call the neighbor, but he wouldn't. When we were finally done I told him, "I can't believe you did that by yourself year after year."

"I sure did," He said with a bit of pride.

A week later we had our first snow, but didn't have the chains on the tractor. The tractor was on the wrong side of the barn, so we had to drive it out across the lawn. It got stuck in the snow. My father and I worked trying to get the chains on. That was a three-nitroglycerine job for my dad.

By the time Thanksgiving came around, I was doing half of the driving when my parents and I went out. Without money I had **no** freedom at all. My days consisted of trying to find an odd job to do in the house. I had my computer set up in the dining room while I was sending out resumes. I'd get up, check the paper, send out my resume and cover letter, and then wait for the mailman. On the days we didn't go out, the mail delivery was the highlight of the day. It was a break for me to take Brittany for a walk.

We would usually go out on Tuesday, Thursday, Saturday and Sunday—we had a regular routine. Tuesdays and Thursdays were senior luncheon days. The food was always good, but not being a very sociable person, I usually kept my nose in a book while my parents socialized with their friends. I hungered for fellowship I could identify with. Yet in my spirit, I knew that I was where the Lord wanted me. Then on Saturday and Sunday we would go out for a ride and stop at a restaurant to eat and then run errands.

I had no contact with any of my friends and didn't feel I could give out my parent's phone number. I couldn't talk to Greg either, because his name was not a household word. Greg's and my communication was strictly through letters. Hour after hour and day after day the boredom, even with playing solitaire on the computer (which I did not learn until then), wore on me. I would cry myself to sleep nearly every night. I was grieving inside about my situation in general. My spirit was aching to talk about Jesus to someone who knew Him as I did. I had to have some escape route, but without funds what could I do. Brittany was a godsend indeed. She helped all of us during those days when my father was slowly dying. The air of depression in the house was horrible and when my father's dementia would kick in my dad would say harmful things he didn't mean.

Since job hunting was going so badly, I decided to get a part-time Christmas job. I had worked at J. L. Hudson's before, so I applied there, and they hired me right away. I worked anywhere from 25-35 hours a week. That put gas in my car and got me out of the house. Now at least I had some source of communication at work, though I had forgotten how difficult it was for me to be on my feet for long periods of time.

By the time Christmas arrived, I was doing all of the driving when my parents and I went out. Christmas Eve marked my father's 81st birthday and he was still doing ok—not great, but ok. As usual, I was dreading Christmas. It had been years since I had spent Christmas with either of my sons. I was tired of being the "fifth wheel" with my parents and my sister's family although I know they didn't feel that way.

We were sitting around taking turns opening gifts when suddenly, from behind me came two strong hands grabbing my shoulders and a voice whispered in my ear, "Merry Christmas, Mom!" I looked up and there was Bob. He had flown in from Prague, Czech Republic, where he had been living. He had flown in to Chicago and drove from there through a horrible blizzard to surprise me. I was so excited. I cried so hard because my baby had come to see me. Bob was in town for only a couple of days. We went shopping and to the movie. We had a wonderful two days together, however, the gloom of my living arrangements bothered him.

Nineteen ninety-eight brought several changes. I was able to get temporary work at Michigan State University, which was a real blessing. I was to start at a higher wage than I had made for the past ten years though it was still poverty level. I kept my part-time job at Hudson's for gas money until I got situated at MSU. Then the real problems started for my father. Between January and May he was in and out of the hospital with congestive heart failure about six times.

One evening when my father was in need of 24-hour family watch while in the CCU unit, I was talking to some friend's of my parents who pastored a local church. We were on the same wavelength spiritually, so I told them I needed to spend that particular night and minister to my father in song. My nephew, David and I took turns sitting with my father. David took the first watch, and I found a couch to rest on. When I got up and went into my father's room, David updated me—the nurse had been working with my father for the past two hours and couldn't believe that he was still alive. David said his spell was so bad that it scared him. The nurse pulled a table and chair into the room to do her work so she too could watch my father. I sat near his bed for the remainder of the night.

I was trying to figure out how I could minister to him in song with the nurse there. Finally, I just decided to sing until she told me to be quiet. I started by humming my father's favorite hymn, "In the Garden," then I added the words. I sang very softly and was really in the Spirit, so my voice was clear and sweet. Then I went to another soothing song, and another and another, singing each one over and over again until I received release in my spirit. I knew that my father's spirit could hear me and was responding to my singing.

After I sang a couple of songs, my father began to stir. The nurse moved quickly trying to make him comfortable. I continued to sing. The nurse whispered to my father, "Mr. Barnes, are you listening to your daughter? I know where she got her beautiful singing voice (my father loved to sing and had a very pleasant voice). Her music is so peaceful and is really relaxing me. You just keep listening to her singing." I was so blessed, because the music was not only ministering to my father and myself but it was ministering to the nurse too.

The next morning after the doctor made his visit, the nurse came in and started pulling out tubes and preparing my father to move to another unit with plans of going home.

That night my mother, her friend Barb, and I were in the room with my father. Barb and I began singing hymns. Suddenly, my father reached out both of his arms and called us around him. So we hurried to our feet and gathered around my father holding hands. He wanted to pray—my father prayed a prayer of thanksgiving. I could hardly contain the joy coming out of my spirit. Barb said later when she looked at me, "The joy on your face was so beautiful."

The next couple of months were up and down, with my father being in and out of the hospital. Each time he left the hospital, his condition was weaker. He had to go on oxygen 24 hours a day. My mother told us later that whenever her friend, Barb, and I began singing hymns to my father, she would watch his breathing and it would stabilize.

❖

I had been in three different temporary positions at MSU by the end of March. The third position I even received a little raise. This position would last a long time, for which I was thankful.

On May 8, 1998, I had to leave work early to go to the hospital for my father. He was in ICU this time, and his heart was only functioning at 15 percent of capacity. After my sister got there, I went to the house to let Brittany out. While I was home, I began feeling bad, so I hung around the house. I felt the urge to pray, so I got down on my hands and knees and prayed in the Spirit. I asked the Lord to show me what was going on, and before I knew it, I was on my face in travail. In the spirit, I could see a dark pit with a lot of people in it. They were trying to claw their way out, but were unable to do so. They would get so far then fall back down in the hole. What I was seeing were souls. I kept travailing and praying.

Then I realized that there was no time and space in the spirit, so I started crying out to them, "It's Jesus—call out to Jesus. Daddy, call out for Jesus." Over and over again I travailed for the souls and cried out for them to cry out to Jesus. I could see my father's head coming up through the group of souls. Then finally—peace—I had the most incredible peace come over me. I was so joyful and peaceful. The song "There is Something About That Name" filled my spirit and I began to sing it. I sang it all the way to the hospital. I kept hoping that Pastor Bob would be at the hospital when I got there. He was. I stood by my father's bed and I asked Pastor Bob to teach my family from the 91st Psalm.

Pastor Bob began to read, and when he finished he got up and prayed for my father; then he left. Shortly after he left, the rest of us, my mother, sister, nephew, and I said our good-byes to my father and left. I was the last one. I whispered, "Good-night, Barnsey (my pet name for him). I'll see you tomorrow."

My father died while we were all on our way home that night and the blessing was—he made it home. I know that because I had the peace that passes all understanding I received after I battled the devil in the spirit for souls. We won!

CHAPTER XXXV

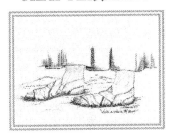

When, God, When?

During the time when I was running my mother back and forth to the hospital, I was not letting up on Gregory's case. I was quiet about it, and only my sister knew what I was doing. I made it a habit to touch base monthly with Jessica Kage. She was impressive. Even if she didn't have anything to tell me, she always returned my phone call.

In February 1998, I received a letter from Gregory telling me of a meeting concerning clemency that was scheduled for the 20th of February with the governor's legal council. They had originally surprised Gregory, but had to postpone the meeting a week, which gave him time to contact me so I could notify people to pray about the meeting.

According to Greg's letter, the meeting went great. Both Ms Kage and Mr. Shriver showed up with a stenographer. They questioned and re-questioned Gregory about his actions the night of the shooting. They also asked him general information questions to find out more about him. They wanted to know what his plans were if the governor did pardon him. Greg was able to answer everything comfortably and some questions tearfully. He was also able to enlighten them about the man, Gregory Oliver. He was able to tell them about the Associate's Degree he earned as a paralegal while incarcerated. An even bigger surprise was the fact he had two honorable discharges from the army. He was able to share his ideas for ministering to the men while in prison and followed up his ideas with the paperwork that we had already put together for the program so they would know he was sincere.

Greg said he broke down crying a couple of times when he was sharing about his brother, Ron. They asked if he had ever asked Ron why he shot those people, to which he replied, "Yes" and continued to answer their question about Ron's response, "He just looked at me with a hurt expression in his eyes. You see in Ron's mind, he thought he was protecting me," Greg said. At that point, the interview had to pause until Greg got his composure back and was ready to go back "on the record."

When asked about the gas can he had with him that night, Greg's response contained an air of humor with the truth to dispel the inferences that the prosecutor was trying to inject. He said, "Ms. Jessica, if you were taking a young lady out...Oh no, Ms. Jessica, you can't take no young lady out [They all laughed.] If a young man was taking you out, would you like to sit in the back seat with a gas can?" He answered their question with a question that they couldn't argue with. When Ms. Jessica and Mr. Shriver got up to leave, Mr. Shriver looked Greg square in the eyes and shook his hand. As Greg tried to pull his hand away, Mr. Shriver grabbed it firmer and said, "I want you to know that your case is the only one we are working on."

I had a chance to talk to Jessica about the meeting a week later. She told me Greg was very straightforward with his answers. She said that they had a stenographer there so they could have transcripts for the governor to read what Greg had to say and not have to go by hers and Mr. Shriver' interpretation. "The governor is a fair man," she said, "and we can be thankful that Missouri has a governor who will even consider looking at clemency cases. We don't just sit down with the governor and make recommendations, and he says, 'OK.' He goes over each case with us, because he does not want to make a mistake. He really wants to do what is right, Bonnie."

Over the next couple of months Jessica shared other things with me that didn't divulge too much information. She shared just enough to let me know that she was really into the case and concerned about the right outcome. Their legal position while reviewing the clemency cases is more like that of a judge versus lawyers, which it would have to be in order for them to nullify a decision that came from the courts and went through the full process. After meeting Greg, she knew what I knew and what everyone else knows who meets him. Several times she said to me, "He is really a nice guy!" She also agreed that the man she met and talked to with Mr. Shriver was not the man in the transcripts.

At the end of April 1998, I made my regular follow up call to Jessica. She shared some upsetting news with me. Jessica was going into private practice and getting out of criminal law. That Friday was to be her last day working for the state. Part of her reason was because criminal law and her job were just too emotional. She had been studying the death row cases that were coming up for execution, and there had been one execution scheduled each month in the early part of 1998. She assured me that she was leaving Greg's case in a very good position and that Mr. Shriver and Mr. Dodger were the only people handling it now. She assured me that she worked well with both Mr. Dodger and Mr. Shriver. She told me I had been a good advocate through this whole process.

❖

My father had been dead for three months. Frankly, I was amazed at how well my mother was doing emotionally. Then one night when I was coming into the house through the laundry room, I had a quick flashback vision. About one month before my father died, he had fallen in the laundry room; but even though I saw my dad in the vision, I knew my mother was going to fall.

During the night Brittany woke me up to go out. While she was outside I used the bathroom my parents usually used. While I was in there I had another flashback vision of another fall my father took in that bathroom. During that particular fall, he broke his back. That vision, like the earlier one, was telling me that my mother was going to fall and break something. Before I left for work in the morning, I told my mother to "Be careful."

The next day at work, I received a phone call from my mother. "Bonnie." I heard my mother's very weak voice. "I have some bad news. I fell in the garage and I think I broke my arm."

"Mom, I'll be right there," I dropped everything and went to my mother's house to take her to the hospital. Indeed, she had a very bad break in her upper left arm bone. The prognosis, after three days in the hospital was six months to heal and severe pain for four weeks. She had to walk with a cane because she was not stable enough without it. Because she couldn't lie down, we had to get a hospital bed for her to sleep in. The hours dragged by for her as she battled pain every moment of the day. A nurse's aide came in to bathe her and an occupational therapist came in two or three times a week to check up on her.

On weekends, I took her for her usual rides. Except now I had to be even more careful driving because of the pain. She couldn't get dressed so she wore her hospital gown and cotton robe in the car. I did all of her running. My mother was laid up for six months, because she didn't heal and had to go into surgery after three months.

❖

My son Bob was getting married in Prague, Czech Republic. The Lord blessed me with a way to get there with a dollar or two extra. So I decided to make a real vacation out of it and go to visit Greg for our fourth anniversary. While down in Missouri, I decided to visit Mr. Shriver or Mr. Dodger. Mr. Shriver was on vacation, but I managed to set up an appointment with Mr. Dodger on the day of Greg's and my fourth anniversary and the day before I was to fly out to Prague.

❖

I really didn't go as prepared for the meeting as I had been for the other meetings. Mr. Dodger was his cool conservative self and was probably wondering what I wanted. I began by saying, "I'm not here to slap a lot of information down that I have discovered about the case. I have done that during the 11 years I have been studying this case. But I've discovered that Johnny Lee Wilson's case was studied for one year, before he was released, and so too with Gayle Boone's case; now Gregory Oliver's case has been studied for over a year. It is time to make a decision, and I am here to see if there is any information that you can share with me?"

His response was cool, "No."

"You know when I presented this case to Jessica for four hours last October 2nd, my ten years of study was laid out. She was a delight to work with. She responded to every phone call whether she had anything to say or not, but at least I knew that there was movement on the case. When she left in April, she told me that she was leaving the case in a good position. Now whatever that means I don't know. What I do know is that she read the information, then did her information gathering, whereas Mr. Shriver did his information gathering before reading the transcripts in March of this year. Jessica didn't know if he had finished them or not when she left in April."

Mr. Dodger was fairly quiet as he listened. I continued with some more things that Jessica had told me, so that he would know I was staying on top of everything. Finally, he said something that added to the conversation. "A couple of week ago Mr. Shriver told me he had to do something with the Oliver case," he finally said.

I really don't remember how the conversation got started, but I found myself talking a little about myself after all of these years. I told him about how I discovered that many of the men in the prison had learning problems like me and were told they didn't have what it took. I let him know I had been on academic probation a lot, but always managed to succeed just as these men can. I also told him that Greg and I already began putting together a curriculum for troubled people. Then I got emotional and started crying.

"You know," I said, "the only thing that stirs me other than the Lord is the American flag and what it stands for. From what I see going on in this country today, it makes me sick. Even our president is not above the scrutiny that is going on." He listened attentively as usual and I was not embarrassed about crying over my feelings about our country. Then I finally said, "I was hoping to hear something more positive."

Then he reemphasized to me, "I said, Mr. Shriver told me two weeks ago that he had to do something with the Oliver case. He knows when to approach the governor on the issues. I promise you I will get with Mr. Shriver to see what his plans are."

"Does he handle all of the governor's legal matters?"

"Yes."

"Then he is a busy man. What about session?"

"They don't meet until January."

"Then we don't have to worry about that taking up time."

"No, but the governor is a busy man."

"I know that, but he doesn't have to concern himself with what the legislators are doing right now."

"Based upon my knowledge of the case, this is my recommendation. I recommend that they commute the sentence to life and bring him up for parole and probation. He would still be accountable for the 50 years."

"If that is the case, then what laws govern when he would be eligible?"

"The laws that were in effect when he was arrested."

"That was June 1985."

"Then he would be eligible in 12 years."

"He's already served 13, so he is ready. How often do they have parole hearings?"

"Everyday," he said.

"I mean at Jefferson City once a month?"

"Yes."

"Now if it goes that route, can he go to Michigan?"

"That depends on whether Michigan will take the case."

"Who does the leg work to find that out, you or me?"

"We do."

"Can I go to the parole hearing if they have one?"

"He is entitled to a representative."

"Does that person have to be a lawyer?"

"No."

"Good, but we still want clemency and that is what we are praying for. Can he go to Michigan with clemency?"

"He can go anywhere because it will be as though nothing ever happened and his record will be clean."

"That is what we are believing for."

"I don't know what Mr. Shriver's recommendation is he knows the case better than I do, but I promise you I will get with him."

"I'm going out of country tomorrow and I will be back in the States on the 21st. Can I call you to follow up and see what he says?"

"Yes."

"Whom should I call, you or Mr. Shriver?"

"You can call me."

"The soonest I can call will be the 22nd—will you be available?" I really didn't want to call and not be able to talk to him and play phone tag for days.

"No, not on the 22nd, or the 23rd." He said as he checked his calendar.

"Then when can I call? When you will be available?"

"I'll be available to talk to you on the 25th."

"Good, I'll call you then—morning or afternoon?"

"Anytime is fine."

I was feeling good about the meeting when I left because I had gotten another promise from Mr. Dodger, who up to that point had never let me down when he promised me something.

I surprised myself with how direct I had been. Somehow I had learned through my years of sales experience to close the sale by asking for the order, which in this case was Gregory's freedom.

In Chicago, I stayed with my girlfriend Joyce and her husband. I had gotten permission for Greg to call collect to her phone. I was running late, because I stopped by to update my friend Kathy before I left Jefferson City. I kept hoping that Greg wouldn't call until 7:00 P.M. so I wouldn't miss him. I got in just in time to talk to Greg. He sounded sort of matter-of-fact on the phone, but I knew the men were teasing him about not being able to be on the flight with me. He had told the men he was going to Prague with me. He had to deal once again with harassment because of his bold confessions of faith.

❖

Prague was wonderful and the wedding was beautiful, though not without tension. Tradition in the Czech Republic dictated that the persons with the places of honor are the parents. The mother of the groom walks the groom down the aisle. Then comes the father of the bride. The father of the groom escorts the mother of the bride and is third in line walking down the aisle. The mothers carry bouquets that are tied upside down.

During the ceremony, which was in Czech and English, the parents of the couple are the only ones who sit in the front row—not stepparents. When the time came for us to take our seats, Olina's parents grabbed me and had me sit with them so I would not be sitting with Bill. He sat alone and his wife had to sit behind him. At the dinner though, we had to sit together, leaving me very uncomfortable, while his wife had to sit elsewhere.

❖

The flight from Prague to Warsaw was on a small commercial turbo prop aircraft, which was parked away from the terminal. We all had to be bussed out to the plane for boarding. I was the last one in line. As I was waiting, I got a glimpse of the sunray shining down through a mostly overcast sky. When it hit me, not only did I feel its warmth, but also I felt the Lord was saying to me, "No more delays!" The impression I got was that there would be no more delays in my life, but I thought I would wait to see whether I was indeed hearing from the Lord.

In Warsaw, the flight was held up because of connecting flights. As the loaded plane sat waiting, the air in the passenger compartment was getting stuffy, and I was feeling really tired. I just closed my eyes to rest them and was caught up right away in the Spirit. I was aware of what was going on around me, but was mesmerized by the Spirit world. This is what the Lord said as I saw in the Spirit angels all around me, comforting me. "This crossing of the Atlantic physically," I heard, "is going to be your crossing of the Jordan. When you land in Chicago, you will be in your promised land. Your anointing will be greater and you will be able to minister better to my people. Your own family will begin to view you differently and accept who you are."

I was weeping from down deep inside me and I could feel the tears running down my cheeks. It was incredible. As soon as I was released back into the world of the flesh, I grabbed my journal and began writing with an almost uncontrollable speed. I didn't want to lose those minutes I had just had in the Lord's presence.

As we began our decent to land in Chicago, I was reminded of the promise I had received just nine hours earlier as the plane was taking off from the airport in Warsaw, Poland. I sought the Lord and confirmed what I believed He told me while I was in Eastern Europe. This was my crossing of the Jordan. Ahead of me were my Jericho, Ai, Bethel, and more.

My friend Joyce met me at the airport. I shared my incredible flight with her. I read her my journal entry, and she agreed with me that it was of the Lord. Now all I had to do was to continue to seek the Lord for Him to take me through the next steps one step at a time. I was not looking forward to the weeks ahead, because I was not going to have a job until October 12th and the days were going to be long.

On Friday September 25, I decided to go to Grand Rapids, have lunch with my sister, and then go on a short trip. It was my day to contact Mr. Dodger. My first phone call found him in a meeting. Because I was on the road, I gave my sister's work number if he were to return my call. I tried four times that day, finally making contact at the end of the day. Mr. Dodger told me he had talked with Mr. Shriver and that they were going to get together either the first or second week of October to determine how they were going to handle the case.

"Not to be a pest, when can I follow up on the case?"

"Try the end of October."

"Who should I call, you or Mr. Shriver?"

"Call me."

"That makes sense I started the process with you and I will finish it with you."

Now the waiting game was to last at least four more weeks before I would be able to follow up.

❖

On October 28, I contacted Mr. Dodger to see how his meeting with Mr. Shriver went. The Scripture that summarizes that phone call is, *"Hope deferred maketh the heart sick; but when the desire cometh, it is a tree of life."* (Proverbs 13:12) Mr. Shriver had to postpone their meeting for something else, but Mr. Dodger said that he was good about getting back with him. I was to call back in two weeks. More postponement and delays lay ahead. Dealing with the bureaucracy is a draining process. Oppression is almost continual and delays are inevitable. I don't know why I had my hopes up that I might hear something encouraging when I called. After years of bad judgements, delays and disappointment, I guess I should have known better.

❖

Thanksgiving was near and there was no encouraging word about Greg's case. I decided to go down and visit Greg. I dropped my mother off at my niece's house and hit the road. Greg was thrilled to see me and was even more thrilled when he found out that I was going to visit for three days. It wasn't until our second visit that Greg told me a story that he had been keeping quiet for two months. He said, "I couldn't write the story to do it justice, so I waited until I could tell you in person."

"The NAACP here at the prison requested that the Parole and Probation Office send an officer in to talk to some of the men who would one day be eligible for parole and probation. They videotaped the meeting. One of the guys was complaining about what they had to say, so I asked if I could see it. The representative was telling them everything that you have been telling me," Greg said.

"What sort of things did she say?" I asked.

"The woman they sent in was new to the office. She told the men that the committee goes over the record very thoroughly. The men were not happy about that and one of the men was complaining to me about it. I was excited because that's what we need for them to do is to go over the record," Greg continued. "One of the men even asked if he could go to another state once eligible for parole. She answered by using an illustration: 'There is a case of two brothers. One is innocent and the other had something mentally wrong with him. Let's say the innocent man wants to go to another state like Michigan. In a case like that, we have to check with the other state to see if they will take the case; if they will, then we will transfer him there.'"

"She actually said that?" I questioned, thrilled.

"Yes."

"And she used the example of the two brothers and actually mentioned Michigan?"

"Yes!" I almost shouted forgetting where I was. "That's no coincidence. That's God. They are actually working on your case. A new person only has those cases to fall back on as examples that they have knowledge of. You have been sitting on this for two months? Shame on you!"

I continued, "You know, at the end of my last telephone conversation with Mr. Dodger he said, 'Take it easy.' At the time, I thought it was unusual and not quite as professional as he usually is. I felt that comment could have been interpreted in a couple of ways. The way I interpreted it was that he was telling me that he and Mr. Shriver hadn't met yet and to avert my getting angry, I needed to take it easy and not panic. He probably remembered the day I barged in on him. Now this Parole and Probation officer is talking about your case on videotape? That confirms that they are already laying down the groundwork for paroling you if the governor doesn't pardon you! Yes!"

Mr. Dodger had told me that if they have a hearing I could be present at it. But there is a possibility that they might not have to have a hearing because there are transcripts of how Greg responded to the same kind of questions that the board would ask from when Jessica and Mr. Shriver met with Greg earlier in the year. In those transcripts, both Mr. Shriver and Jessica told Greg what a good advocate I was; therefore, the one person besides Greg that would be allowed in the hearing was also identified. There were high recommendations from the two lawyers and possibly from Mr. Dodger. All of this was encouraging. But still we wanted Greg's name to be cleared, and only the governor can do that.

❖

I was tired of the hold-up on Gregory's case, so I began sending countdown flyers through the mail to the governor's office. At first I sent daily a bar graph with the actual days and business days left until the different holidays, such as Hanukkah, Christmas, New Year's, and the beginning of the 1999 Congressional Session. I didn't know how they would receive it, but I felt they needed someone to encourage them along.

After a couple weeks of sending the flyers, I decided to call and talk to Mr. Shriver's secretary. When she answered, I said, "This is Bonnie Stuck, the Michigan pest" The way she responded to me was as though I was a long-lost friend. She said that she had been getting the flyers and thought they were cute. She assured me that Mr. Shriver was getting them and that they did not turn him off. Being limited in what she can say, she was cautious, but I was able to get some information out of her after she told me that they wish everyone was as patient and nice to work with as me. She said, "We need more people like you."

I received confirmation that there were no executions scheduled in the near future. Then I reaffirmed that the study on the case was complete and that Jessica had done a good job. I let the secretary know that the Lord guided every move I made on this case and that we had decided to do it His way. So I did a little witnessing too. She told me, "I can tell you this, that the case is in his office, which is a good sign."

I told her that I was really hoping that something would happen before the holidays. She was very sympathetic towards that, but of course didn't have any answer.

I also reminded her of something that Mr. Shriver had said, that if there weren't credence to this case, they would have kicked it back a long time ago. She responded with strong agreement and reassured me that was indeed the case. She made sure she had my phone number and contact times to reach me. So I asked her if she would let Mr. Shriver know I called and that the flyers will continue to come also. She laughed and assured me that he would get them.

I felt as if I had a strong advocate in the governor's office. Secretaries do have a strong influence, don't they? Even with the rapport that I was establishing, we still had to endure the waiting game through another holiday season. We continued to wonder and question "when, God, when?"

CHAPTER XXXVI

God's Timing—God's Signature

Weeks passed and still there was no news about Greg's case. My temporary assignment at Michigan State University was nearing an end. I decided that I would take a short trip to Missouri between assignments—that is, if my assignments would allow it. I had been sending my flyers on a regular basis trying to keep Greg's name in front of them daily. I had received positive feedback from Mr. Shriver's secretary, so I knew they weren't tired of me yet. I knew as long as I kept my flyers versatile, it would keep their interest up. I was running out of cleaver ideas, however, and wanted something that would drive my point home—hard.

One morning I woke up laughing with an idea. I laughed all the way into work and finally decided that this had to be the Lord's idea. I stopped and bought some toilet paper and picked up a small box to mail them in. Each roll of toilet paper represented an aspect of the case that was faulty and filthy with constitutional error. One was the judicial area, another was the prosecution, still another was for the ineffective assistance of council, and the fourth was for the stacked jury and the other things that confirmed the manipulation of the case. I covered the toilet paper with gold tissue paper and then laid a note on the top saying, "This is a little something to help you clean up the mess that the state of Missouri v. Oliver left in the judicial system." Then I wrote Mr. Shriver's secretary, a note asking her to discard the package if I was stretching it too far. I didn't get any feedback one way or another, so I had no idea whether it was received in the humor that it was intended.

In planning my trip, I wanted to make sure I could set up an appointment with Jeramy Shriver. I called to see if I could meet with him while I was in town. I waited a week and received no answer, so I called back. Janet put me on hold when I told her why I was calling. To my surprise, Jeramy Shriver picked up the phone, "Hello!"

"Oh!" I said surprised, "I wasn't expecting you to answer."

"I really don't think you need to come down here right now. I have the case here and I am working on it." I knew that was the proverbial put-off.

I re-emphasized the length of time it had been and some of the things that Jessica had told me back in April 1998, but he was consistent. We talked about the up-coming executions and he mentioned Darrell Mease and a couple others, which would demand the governor's time and energy. So I knew we had more of a waiting game ahead of us, and my tone reflected my disappointment.

Then he said, "I can assure you I am sitting here right now and Greg's case is in my box. I am sitting here looking at it."

"Well," I said, "Are you looking at it favorably?"

"You know I can't answer that!"

"Well, you can't blame a girl for trying—can you?"

"I assure you that Greg's case is getting looked at."

Two days later I received a phone call from my friend Fran. "Did you hear the news?"

"What news?"

"The governor of Missouri commuted a man's sentence on death row at the Pope's request."

"You're kidding!"

"No, I'll bring the article down; we have a couple of copies."

So when Fran came around delivering the daily news for the University, she brought the article. I made a copy of it and couldn't believe what I was reading—Jeramy Shriver's name was even mentioned as being present when the Pope met with the governor and pleaded for Darrell's life to be spared. But I still didn't know where the governor was coming from now with his gesture in honoring the Pope's request. What would that mean for Gregory?

❖

One week later I received a letter from Gregory. He reminded me of the picture I had of Greg, Ron, Darrell, and one other man. Two of the men were dead, and only Greg and Darrel were left. Greg and Darrell had become pretty good friends while they were at Potosi. Greg wrote,

"The other day before I was even aware of an execution, an inmate who scoffed me quite often because of my stand made the statement, saying 'You ain't going nowhere and they are

*going to execute Darrell.' I immediately turned around in sur-
prise because he mentioned Darrell's name and I said, 'I rebuke
that.' I know without a doubt the enemy was trying to sneak
away Darrell's life, but God took the opportunity of the Pope's
visit to save the life of a friend. Darrell has told me he also is
innocent of this case of his. Even though I believe him it all rests
in God's hands."*

Greg also included a letter that Darrell had written him back in
1997. I was told that Darrell has said all along that the Lord was going
to intervene on his behalf. As I read the letter, I realized that Darrell
was indeed a man of faith. His guilt or innocence I cannot determine.
I just know that the Lord was working in him and around him in a
mighty way. To what end, I do not know. I have included his letter just
as he wrote it.

No Longer CP [Capital Punishment]-*83*

1-12-97

My Brother!

*A most excellent letter, you 'out did' yourself this time—
smile–Thanks–I send it on to Mom.*
*I had been praying for you & a couple of other prisoners recently
that God will free you from prison & that you & Bonnie—&
the others, will have abundant life & full joy. I have amended
that slightly by the addition of NOW! in your case. (Job 42:10)
As to wht yo said concerning to beware of satan trying to cause
doubt, I'll quote you from a letter I got from me Mom first, wh
was rote the 1-5-97: ... These are Norman's words about these
verses! Abram obeyed God, laid out his sacrifices, & was waiting for God to move & here came those old buzzards of doubt
to eat it up & Abram drove them away. Didn't allow them to
steal his faith. Don't noe how many times he had to chase them
off, but he didn't give up. Then God spoke to him in his deep
sleep!—Then he applied it to our standing in faith on something that we noe only God can do for us & keep those buzzards
of doubt chased away & God will do what He says He will do.
Yours was a second confirmation & soon afterwards, I got....
The fact (That's a multiple, double confirmation!) that god has
freed me (& you & all others who will receive it) from prison is
confirmed numerous of times in His Logos or ritten Word. God*

has also confirmed my salvation, deliverance, and freedom <u>from</u> prison at least 4 times in His Rhema or spoken Word. So Gregory, like we used to say, 'It's a done deal!' The only thing left is for our freedom from prison to manifest in the natural–to God's glory (Jn 11:40, 14,13) & our <u>full</u> joy (Jn 15:7,11). Ain't it 'hi time' we went!!! Yes! Quickly Lord, quickly! David (Acts 13:22) said that a lot; "Save me Lord god! <u>Hurry</u> & help! (Psa. 70:1-5)

...So Gregory, when I suddenly got a NKJV the next day, I immediately, or soon after (my first impolse was to cluth it fer myself–smile)... ☺

New that it was for him, not me & that he needed it more than I did & also that I will be out there w/my leatherback KJV w/Copeland's notes in it rite SOON!...

I'm in 2B-21 now, working my way towards the front door. Or else I'm home time you gets this! Tell Amrone I said, 'Hi! & stay strong in our Lord!'

As he went thru cold bath fields he saw a solitary cell and the devil was pleased, for it gave him a hint for improving his prisons in Hell

Samuel Taylor Coleridge

It's very interesting that you mention Corrie 10 Boom. I had just rote about her in a letter to the Christian penpal. I have Corrie's book at home, but I've yet to read it.

In 1946, the year I was bor, & soon after God had delivered Corrie 10 Boon from the Nasties in Germany, she flew over Branson in a small plane & saw a vision of Angels hovering over Branson & God told Corrie 10, 'I will bring mutitudes here! So Gregory, millions & millions of people come thru Branson every year & more & more Christian shows, Christian singing & Christian ministries are setting up shop at Branson. It's set up for a Gospel Explosion, Big Time! I do not noe why God chose...

David ran towards Goliath of Gath! ... As you & me & the poet noes, it was Goliath of Gath who didn't have a chance, but it wasn't about weapons, it were about who each of them served. David cd have tooken him bare handed (or even w/out laying a hand on him) after all David was used to grabbing lions & big ol grizzly bears by the thoat & killing them & so Gregory, you and I both noe that ain't natural! — That's supernatural! It was good what you said about the gates around Potosi too.

Also I believe you are rite when you say you were delivered from Potosi. Evilness is in control more & more here, for those who don't have our God for a shield.

You noe me better than that Gregory!!!! I don't even let up I ain't giving up no grounds. 'Quit ain't in my vocabulary, that is I ain't a quitter, never have been, never will be & I have no use for em. I am more than a conqueror (& that's a lot!!) through Jesus Christ, my Lord & Savior. I am victorious in everything God & I plan to do according to His Word. God is my Partner in every area of my life & so Gregory, I think BIG! Those who noe the Lord will do great exploits! (for God). It would be crazy to give up when God has already assured me of total victory! Your letter was a blessing, thanks. Tell Bonnie I said, "Hi & keep up the good work, there's a great payday on it's way!"

He Rode On! Darrell

❖

Try as I might to discover the many answers to the question "Why" I can't, but the Lord began showing me as I began to think about the circumstance around Darrell's commutation of sentence and all of the executions that have taken place. The question that so many people ask, "Why do bad things happen to good people? Why must a child suffer brutal treatment at the hands of a murderer? Why must a person die because of another's careless drinking and driving problem? Why must so many young people be sexually victimized by so called caring adults? The list can go on and on even with less dramatic questions. The answer that I have gotten is summed up in two phrases, *Relationship with the Lord* and *Salvation of the soul*. "What does 'relationship' have to do with it?" one might ask.

The Lord's chief concern for humanity is that they all come to the saving knowledge of Him so that their souls can stay in beautiful fellowship with him. There is nothing that we can do outside of blaspheming the Holy Spirit that the Lord cannot forgive. So why does the child have to suffer? It is about the souls of the lost, even those lost souls who don't know that they are lost because they are basically good people. They are, what I was a "saintly sinner" and don't know they are, because self-righteousness is part of their fleshly and worldly make-up. Like my situation where I was so full of myself that I couldn't see the forest through the trees. The revelation that the Lord showed me about this is difficult, very difficult, but if viewed from the Lord's view, I think it is *an* answer I can live with.

When anyone, especially a young person, has to suffer at the hands of a malicious attacker, the shock waves rock the lives of not only the victim's friends and family, but also the friends and family of the attacker. We cry out, "Why, God, Why?" and we spend years and life-times trying to answer that question. But there comes a time when we have to sit back and listen for the answer.

What purpose does that unnecessary death or catastrophe serve in God's scheme of things? A child dies unnecessarily and the family wants vengeance; they want an "atonement" that humanity cannot give. Their pain, anguish and feelings are understandable and we have sympathy of them. The victim's family continues to grieve and seek answers even after a conviction is rendered, but there are none. The criminal is executed and still there is no peace. There might have been a moment of tempo-rary satisfaction, but their loved one is not brought back—they are only temporarily vindicated, but they still can't understand, "Why" they had to suffer so.

In the meantime, the perpetrator of the crime who realizes his/her guilt, repents and develops the relationship with the Lord that He has always wanted. The death of that child resulted in someone who might have been lost to come to the saving knowledge of the Lord. Therefore, in that child's short life they are responsible for the salvation of another's soul and possibly that attacker's family's soul as well as s/he shares his/her new life in the Lord with them. In the meantime, if the family and friends of that child develops a relationship with the Lord much like the criminal and his family did and they learn to forgive the criminal or inmate on death row, then they too have obtained that sal-vation, sanctification and relationship that the Lord wants for **_all_** of humanity.

That innocent child in its brief life was responsible for the salvation of several souls. This child will hold a higher place in eternity for its role on earth than people who go to church week after week and year after year and never once share their faith and love for the Lord Jesus Christ. It's a martyr's life indeed.

This is a hard lesson and it brought tears to my eyes when the Lord began to reveal to me the pain that both families go through for what appears to be unnecessary deaths and catastrophes. This is *not* the answer to *all* suffering I know, but it did help me to understand this aspect of it better. Ultimately, however, vengeance and vindication is totally the Lord's because He is just—man falls short.

My prayer is, "Let my life, O Lord, be one that you can look on and say, *'Well done, thou good and faithful servant.'* Let my life be one that encourages people to want to seek your love and to find their place in the kingdom of God by fulfilling your plan and purpose in my life. Let me walk in forgiveness, let me live in your peace, let me love your people from the oldest to the youngest, from the richest to the poorest and from the best to the worst, because they are yours and you, O Lord, have a purpose for them as you have for me. Allow each person that reads this book to have a heart experience with you as I have and allow them to begin to seek your 'perfect will' for their lives and give them the courage to *'Walk a Mile in Your Shoes!'* In Jesus name let it be so." Amen. *For, without a test there is no testimony!*

❖

I couldn't let the commutation of the sentence detour me, however, I had to follow through with my next plan. I began putting together a large presentation board that I was going to hand-carry to the governor's office when I went to Missouri. I had no intention of bothering Mr. Shriver; I just wanted to give it to Janet, his secretary, and let her pass it on. I knew that they were enjoying the flyers, but I didn't know about anything else. This presentation, size-wise, would overshadow anything else I had sent.

I picked up a tri-fold presentation board and began putting my idea in action. On the center of the board I staged the courtroom with all the identified players in place, including witnesses, evidence, and the eyewitnesses that were not brought forward. Below that I had a brief summary of Ron's mental condition and my theory that he was both sane and insane when he shot the victims. On the right wing of the board I had different classifications of topics and questions to ponder listed. I even had some quotes from politicians from both parties in reference to legal issues, some relating to the president's misconduct. The left wing had a picture of the crime scene and a description below it. Then on the bottom left I had a flow chart depicting how the case went through the system and every person that saw the case legally— *but not really.*

My job situation worked out so I could have the week off and would begin a new assignment the following week. I left early on Monday morning, February 15, for Missouri. Once I arrived, I called my friend Fae and spent the night there. She was impressed with my board and from it got a clearer understanding of the case. She could see the relationships between the witness, juror and deceased. She could see plainly the relationships in the judges and the changing of the victim's ages, which is what I wanted to be seen.

The next day I got up and went to the mall to walk and pray. The Lord gave me a message to contact my friend Kathy and have her pray for the meeting; because Greg had no idea what I was doing, I wanted more prayer covering, so I took pizza over to Channel 25 for lunch to share with all the people there; we all had a chance to pray. On the way to the governor's office I was praying and asking the Lord to not let me go there alone. I also asked Him to have a parking space for me right in front, because my feet were sore and I didn't want to walk too far. I can't say that I was nervous at all; when I pulled up in front of the Capital Building to find one lone free parking space open, I knew that all of this was ordained of God.

Inside the capital I climbed the many steps to the governor's office. I was so out of breath that I had to sit a while until I could walk in calmly. There was no one but the receptionist at the desk. I tried to speak confidently as I said, "I have a delivery for Janet, Jeramy Shriver's secretary."

"Who should I say is here?"

"Well," I started to stumble, "Let's make it a surprise."

"Oh, then it's a present?"

"No, it's a presentation." I was getting myself in a corner. "Well, you better tell her it's Bonnie Stuck—no, tell her it is the 'Wacky Michigan Resident.'"

She laughed at that as she picked up the phone and said, "The 'Wacky Michigan Resident' has a delivery for you." She was laughing as she hung up the phone as she said, "I don't usually announce people as 'wacky.'"

"Did she laugh?" I asked.

"Yes, she did!"

"Good."

The large door opened that led down to Jeramy Shriver's office and Janet peeked her head around saying, "You have got to be Bonnie Stuck!"

"Yes, I am," I said as she came over towards me. She reached out to shake hands. Not being one for small talk, I immediately jumped into my reason for being there, "I haven't sent you any flyers for the past couple of weeks, and here is the reason why!" I lifted the board up and opened it in one gesture. She just looked at it and laughed approvingly. "I put this together hoping that Mr. Shriver would use it to present the case to the governor. I have tried to be respectful, yet lighthearted while driving my point home about this case." She indicated to me that I had been. I let her know that I was going to be in town for the rest of the week and that if anything happened I could be reached at the prison during visiting hours.

Her response surprised me. "Bonnie, while you are in town, please come back by."

Shocked I said, "Really?"

She assured me "really" and said, "Please call or stop by while you are here."

I was floating by now and so thankful for her wonderful grace and reception. I don't think my feet touched the ground all the way out to the car. I hurried over to my friend Kathy's beauty shop and let her in on the news. Kathy felt confident there was something, on the board that was going to jump out at someone. I was uncertain what I was going to do about going back to the governor's office, but I knew that the Lord would guide me

That evening I had dinner with Fae and Beth and we talked about my wonderful day. We decided that the game plan should be to call the next day, Wednesday, after visiting Greg and checking to see if Friday morning was a good time to stop in. That way if I got in to see anybody I would have a chance to not only tell Greg, but also to let him see the new hairdo Kathy was planning to give me.

I was anxious to see Greg the next day. Beth was visiting her husband too, so we got to go in together and sat by each other. As usual, Greg took longer than anyone else did to get up to the visiting room. I made good use of the time because Beth wanted me to update her husband, Ray, on Greg's case. I was just finishing the update when Greg came through the door of the changing room. We had a good visit. Needless to say he was thrilled. I informed him that I was going to call after the visit and would update him some more the next day.

I rushed right over to the library to update everyone via e-mail and to call the governor's office. When Janet answered, I asked how Friday was looking for me to stop by. She told me of the morning staff meeting and asked me to be there at 10:30 A.M. "I can't promise you anything, but we will see what happens."

"I'll be there," I said.

Thursday I went to get my hair done and styled for the first time in twelve years. Up until that time, I was like a Nazirite and came under heavy conviction at the thought of doing more than trimming and perming my hair. Kathy hadn't really done any cutting other than taking the length off the back and already I knew I was going to like it. She did a beautiful job. I had a new, more youthful, sassy, yet professional look.

That evening Kathy and I had so much fun. We decided not to talk about anything that would drag us down and just enjoy the evening. We laughed and giggled the whole evening. I had Kathy laughing so hard at this fine restaurant that looked like it was filled with lobbyists and politicians, that when she went to wipe the tears away from her eyes she smeared mashed potatoes all over her eye. Needless to say, that broke us up more, and Kathy finally had to excuse herself.

Friday arrived. I was promptly at the governor's office ten minutes early. When I walked in, another woman was also there. The woman at the reception desk said, "I don't believe it, I seldom sit at this desk and both times that I have this week I get to announce you. What was that word we used again?"

"The wacky one!"

"Oh yes," she said as she picked up the phone to announce me again and went on to say the other woman's name and mentioned that she had a 10:30 appointment with Jeramy Shriver. My heart sunk. But I waited patiently. Janet came out and told the other woman that her meeting had been cancelled. Then she looked at me and said that Mr. Shriver was still in the staff meeting and that they would be finishing up pretty soon; then he would be right with me.

As I settled in for the meeting, I kept telling myself, "What am I doing here? I don't have any new information or anything else to say. I have said it all."

But that still small voice said, "I will take you before governors and kings and I will put the words in your mouth."

"Thank you Lord." I whispered to myself. Then I started a conversation with the receptionist. "You know, as I was walking up to the Capital Building I was sensing the awesomeness of being here and was wondering if the regular employees are ever complacent about where they work?"

"I don't," she said. She told me that she was the office manager. About that time the receptionist came back from break. At that, the office manager, who was only filling in while the receptionist was on break said to me, "Follow me." She escorted me into the governor's office (he wasn't there). She was showing me the remodeling job that had been done on it. She told me that the conference table that was in there was one of the only pieces of furniture that was left after the capitol burned, which was a bit of history I didn't know about. Then we went back to the lobby.

Jeramy Shriver finally entered the lobby after a long staff meeting, smiling from ear to ear. This was not the sober, straight-laced man I remembered from three years earlier. He invited me into the conference room. As we were sitting down the first question out of my mouth was, "What was it like meeting the Pope?"

"I didn't meet him. I've seen him twice."

"Oh, the *New York Times* said that you were with the governor when they talked."

"No, I can tell you that seeing him you knew that there was something very special about him."

"While we are mentioning it, politically, what impact will it make on other cases—what the governor did as far as honoring the Pope's request that is?"

"What the governor did was just an act of respect for the Pope's request. There was nothing political about it," he said.

"When Johnny Lee Wilson was pardoned, what were the political implications?"

"When a decision like that is made, we have to make sure that the law is on our side. There was an audiocassette of the police interrogation that was very convincing as to the reasons he pleaded guilty to a murder he didn't commit. The only repercussions that we received were from the county where Johnny lived. Once they saw him on a press conference and realized how simple-minded he was, they stopped, and we haven't heard anything else."

"So as long as the law is on your side, you can make those decisions," I paused. "You know, when I first started working on this case I knew nothing about the law. I was studying exegesis and hermeneutics and I knew Biblical law. Every time I ran into something that violated that law I looked deeper. Consequently, I saw things that a lawyer wouldn't see, because they are only looking for points of law and I wasn't—I was looking for truth."

"That is why they don't want lawyers on juries," Jeramy said. "It's like the story of the child that went away for the summer and wrote her uncle about all of the wonderful things she was experiencing. She described in detail everything. The uncle was so excited with the letter that he showed it to others, and all they saw were the spelling errors and the grammatical mistakes."

I knew when he told me that, that he was also telling me that I have showed them what the record says, which couldn't be gotten from the points of law and from a lawyer's perspective. I was so excited. The meeting was an absolute blessing. I then reminded him that it had been a year since he had met with Gregory and his response surprised me. "He is very impressive," he said.

"Then you understand why I have hung in there so many years?"

"Yes, I do."

Then I informed him of my reasons behind keeping quiet about this case and not putting it on TV, which he knew I could have very easily done, seeing I had been working for Channel 25 TV station in Missouri. "We have kept quiet because we believe in the integrity of the system. We know that all the people in the system don't have integrity, but we believe the system does and we will continue to believe that." I could tell from his reaction that he received what I said very well.

I asked him if he was going to use my presentation board when he presented it to the governor, and his response was, "Yes!" This was not the same man that was so somber three years earlier. He was gracious, good-natured, personable—everything you could ask for. He wrapped the meeting up by telling me that he had an agenda for the case. He wasn't going to tell me what his timetable was, however, because his schedule was so hectic that he had to change meetings all the time. I really couldn't have asked for more. The finale was worth the wait. He told me that he had already started talking to the governor about the case."

My response was, "You mean the governor knows Gregory's name?"

"Yes, he does."

"Does he know my name too?"

"Yes, he does, and he has seen the toilet paper!"

❖

One cannot imagine the cloud I was on when I left the governor's office. In my mind, there was no doubt that Gregory's case had favor and that he would be released soon. I could hardly wait to tell Greg the news. I arrived at the prison just as they were counting the inmates, so I had to wait over an hour for Greg to come up. In the meantime, I was telling one of the correctional officers about the meeting and that Greg would be getting out shortly.

When Greg came out of the change room, he had the biggest grin on his face. As soon as he was close enough, he said, "It's good news, isn't it?" The CO had gone back to the change room and broke the news to Greg by saying, "I understand you are getting out real soon." At that Greg did a little dance. Then the CO went on to say, "In the seven years that I have watched you, you have never given us a bit of trouble." He was sincerely glad at the thought of Greg one day being released. I went over the meeting in detail with Greg, and we prayed for Mr. Shriver and the governor. Greg loved my new hairdo too.

This trip was one of the most memorable ones I have ever taken down to Missouri. I can't remember a trip where every day was filled with something special that the Lord had done. We still had to wait upon the Lord to complete the miracle, but somehow we didn't have the let-down we usually had with waiting. Every time we both thought about the trip, we were in awe of how the Lord had put the players together.

❖

I came back and settled into another temporary job at Michigan State University. This assignment was a short one; then I moved on to another assignment that would last a couple of months. New people and new positions—and with each assignment I was broadening my knowledge of computer software. No two divisions on campus used the same exact software so I was the benefactor. I liked the people I worked with, and they all treated me well.

❖

It was nearing the end of another assignment, and our 5th anniversary and my birthday were near. Thus, I decided to take another trip to Missouri to visit Greg and see if I could set up another appointment with Jeramy Shriver. I wasn't excited about this visit, but I knew I had to go. It was the same feeling I had when I made the three-day trip with $40 in my pocket and a full tank of gas.

The drive to Missouri wore on me. It was anywhere from 11-12 hours one-way, depending on traffic, and I always drove it in one shot—usually leaving in the wee hours of the morning so I could get around Chicago before the morning rush hour. Leaving at that time also put me through St. Louis during mid-afternoon before evening rush hour there.

As the time for me to make this trip came closer, I really didn't have anything original to present to Jeramy—actually, I didn't want to go. I couldn't afford the trip, and it didn't look like I was going to have an assignment when I got back to Michigan.

In spite of my negative feelings, I made up a list of questions. That is all I could come up with. I decided that this time I was going to be more confrontational than in the past. I shared with my mother what I was doing.

The trip down went without incident, at 10:15 A.M. the next day I arrived at the capital building in Jefferson City. There was a lot of commotion. I mounted the steps to the second floor and could see from a distance a crowd of people mingling and mulling around the governor's office. They looked like legislators to me and I knew something important was going on. I hung back until I got the courage to walk by the crowd. Once inside the reception area the atmosphere was different. There were only a couple of people there. I announced myself and took a seat asking the receptionist if there was a press conference scheduled. When she replied in the affirmative, I knew then that my appointment was going to be cancelled. I waited anyway, and within seconds the reception area was flooded with members of the media. I was wishing that I was invisible at that time.

Just then the door to Jeramy's office area opened, and he moved with purpose in his step. He paused to talk to someone and as he turned he saw me sitting there. I knew he recognized me, but he didn't say anything. Shortly after that Janet came out and told me that the meeting was cancelled and asked if I could come back at 11:30 A.M. I kept myself entertained during the press conference and the wait by roaming through the Capital Building's Museum. The press conference was about the abortion issue; again, thoughts of the insignificance of my being there flooded my mind. *Who did I think I was daring to think I could meet with the governor when he had so many other important issues on his desk?*

Eleven-thirty came and Jeramy was right on time. He led me through the corridor leading to his office area. I figured he was going to take me back to the first conference room that we had met in. But to my surprise he let me to his office. His desk had two piles of work stacked up about two feet high on either side. Instead of him sitting at the desk and viewing me through the window of paperwork, which confirmed his horrendous workload, he sat in one of the two side chairs and I sat in the other. There was no barrier between us, just a casual seating arrangement.

I began by expressing my thoughts, "Do the people who work in this building even comprehend the authority that they have—the authority over even life and death?"

"We like to call it responsibility."

"Do they realize their responsibility then?"

"Some do—others don't"

I asked him several questions in a leading fashion trying to find out how far the case was, whether he and the governor were talking about it, and how close they were to a decision. Jeramy knew what I was doing and he was a master of giving answers that didn't reveal what I wanted to know, which was discouraging. Frankly, I think he was tickled by my approach. Bonnie, the novice was asking leading questions to one of Kansas City's ex-Prosecutors.

One of the directions that I went in was using the timing element with all of the executions that Missouri conducted so far that year— nine, to be exact. This was more than in any other year. I argued that they were able to make a life-and-death decision in an average of three months, and yet they couldn't give a man his life back in five and a half years of study.

The conversation took an interesting turn after I told Jeramy the story of when I was a child and I was told by one of my teachers that people do their best work in their fifties. Then I let him know, "I'm doing my best work, Jeramy. It's not going to get any better."

He acknowledged that he was aware that my life's blood was in this case. At that point, I let him know that the book was written and that I used their real names.

"Oh, don't do that!" he said abruptly.

"Jeramy Shriver," I said in a motherly fashion, "do you think if I were saying anything derogatory about you, Michael Dodger or the governor that I would use your real name?"

"Oh, my daughter will love that."

I was fascinated when he began to tell me the story of his role model, which let me know that he was comfortable with me. He said when he was a child, he met Robert Kennedy and that he was so impressed with this charismatic man that he became his role model. His reasons were simple. "Robert Kennedy, we agree on, was smarter than John." To that I agreed. Then he went on to tell me why: "Robert Kennedy had a real heart for the little guy and defending their constitutional rights."

I had all I could do to stay seated. I was ready to do a "joyful jig," but I managed to contain myself. Just think, an advocate for the poor was his role model, but who was the "we" in his conversation? Did he mean that both he and the governor respected Robert Kennedy that much?

I found out, too, that Jeramy was not going into politics and that it was certain that the governor was going to run against the Republican candidate for the Missouri Senate Seat. He told how old he was and that a decision would be made by January 1, 2001 and no later than January 6, 2001 when his desk had to be cleared off. Needless to say I was disappointed.

It was time for my last question, which was the most confrontational one of all. "Jeramy," I began, "you know after all this time I have family and friends that are beginning to think that this is a no—win situation and that you are doing nothing by yanking my chain." I paused for effect. "Are you yanking my chain?"

Jeramy looked me right in the eye and said, "Bonnie, if I were yanking your chain, do you think I would give you," he looked at his watch, "45 minutes of my time?"

"That is what I thought, thank you."

He walked me to the door to say, "Good-Bye." I turned and pointed my finger at him as a mother does to their children when they are giving instructions. "Jeramy Shriver," I said, "you, young man, have yet to do your best work." He just smiled and I left.

The full impact of the meeting didn't hit me until I was telling Gregory about the meeting. As good as Jeramy was at giving me non-answers, he was just as good at giving me signals that indicated that Gregory's case had some favor. As far as we were concerned we had an out-date of no later than January 6, 2001.

Even though I did not want to go, the trip was again a success. And the best part was that I got past the outer office, the stuffy back conference room, and the executive conference room, and found myself in the private office. That is favor in climbing the ladder of executive advocacy.

I wasn't sure when I could make another trip because my car began acting up on this trip so bad that I had Gregory praying for it so I could get home safely.

❖

Back in Michigan I didn't have a job to go to. So Monday, October 4, 1999 I headed out with flyers to post around campus, trying to get some freelance work. As I neared one of the shopping hubs, that still small voice spoke to me like it use to when I was a young Christian: "Go to Family Christian Stores and get a part time job."

I looked at my watch and said, "But, Lord, they aren't open. It is only 9:00 A.M."

"Go over to Family Christian Store and get a part-time job," that still small voice said again.

"Ok, Lord," I said as I drove over to the shopping center.

I didn't have any trouble finding a parking spot right in front because every store was closed. I went up to the door anyway and sure enough it opened. Mike the manager was right there in front. I asked, "Are you doing any hiring for Christmas help?"

"Sure, go ahead and fill out an application."

I filled it out and went about my business. I decided to call into Office Services at Michigan State University just in case they had a new temporary assignment for me. They did. I made the contact I needed to and agreed to start the next day. Not having to worry about a job any more, I went home. When I got there I got a phone call from the Family Christian Store's manager, asking me to come in for an interview. A day that started out with no job ended up with two jobs.

The next morning I reported into my new temporary job and found out about the previous temporaries. Neither temporary could handle the assignment. One never showed up the next day after training and the other told them after four hours of training that it was not a temporary job and that it was too much for her to handle. Every so often when I was training, someone would pop his or her head in and ask, "Are you going to be here tomorrow?" I made it through the first week.

The same day that I started my temporary job I also started my part-time job. Twelve-hour days were to be the norm for the next fourteen months, and still I was near poverty level income.

The next week I was going to be on my own with my day job. Midweek I was driving to early morning prayer when my car acted up and my transmission light went on. I had just put $2,000 into the car, and now the two-year-old rebuilt transmission I had put in was quitting on me. I called AAA and my initial plan was to have the car towed to the dealership. While waiting for the wrecker, I called my niece Randi. Her husband is part owner of a GM dealership in Western Michigan. Randi and I decided to have the truck tow me to her in-law's farm about 80 miles away, then Sam would come by and pick it up with a truck. Once the wrecker had the car loaded up and we were on the road, I received another phone call from Randi. Plans had changed my 30-mile, then 80-mile tow wound up being a 130-mile tow all the way to Sam and Randi's dealership. I was not going to put another penny into this car, and the place I felt I could get the best deal was with Sam and Randi.

All morning long was spent looking at cars that I couldn't afford. In the meantime, the dealership was contacting loan companies to see if they could secure a loan for me. I was so discouraged by the time we finished lunch. I still didn't have a car picked out and feedback from lending companies was looking grim, plus the interest rate was high. Finally they asked what I could afford. "Nothing really—in a pinch, I guess I could possibly swing $200 if I can keep my part-time job."

There was only one car in the lot that we could get the payments manageable, so we checked with the finance companies. One by one I was rejected. Finally we heard back from my credit union. Not only did they approve me with an automatic deposit, but the interest rate was two points less than what the dealership could get.

As I was driving my '97 Cavalier with 29,000 miles on it home, that still small voice began speaking to me again. "What was the last conversation that you had with Jodi before you left your last job?"

"Well, Lord, I was admiring her car and asking her about it."

"You're driving it."

I began thinking about Jodi's car. Sure enough, I was driving a car like hers. The only difference was that hers was a four-door and mine was a two-door model. Everything else was exact—including color. Then the Lord continued: "I got you your Toyota, which was the desire of your heart; then you made the deal on the Chrysler and had nothing but trouble with it. Now I got you this car and it will perform just as the Toyota did." Again I was driving God's car with His signature on it.

❖

My new temporary job at MSU was the most demanding job I have ever had. It was not a typical temporary job, but I lasted the full four-month period of time plus a two-month extension they requested.

One of the most devastating things that happened during this season of delay was the brutal stabbing death of Mary Thomas the alleged kidnap victim. She was the only witness with a consistent testimony, and she was the only person who could identify the stacked jury members. She also exposed some newly discovered evidence about how the gun got reloaded without Gregory knowing it. Thank God, I had her interview on videotape for anyone to see. Once viewing it anyone would know that this woman was not only consistent with her testimony, but the key to exposing the real travesties in the Oliver case.

❖

In November, the thought of the holiday depression that was ahead was weighing me down. I had started going to early morning prayer every morning before work and the drive there was my prayer drive before prayer. One morning I was seeking the Lord and He spoke and said, "This holiday season I want you to bless as many people as possible."

"Ok, Lord, but where do you want me to begin?"

"Begin with your mother."

I tried to figure out how I could start blessing my mother. The first thing I did was to pick up a couple of things from the Dollar Store and make a lighted potpourri container for her for the holidays. Then I fixed up a dish of candy for her. The next day, Sunday, I bought her favorite roasted chicken. I called her and told her I had a surprise and not to cook. I also bought some icicle lights to place around the porch for Christmas. I had the next Monday night off, so I decided I would hang the lights, then make an excuse to take her out. I knew if I turned right at the drive that possibly she wouldn't see the lights and I could drive around looking at the other lights, then drive home and she would get the full impact. We wound up going on a long drive looking at the Christmas lights, and we both enjoyed it.

The next night, Tuesday, I went into the bookstore and saw a box of the "Book of the month value book" in the back room. The book happened to be a book I had given away many times, but had never read it from cover to cover. It is the classic entitled *In His Steps*. Amy, one of the girls I work with, suggested that I send that book to the prison. That is exactly what I did. To bless as many people as I could, I sent over 500 books to J.C.C.C. that Christmas. That following year as my Y2K project I sent over 2000 new Christian books to Missouri and Michigan prisons.

❖

Delays seemed to be the name of the game in the State of Missouri v. Oliver case. With the governor running for the U.S. Senate, I knew that attention to Gregory's case would be avoided until after the election.

October 16, 2000, just three weeks prior to Election Day 2000 the news from Missouri was devastating on the eve of the third presidential debate that was being held in St. Louis. The Missouri governor was killed along with two others in an airplane crash just south of St. Louis.

At first, I was crushed. My thoughts were selfish—thinking only of the fourteen years it had taken so far to fight Gregory's case. The thought of starting all over again was devastating. I don't know if my tears were for the governor or for Gregory and me. Without the governor, I felt our plight was hopeless. Almost immediately, the Lord reminded me that He was on the throne, and my thoughts immediately began focusing on the governor's family and the tragedy they were living. I went to the St. Louis Post Dispatch on the Internet looking for conformation of what I had just heard.

Already the media was talking about swearing the lieutenant governor into the highest state office. He had decided not to run for governor and was getting out of politics completely. Prior to his political life he had been a teacher and school principle. One of his main reasons for him getting out of politics was his family life—he wanted it back. He had a tremendous amount of respect for the governor, as did all of his staff. The article stated that the new governor's course of action would be to continue in the path that the preceding governor had chosen.

Had the governor made a decision on Gregory's case? I wondered. Only Jeramy Shriver knew the answer to that question, and only Jeramy could present Greg's case to the new governor in the proper fashion. Time was the only thing left now and there were only 108 days left of his term.

❖

I was concerned about how Gregory would react to the tragedy especially seeing I was saddened for the family and staff, and not thinking of the clemency. I was very peaceful about our whole situation during this time. Four days later I discovered that Gregory was fine and his concern was for the governor's family and the families of the other victims. While I was sending a sympathy card to the governor's staff, Gregory was sending a card to his family with his a few extra words of encouragement.

❖

One of the beautiful things about moving around Michigan State's campus was that every place I went I was able to minister. Shyness about my faith is not one of my weaknesses so I always put "Jesus is Lord" on my screen saver that floated across my screen whenever the computer I was using was inactive. Sometimes I would format it boldly and other times I was subtler because of the environment and the personalities I was dealing with. Regardless, Jesus was part of my office space and I wanted people to know it. Recently, to my surprise, a scrolling marquee was on the new computer I was using that said, "Whisper a Prayer in the morning..." I added to it, "because Jesus is King of kings and Lord of lords." My boldness brought some closer Christians out, and I found that there were pockets of Christians all over campus.

I was fortunate enough to be on campus when Michigan State University made the final four and ultimately won the NCAA Basketball Championship in the year 2000. The energy was great, I have to admit I even put on my MSU hat to watch the final games. I gave my mother an MSU wand to wave, and I let her know when it was time to cheer and wave her wand—especially for MSU's three-point baskets.

I wish people would get that excited over Jesus when he scores a point by winning another soul to the kingdom of heaven. Christians get mocked for getting excited over Jesus, our star player, but they don't mock fans when they gang up at the airport waving and cheering the victorious MSU Spartans when they came home.

Who will line up for Gregory when the victory is won and the truth of his wrongful incarceration is exposed—giving God all of the glory?

❖

The new administration was sworn in on January 8, 2001 and only one player remained the same, Jeramy Shriver. He was taken over into the new administration for a season because of his involvement in some of the pending legislation. He had called me and told me that he was going to discuss Gregory's case with the new chief legal council. So now Gregory's case is in a new administration after spending six years in the previous one. Again, I was promised that I would be contacted and again the waiting game took place. Over half of 2001 is over and still there is no word, but there is something very special about my feelings towards this case. Greg and I are at peace knowing that the Lord has everything in His hands. Whether or not Greg's deliverance is today, tomorrow, or next year, I know that God is in control and He will deliver Gregory *"in due season if* [I] *faint not."*

As of April 2001, Jeramy Shriver went into private practice. Now none of my contacts are in place anymore. Leaving only God to do His work. And only He will and can get the glory, while both Gregory and I wait in peace on the Lord's deliverance.

Delayed answers to prayer are not only trials of faith, but they give us opportunities of honoring God by our steadfast confidence in Him under apparent repulses.

C. H. Spurgeon

GREGORY'S PERSPECTIVE

Walking Free!
by
Gregory Oliver

It became very clear that listening to God's directives was going to be paramount if Bonnie and I were going to secure the final stages of this miraculous deliverance and vindication for both of us. This deliverance would prove that I was truly the innocent man Bonnie believed me to be those many years ago.

Each year that passed took an abundance of God's grace, love and precious promises to keep us focused and free from becoming bitter over the injustice that seemed to have no end. I learned long ago that everybody's situation appears, to themselves, to be the worst that ever happened to anybody—in the world. Bonnie and I had to learn to see this whole thing from God's view, to keep it in the right perspective and to learn from the experience what the Lord wanted us to extract from it so that our experience could benefit others.

As a child of God, I know the Lord never gives us more than we can bear, but when a person comes into a prison setting it is totally unlike the culture he or she has just left. It is even different from jail because in the jail setting people must prove themselves, whether they will stand or fall prey to the vicious, more aggressive prisoners. From this jail reputation, which precedes the inmate to his/her prison home, the prison reputation is established—in most cases, that is.

I had a few fights during my stay at St. Louis City Jail. One in particular was with a guy that had been bullying guys out of their telephone calls. I had warned him ahead of time not to try on me, but he tested me anyway and wished he hadn't. We both got a few days "in the hole" for the incident.

Another time a guy challenged me because I refused to participate in their escape plan. I told him, "I am innocent. I don't have to do something like that." He considered me a risk and felt that he had to try and force me to change my mind for fear that if I wouldn't help them, I would hurt them by snitching. Two years later I found out that an escape on a person's jacket (record) would cancel all appeals and destroy his or her chance to prove their innocence. The escape plan was hampered by the loud noise they made with the radio to drown out the sound of the grating hack-saw that grated day and night trying to penetrate a one inch steel bar near a window. One of the lieutenants on duty became suspicious and called for a cell search and found the worn out hacksaw blade, which was almost unrecognizable. The lieutenant gave all of us a conduct violation for having sharp instruments in the cell area, because he didn't know whose they were. When I got out of "the hole" for that incident, I was moved to another walk (the cell tiers are called a walk).

On my new walk, I was housed with one of the well-known mob bosses in the St. Louis area—one of the Leisure Brothers. He was being held over for trial on racketeering and car bombing. Inside and out the Leisure Brothers had people who did things for them, i.e., their dirty work. We became pretty close because I would talk to him on occasion. Bonnie told me that on the day of my sentencing, the courthouse was full of heavily armed officers. When she asked, "Why?" they told her the Leisure decision was coming down that day and they didn't know what to expect, so they were prepared for anything.

It wasn't until sometime later that they moved another guy on the walk who couldn't stand the fact that Leisure kept opening the window during the cold winter months, selfishly freezing the whole area. Even though he respected me, he totally disrespected other men on the walk until I saw the need to say something to him. He responded by saying, "That Nigger can move if he don't like it on this walk." Their verbal war continued for several days until the man was threatened about the closed window by one of Leisure's henchmen, who jumped him.

I told Leisure, "That was uncalled for!" and asked if they couldn't come to some type of compromise for the entire group of men on the walk.

Leisure then said, "You both can get off this walk."

I assured him that I was not going to move, so he called me out as soon as they unracked (opened) the cells. When he reached up to me, he was surprised and realized how fast I was and that I was much stronger than he was. I overpowered him, and his henchman was warned by some of the other men to keep it fair and stay out of it. People were not known to get into it with a Leisure and walk away and tell about it. I didn't think about that then, but I did many times afterwards because that reputation follows a person throughout his or her prison stay. For me it was an exception because of my maturing in Christ, and this became more obvious than those old reputations.

After I had moved to the prison, while on a visit with Bonnie, Leisure was also on a visit with his wife. I told Bonnie who he was when he acknowledged me in the visiting room. She was impressed with my rapport with him. So the respect lingered even after the jail incident—even in the criminal world.

After Ron and I were sentenced and turned over to the D.O.C. (Department of Corrections), we were transported to the diagnostic center. We went through the routine of being herded in like cattle, stripped bare and examined for contraband, before and after the shower, disinfectant spraying and doctor examination.

I knew Bonnie's and my communication was going to be somewhat limited because phone calls were not going to be allowed at all because of the strict rules of the reception center. We both looked forward to the transfer to M.S.P. (Missouri State Penitentiary) so we could have our first contact visit. It was clear we were more than fond of each other and our friendship and love for one another was increasing more each day.

Ron and I finally arrived at M.S.P. two months after leaving city jail. We had to go through the three-day orientation before being assigned to general population with the other inmates. The nightmare stories we had heard so much about M.S.P. were now about to become first-hand experience for us, but I continued to stay prayed up, which kept us strong throughout this whole ordeal.

The moment of truth arrived as they paraded us out into the general population, which was normal routine for the new inmates. This was also the time that the old convicts would choose up the "fresh meat," as they called the new arrivals. As we approached the ground area of general population we noticed a soon-to-be common sight, in which a man who had been badly beaten and stabbed was being escorted to the emergency infirmary. I don't believe culture shock would be a strong enough term to explain the transition we were about to make.

We quickly assessed the lack of concern and callousness that was shown toward human life in a place like this. For instance, a friend of one of my brothers had heard that the Oliver brothers name carried a reputation and asked if we would help him out of a serious jam. He owed a guy some money that was threatening to collect it—or him when he came for it. I told my brothers [Greg's brother Curtis was also at M.S.P. serving three years] we weren't getting messed up in anything like that, but that I would pray for this guy. I did just that, and when a certain inmate came to the guy to collect the money, he reinforced his threat by saying, "I'll be right back and you better have my money or else." Not even fifteen minutes later this same inmate went out to the TV room to collect from another man who owed him money. They got into a knife fight, which resulted in his death. When my brother's friend came and thanked me for praying for him, I had mixed emotions. I was glad that my brother's friend wasn't hurt, but I was also saddened over the senseless loss of a life over money. Later I discovered that during the knife fight the one man was going to spare the other one's life, but he insisted that the man finish the job and kill him. So he did.

❖

I had my first visit with Bonnie, and it was like being in another world. She told me how much she enjoyed visiting without being in city jail's classroom setting, where we really couldn't communicate. We continued to enjoy our visits, telephone calls and letters while we awaited the post-conviction motion and appeals to go through in the hope that they would throw out this wrongful conviction.

I kept busy by working, attending college, studying in the law library and attending chapel services. Time really flew by at times and nearly two years were gone and still no word on my appeal. The post conviction motion was received hard, denied and later co-joined over to the appeal.

Bonnie continued her letter campaign to the courts, her prayer, fastings, and meetings whenever she felt led by the Spirit. For example, the appeals hearing that she attended secured some vital and much needed evidence for future use.

When my appeal was denied, it was very disappointing; but we kept the faith, pursuing the next stage which was the Missouri Supreme Court and from there the Federal Court. But these brought no resolution, although vital evidence was collected to our advantage at each stage of the legal journey.

The state had built a new prison for what they called the "worst of the worst." Because of the type of sentence that was handed down to us, Ron and I were transferred to Potosi. The prison warden was an ex-Vietnam vet whose attitude about executions was conveyed in a message saying, "Someone has to take out the trash." The Lord knew that I was angry over something that the warden had said about the men. I believe the other men had him approach me and disavow his negative statement and vow that he was going to support the new legislation on getting rid of the long sentences. That let me know even this hard-hearted man could be moved by the Lord.

I was shown in a vision that we would be going on a visit, but instead I would be coming out of prison. It wasn't long after that as I continued to confess *I was out of there* that we were delivered from Potosi. On the 13th of April 1992, the beginning of Passover, which commemorated the Israelites deliverance from bondage in Egypt, I was delivered from my Egyptian bondage in Patosi.

Because there were so many of us leaving at one time, they had to process us out via the visiting room, which was consistent with the vision the Lord had shown me. This was the stage of God's delivering work that took us from Potosi back to M.S.P., which was now called J.C.C.C. (Jefferson City Correctional Center). To me this was a modern day Exodus as God brought eighty of us out of that horrible place. I was unable to contact Bonnie who was already on her way to Missouri from Chicago to visit me, and I knew she would have one hundred more miles to drive in order to get to Jefferson City, because she didn't know of the transfer.

❖

My wife, Bonnie, is an extraordinary woman, and I thank God for her sensitivity to His Spirit, because she suggested that I refile a petition for pardon, which the Lord in turn confirmed to me, and after her tenacious follow-ups we have received favorable response and review. Ecclesiastics 5:8 says,

> *"If thou seest the oppression of the poor, and **violent perverting of judgment and justice** in a province, marvel not at the matter: for he that is higher than the highest regardeth; and there be higher than they."*

We expect that any day now that I will be "walking free" and authoring a book by the same title and producing an album of the songs I wrote while incarcerated. Why? Because God chose a woman named *Bonnie* to champion a case of injustice that would have gone unnoticed had it not been for her willingness to pay attention to the "tug" of the Holy Spirit.

> The Lord said to Isaiah [Bonnie], *"Whom shall I send, and who will go for us?"*
> And Isaiah [Bonnie] said, *"Here am I, send me."*
>
> (Isaiah 6:8)

APPENDIX

Freedom Express

(In Brief)

The Oliver Brother's Story—For We Trust the Lord

Behind Bars

❖❖❖❖❖

The blue Ford Mustang sped to an abrupt stop one rain slick night. The St. Louis City police officers rushed the car to apprehend its two occupants. The instructions had been, "Shoot to kill," but the passengers created no problems for the officers on the roadblock. Gregory, a tall brown skinned young man was driving his brother Ronald's car when apprehended.

"Pretty good driving," one officer said to Gregory as the Oliver brothers assumed the position. The brothers were frisked and read their rights before being escorted down to city jail for questioning. Ronald Oliver, Gregory's younger brother, had just tripped out mentally, which resulted in the death of one man and gunshot wounds to two others.

Gregory was questioned as a witness to the crime without the presence of a lawyer. After questioning, Gregory was confused when the police officer said, "Book 'em!" Both Gregory and Ronald were booked for the same first-degree murder charge, the same two first-degree criminal assault charges; Ronald was charged with additional charge of kidnapping.

At Ronald's arraignment, the judge told the boy's mother that there was no evidence against Gregory.

At Gregory's arraignment, however, the story was different, and he was shocked when the judge held him over for probable cause. He was even more shocked when the grand jury came back with a "true bill" for the charges. ■

The Crime

❖❖❖❖❖

On the morning of June 6, 1985, Gregory received a collect call from an old girlfriend, Sandy. She told him she had just gotten out of jail (for an auto theft charge) and asked if he would pick her up and either take her to get food stamps or to another party's house to borrow some money. Gregory was unable to help her at the time, because he had a moving job to do that day. Gregory then called his brother, Ronald, to see if he could give Sandy a ride. Ronald was also unavailable. So when Sandy called collect a second time, Gregory let her know neither he nor Ron could oblige her.

Gregory went about his business for that day by taking care of the moving job he had lined up. His car was out of commission, so he called a cousin to help him. When the job was completed his cousin was not able to take Gregory all the way home; so Greg asked to be dropped off when he saw a couple of familiar faces. He happened to be by the home of an old family friend, Mary Thomas. Mary used to go out with Gregory's older half-brother, Charles.

While at Mary's, Gregory called his mother's house to see if one of his brothers could give him a ride home. No one was available at the time, so he stayed at Mary's apartment all afternoon. Others were already at the apartment playing cards, so Gregory joined in the game. Mary and her friends had already been drinking a little. With some of Greg's winnings he sent out to get something else to drink. Mary tried to call Mrs. Oliver again to see if anyone was available yet to give Greg a ride. Then Gregory called a third time and found out that Ronald was on his way. When Ronald finally arrived, no one seemed to be in any hurry to break up the game, so Ronald sat down to observe. (843-870, 332, 334, 716, 717, 723, Trial Transcripts [TT])

While playing cards, someone suddenly flicked the lights off and on about three times. This caused Ronald to "trip out." He pulled out the gun he was carrying and began shooting randomly into the ceiling. He then kicked out the window and told everyone not to move. (335 TT) Fortunately, no one was hurt during this incident.

Immediately after that, Mary and Ronald went outside and began arguing over the shooting incident and another incident involving a young neighbor boy who happened to be in front of the apartment when Ronald went outside. Gregory joined them after the argument between Mary and Ron was completed. Mary had told Ronald that she would go with him. (341, 680, 730 TT)

The three of them, Ronald, Gregory and Mary got into the car (The transcripts are not clear at that point as to all of the circumstances around it.) While driving Ronald began acting up again and held the gun to Mary's ribs. After heated discussion, Ronald gave the gun to Gregory who was cramped up in the back seat of the car. Gregory began unloading the gun and throwing the shell casings out the window (The shell casings were found, by the police, where the testimony indicated they would be found.)

Unknown to Greg, a round was left in the chamber and the gun discharged accidentally making hole in the inside side panel of the car. This angered Ron and he insisted Greg give him the gun back. Gregory obliged since the gun was now empty.

Ronald, still angry over the last incident, was arguing with Gregory. Ronald said he was going to put the gun away so he pulled over and got out of the car, moving to the trunk to dispose of the gun. (341, 343, 680, 681, 730 TT)

Mary was beside herself with fear. To quote her, "I was pissing and crying and pissing and crying. Pee Wee (Ron's nickname) was acting crazy, you know."

At some point, Ronald had gotten the gun back into his possession (or possibly never put it in the trunk when he opened the trunk) and was pointing it at Mary and Gregory.

Mary was behind Gregory telling Gregory, "Don't let him shoot me."

"No, Pee Wee, man, I'm not going to let you shoot Mary." Gregory said.

"If you don't move, I'm going to shoot you, brother or not," was Ron's reply. (343, 683 TT)

Mary knew for sure that Ronald was tripping out after he said that. (345 TT)

Gregory, annoyed with the whole situation, pretended to be drunk, and began to walk away from both of them. Mary didn't want Gregory to leave but wouldn't leave with him or didn't feel she could leave Ron the way he was acting. (343, 684 TT)

Mary got back in the car with Ronald and they drove after Gregory. When they saw a group of people at Union and Hodiamont, in St. Louis, Mary tricked Pee Wee and told him, "Hey there's Jay (Gregory's nick name)." She really hadn't seen Gregory; she only wanted Ronald to stop so she could get away from his craziness. Mary jumped out and ran into the crowd. After Mary left, Gregory, who really was in the crowd, got in the front seat and the boys drove off. (354, 685 TT)

Ronald had driven a short distance when Gregory asked, "Where are you going?"

"I'm going to Sandy's house," Ron said.

Gregory wanted to go home, but because he wasn't driving he went along with Ron. It was while they were en route that the decision was made to pick up Sandy and a cousin, which would cause the car to be full. In the back seat, where Gregory had been sitting earlier, was a basketball and a partially full gas can with a hole in it. Ronald had brought the gas for Gregory's car, which was sitting empty at his house. All this time the gun was not visible, consequently, Gregory thought Ron had put it in the trunk.

Once at Sandy's apartment, which was a building that was being condemned, Gregory decided to take the gas can up to Sandy's to store it out of the way so that the fumes would not fill the car. He didn't suggest putting it in the trunk, because he thought the gun was there and didn't want to draw Ron's attention to it.

Upstairs they knocked on Sandy Nicholas's door. Sandy was in her nightgown when she opened the door because she had been sleeping on the couch. Two men were with her in her apartment, while five children were sleeping in the only bedroom. Robert Franklin, one of the visitors, woke Sandy up by telling her someone was at the door. She asked him to answer it, but according to Sandy's testimony neither man could move. The two men in Sandy's apartment were Bruce Campbell (the murder victim) and Robert Franklin (a wounded bystander). The smell of drugs lingered from when Sandy and her sister had been drinking and smoking marijuana (actually PCP) earlier that evening. (291-292, 470, TT and Robert Franklin's deposition [FD] which was not allowed at the trial, neither was Hill's testimony, Police Report [PR])

The Oliver Brothers entered the apartment. Gregory, seeing the men and not knowing who they were, started copping an attitude as he often did around Sandy, "I'm Jake the !!!$#@%^%&# Snake and there ain't no one bad as me." Then he asked if she was ready to go. Sandy got off the couch and went to the bathroom as if to get ready to go with the boys. During that time, Bruce Campbell offered Gregory a drink out of the bottle he had in his brown paper bag. (TT, FD) This indicated that the atmosphere that night was not threatening.

When Sandy came out of the bathroom Ronald went in to use it. While Ronald was in the bathroom, Gregory and Sandy went into the hallway to talk for approximately fifteen minutes. (470, 498, 502, 698-90 TT)

Sandy testified that Gregory splashed gasoline all over the floor threatening to burn the place up, while asking for a match to set it on fire when he entered the apartment. Gregory declares that he never did or said those things. (471-72, TT) [This is crucial to Greg's defense.]

❖

In Robert Franklin's deposition, Gregory was throwing lighted matches at the gas can, indicating that "no" gas had been splashed on the floor. Interestingly Gregory, Robert Franklin and the bomb and arson squad's report all supported Gregory's testimony that gasoline was not splashed on the floor, but the evidence and the testimony to support this never got to the courtroom. The jury was only given Sandy's testimony and the gas can was lost in the police property room. There were photos of the gas can, which showed the sizable hole in it.

The Robert Franklin story couldn't hold up either, because of the dangerous properties of gasoline. When throwing lighted matches at a gas can that had a hole in it, allowing the fumes to escape, there *will be* an explosion and/or fire.

When looking at two of the four stories that were told by people who had spent a part of the evening breathing in a hallucinogenic drug and/or drinking it becomes difficult to believe. The third of the four stories had chemical analysis to support it, but was never brought forward as evidence. All stories actually support Gregory's version of the incident. The variety of stories indicates that there was an issue of witness credibility. Therefore, it was not wise, from a prosecutor's point of view, to bring forward too many versions for the jury to wade through when trying to create a motive. Unfortunately the most drastic story was used from the most unstable eyewitness.

If Gregory really appeared to be threatening with the attitude he was copping, then;
1. Why did Bruce Campbell offer him a drink out of the bottle he had in the brown paper bag?
2. If Sandy felt so threatened, why did she voluntarily change her clothes as if she was getting ready to go with Gregory?
3. Why, if Robert Franklin and Bruce Campbell hadn't been drinking or smoking drugs, (according to Sandy) didn't they try to stop Greg?
4. If they were really drinking and smoking (hallucinogenic) drugs in the apartment wouldn't there be a blur as to the events to the occupants of the apartment, and wouldn't that account for why the men were not able to answer the door?
5. If Gregory were really threatening in his behavior, then the children's testimony in the police report would have indicated it because the children were repeating and exaggerating what the adults were saying. None of the children mentioned Gregory; they only mentioned Ronald.

❖

After Greg and Sandy's conversation in the hall, they came back into the apartment. Sandy still hadn't made her mind up as to whether she was going with Greg and Ron or not. Gregory finally told her, "You ain't going, I'm fixing to go, I got to go," he said as he walked out of the apartment saying, "Come on!" to Ron. (694 TT)

In the meantime, Ron had exited the bathroom and was standing behind Bruce Campbell, having words with him (the transcripts indicate that Ron and Bruce Campbell were having angry words).

While Gregory was on the landing leaving he heard the shot. He turned around, ran back into the apartment, and saw Bruce Campbell lying slumped backward over a stool with a bullet in the back of his head, but he didn't see Ron right away. He was trying to figure out how Ron got a loaded gun back in his possession, because he thought it was in the car trunk—empty.

Sandy, who had been in the kitchen, began yelling when she heard the shot and ran out to see. Gregory lost control and "was trying to get Ronald's attention" by yelling at him. Ronald then shot Sandy four times rapid fire and by this time Gregory was hysterically jumping up and down on the floor, telling Ronald, "You can't kill nobody, what is you doing!" (689, 698, 702 TT)

Robert Franklin was the third victim of Ronald's shooting spree. He testified in the deposition that Gregory asked his brother Ron, "What did he do that for," when Ron shot the victims. (FD) This is referred to as "cool reflection" and supports Gregory's testimony of mild hysteria on his part.

The next thing Gregory knew, "Ron ran out the door" and he ran after him asking, "Why he shot those people." Ronald didn't answer he just got into the car and Gregory followed. During this time Gregory began to collect himself as they drove around and finally wound up at their aunt's house. (700 TT) ■

Ron's Mental Condition
❖❖❖❖❖

In the fall of 1983, Ronald Oliver was a young husband with one son. He was an architectural student at Kansas State University, in Manhattan, Kansas. During his first semester there it was discovered that he had a lobule lesion and surgery was performed. After surgery, he was sent back to St. Louis for a convalescent leave for six weeks so proper healing could take place. This healing process required a stress free environment. About three weeks into his convalescent leave, Ronald was caught in a house fire where his wife and best friend were killed. He was found lying over his son's body, suffering from smoke inhalation. His son, Ronald Jr., survived.

From that time on, Ronald's mental capacity was never the same and neither was his temperament. He flew off for no apparent reason and became violent even with family members. Four family members testified at the trial that he tried to hurt them for the smallest reasons. The state psychiatrists also testified to Ron's *uncontrollable* behavior. Even Mrs. Oliver testified that Ronald would become like a "vicious animal" when he would trip out.

In summation, Ronald went from being a mild-mannered college-going student to someone with an IQ of 65-70 with uncontrollable violent outbursts. His change was drastic that the jail and prison authorities kept Ronald on drugs to control his violent outbursts. ■

Contradictions and Evidence
❖❖❖❖❖

During the controversial parts of the testimonies, I sided with Gregory's version, because of the lack of validity of Sandy Nicholas's testimony. During several out-of-jury-range discussions held by the prosecution, defense, and court during the course of the trial, the prosecution insulted and ridiculed Ms. Nicholas, saying he questioned her intelligence; yet he insisted that her character not be an issue in the trial.

Sandy Nicholas (the star witness) was shown by the state to be incompetent as an eyewitness and Gregory was shown to have an unimpeachable testimony. Yet the court and the jury took Sandy's word over Gregory's and nowhere in the transcripts did Gregory's ability to testify ever enter into the conversation in a negative light, to the contrary.

In the out-of-jury-range discussion prior to the prosecutor calling the last rebuttal witness, the fact that Gregory's testimony had not been impeachable after 28 witnesses was a critical issue to the prosecution. That is why it was, in his opinion, necessary to try and discredit Gregory with this last witness. He said he needed a chance to try and impeach Gregory's testimony, too, which he never did. ■

The Trial
❖❖❖❖❖

The Oliver brother's trial began with the pre-trial conference on April 6, 1987, which was twenty-two months after their arrest on June 6, 1985. This lengthy delay violated the Federal "Speedy Trial Act" in the Oliver case. Also the case was not severed, thereby making it impossible for Gregory to be the focal point of his own trial. This hampered Gregory's right to a fair trial because he was the also-ran in his brother's trial. During the summation, the prosecution drew attention to Ronald's mental condition by making numerous comments to the jury to disregard Ronald's condition. Ronald sat through the entire trial with a blank stare because of the sedative drugs he was on.

Prior to the trial, Ronald spent six weeks at the state hospital in Fulton under ideal conditions where he was tested for mental disease and defect. They concluded that he indeed was suffering from Organic Brain Syndrome. (843-924 TT) Since incarceration, originally at Missouri State Penitentiary at Jefferson City, Missouri, Ronald spent over one year undergoing tests, under those same ideal conditions. These tests proved that a portion of his brain was indeed dead from the combination of the surgery and smoke inhalation.

The focus of the Oliver trial was on the "inconsistent statement" of Mary Thomas to four hearsay witnesses, not on the evidence or the mental condition of Ronald. In other words, Gregory and Ronald Oliver were convicted of pre-meditated first-degree murder on a statute dealing with inconsistent statements of the alleged kidnap victim supported only by hearsay testimony.

Mary, the alleged kidnapped victim, had told the court she didn't want to press charges against either Greg or Ron. ***Gregory was not charged with kidnapping.***

Both men received the maximum penalty of life without parole for first-degree murder and life with parole for first-degree criminal assault. Ronald received an extra 15 years for kidnapping Mary Thomas who swears she was not kidnapped. The jury had found Gregory guilty of Count 3, kidnapping, but the judge brushed it aside. (328-29 TT, judge's comments after verdict TT)

The bomb and arson squad was at the investigation scene taking samples, yet they did not testify at the trial. If they had, they would have been able give the information as to whether or not gasoline had been poured out on the floor. If it had been found, the state would have definitely had them as a witness to back up Sandy's testimony. There were no supportive evidence or witnesses to this fact. It was Sandy Nicholas' word against Gregory Oliver's word through the entire trial. ■